BERLITZ W9-AOP-540

European
PHRASE BOOK

**12 key languages
spoken across Western Europe**

Austria, Belgium, Denmark, Finland, France,
Germany, Greece, Italy, The Netherlands,
Norway, Portugal, Spain, Sweden,
Switzerland, Turkey

How best to use this phrase book

This phrase book is designed to provide you with the essential key phrases you'll need for travelling in and around Europe.

● **Colour margins** will help you locate quickly the language that you require.

● Each language is divided into essential **topic sections**. The following content table will help you find your way around:

Basic expressions	Shops, stores & services
Hotel–Accommodation	incl. bank, post, telephone
Eating out	Time, date, numbers
Travelling around	Emergency
Sightseeing	Guide to pronunciation

● Each expression appears with a transliteration next to it. Simply read this imitated pronunciation as if it were English, stressing the syllables printed in bold type. For further help, consult the **Guide to pronunciation** at the back of each language section.

● In the **Eating out** section, a selection of popular traditional dishes are listed alphabetically, followed by brief explanations, to help you decypher dishes appearing on a menu.

● Throughout the book, this symbol ☛ suggests phrases your listener can use to answer you, simply by pointing to the appropriate answer.

Note: Where languages vary slightly according to gender, parentheses ( ) indicate the feminine version.

Danish

Some basic expressions *Anvendelige udtryk*

Yes/No.	**Ja/Nej.**	ya/nigh
Please.	**Vær så venlig.**	vær saw **vehn**lee
Thank you.	**Tak.**	tak
I beg your pardon.	**Undskyld.**	**oon**skewl

Introductions *Præsentationer*

Good morning.	**God morgen.**	goadh**mo͞a**ern
Good afternoon.	**God dag.**	goadh**dai**
Good evening.	**God aften.**	goadh**af**dern
Good night.	**God nat.**	goadh**nat**
Good-bye.	**Farvel.**	far**vehl**
My name is...	**Jeg hedder...**	yigh **hehd**herr
Pleased to meet you!	**Det glæder mig at træffe Dem!**	dᴇ **glæ**dherr migh ah **træf**fe dehm
What's your name?	**Hvad hedder De/du?**	vadh **hehd**herr dee/doo
How are you?	**Hvordan har du det?**	vor**dan** har doo dᴇ
Fine, thanks. And you?	**Tak, godt. Og hvordan har du det?**	tak god. oa vor**dan** har doo dᴇ
Where do you come from?	**Hvor kommer du fra?**	vo͞ar **kom**er doo fra
I'm from...	**Jeg er fra...**	yigh ehr fra
Australia	**Australien**	ow**stral**ēēern
Canada	**Canada**	**ka**nada
Great Britain	**Storbritannien**	**stoar**britanyern
United States	**USA**	oo ehs ah
I'm with my...	**Jeg er her sammen med...**	yigh ehr hehr **sä**mern mehdh
wife	**min kone**	meen **koa**ner
husband	**min mand**	meen man
family	**min familie**	meen fa**mil**yer
children	**mine børn**	**mee**ner børn
parents	**mine forældre**	**mee**ner for**æld**rer
boyfriend/girlfriend	**min kæreste**	meen **kærs**der
I'm on holiday (vacation).	**Jeg er her på ferie.**	yigh ehr hehr paw **feh**ryer

GUIDE TO PRONUNCIATION/EMERGENCIES, see page 16

Questions *Spørgsmål*

When?/How?	**Hvornår?/Hvordan?**	vornawr/vordan
What?/Why?	**Hvad?/Hvorfor?**	vadh/vorfor
Who?/Which?	**Hvem?/Hvilken?**	vehm/vilkern
Where is/are ...?	**Hvor er ...?**	voar ehr
Where can I find/ get ...?	**Hvor kan jeg finde/ få ...?**	voar kan yigh finner/faw
How far?	**Hvor langt?**	voar langt
How long?	**Hvor længe?**	voar længer
How much/How many?	**Hvor meget/Hvor mange?**	voar mighert/voar manger
Can I have ...?	**Kan jeg få ...?**	kan yigh faw
Can you help me?	**Kan De hjælpe mig?**	kan dee yehlper migh
What does this/that mean?	**Hvad betyder det her/det der?**	vadh bertewdherr dɛ hehr/dɛ dehr
I understand.	**Jeg forstår det.**	yigh forstawr dɛ
I don't understand.	**Jeg forstår det ikke.**	yigh forstawr dɛ igger
Can you translate this for me?	**Kan De oversætte det her for mig?**	kan dee oˌˌoerrsehder dɛ hehr for migh
Do you speak English?	**Kan De tale engelsk?**	kan dee tāler ehngerlsk
I don't speak (much) Danish.	**Jeg kan ikke tale det (ret meget) dansk.**	yigh kan igger tāler dɛ (reht mighert) dansk

A few more useful words *Nogle flere nyttige ord*

better/worse	**bedre/værre**	behdhrer/vehrer
big/small	**stort/lille**	stoart/leeler
cheap/expensive	**billigt/dyrt**	beeleet/dewrt
early/late	**tidligt/sent**	teedhleet/sɛnt
good/bad	**godt/dårligt**	god/dawleet
hot/cold	**varmt/koldt**	varmt/kolt
near/far	**i nærheden/langt væk**	ee nærhɛdhern/langt vehk
old/new	**gammelt/nyt**	gamerlt/newt
right/wrong	**rigtigt/forkert**	rigteet/forkehrt
vacant/ occupied	**ledigt/optaget**	lehdheet/optāerdh

Hotel—Accommodation *Hotel*

I have a reservation.	**Jeg har bestilt værelse.**	yigh har ber**stilt væ**rerlser
We've reserved an apartment.	**Vi har bestilt en lejlighed.**	vee har ber**stilt** ehn **ligh**leehehdh
Do you have any vacancies?	**Har De nogle ledige værelser?**	har dee **nō**aler l**ε**dēer **væ**rerlserr
I'd like a...	**Jeg vil gerne have et...**	yigh veel **gehr**ner ha eht
single room	**enkeltværelse**	**ehn**kerldv**æ**rerlser
double room	**dobbeltværelse**	**do**berldv**æ**rerlser
We'd like a room...	**Vi vil gerne have et værelse...**	vee veel **gehr**ner ha eht **væ**rerlser
with twin beds	**med to senge**	mehdh toa **sehn**ger
with a double bed	**med dobbeltseng**	mehdh **do**berldsehng
with a bath	**med bad**	mehdh badh
with a shower	**med brusebad**	med br**ōō**serbadh
We'll be staying...	**Vi bliver her...**	vee bl**ēē**err hehr
overnight only	**en enkel nat**	ehn **ehn**kerlt nat
a few days	**et par dage**	eht par **dae**r
a week (at least)	**i (mindst) en uge**	ee (meenst) ehn **ōō**er
Is there a camp site near here?	**Er der en campingplads i nærheden?**	ehr dehr ehn **kam**pingplas ee **nær**h**ε**dhern

Decision *Beslutning*

May I see the room?	**Kan jeg se værelset?**	kan yigh s**ε** **væ**rerlserdh
That's fine. I'll take it.	**Det er godt. Jeg tager det.**	d**ε** ehr god. yigh tar d**ε**
No. I don't like it.	**Jeg kan ikke lide det.**	yigh kan **igg**er li d**ε**
It's too ...	**Det er for ...**	d**ε** ehr for ...
dark/small	**mørkt/lyst**	**mør**kt/lewst
noisy	**støjende**	**stoi**erner
Do you have anything ...?	**Har De noget ...?**	har dee **nō**aert
better	**bedre**	**behd**hrer
cheaper	**billigere**	**bee**l**ēē**errer
quieter	**roligere**	**roal**ēē**errer
May I have my bill, please?	**Må jeg bede om regningen?**	maw yigh b**ε** om **righ**ningern
It's been a very enjoyable stay.	**Vi har nydt opholdet meget.**	vee har newt op**hol**erdh **migh**ert

DAYS OF THE WEEK, see page 15

Eating out *Restauranter*

I'd like to reserve a table for 4.	Jeg vil gerne bes-tille et bord til 4.	yigh veel **gehr**ner ber**stil**er eht boar til **fee**rer
We'll come at 8.	Vi kommer klokken 8.	vee **komm**err **klogg**ern **oad**er
I'd like..., please.	Jeg vil gerne have...	yigh veel **gehr**ner ha
breakfast	morgenmad	**moa**rernmadh
lunch/dinner	frokost/middag	**fro**akoast/**midd**ai
What do you recommend?	Hvad kan De anbe-fale?	vadh kan dee **an**ber**fal**er
Do you have any vegetarian dishes?	Er der nogle vege-tariske retter?	ehr dehr **noa**ler **vehgeht**arisger **reh**derr

Breakfast *Morgenmad*

I'll have a/an/some...	Jeg vil gerne have...	yigh veel **gehr**ner ha
bacon and eggs	bacon og æg	"bacon" oa æg
boiled egg	et æg	eht æg
bread	brød	brødh
butter	smør	smør
cereal	cornflakes	"cornflakes"
eggs	æg	æg
fried eggs	spejlæg	**spigh**læg
scrambled eggs	røræg	**rør**æg
poached eggs	pocheret æg	po**sher**erdh æg
jam	syltetøj/marmelade	**sewl**dertoi/marmer**ladh**er
rolls	rundstykker	**roon**stewggerr
toast	ristet brød	**reest**erdh brødh

Starters (Appetizers) *Forretter*

blandet hors d'oeuvre	**blan**erdh "hors d'oeuvre"	assorted appetizers
fyldte tomater	**fewl**der toa**mad**err	stuffed tomatoes
omelet	oamer**leht**	omelet
sildesalat	**seel**ersalat	herring salad
kyllingesalat (**kewl**eengersah**lät**)		chicken meat, macaroni, tomato slices, green peppers, olives, green pees, lettuce and mushrooms, covered with a tomato dressing
smørrebrød (**smør**erbrødh)		large, buttered open-faced sandwich covered with one of a variety of delicacies and garnished with various accessories

NUMBERS, see page 15

Dansk

Fish and seafood *Fisk og skaldyr*

cod	**torsk**	torsk
perch	**aborre**	ahborer
pike	**gedde**	gehdher
smoked herring	**røget sild**	roierdh seel
sole	**søtunge**	søtoonger
trout	**forel**	foarehl
ålesuppe (awlersoobber)	sweet-and-sour eel soup, with apples and prunes, served with dark rye bread	

boiled	**kogt**	kogt
fried	**stegt**	stehgt
grilled	**grillet**	greelerdh
roast	**ovnstegt**	o°°nstehgt
stewed	**stuvet**	stooerdh
underdone (rare)	**letstegt**	lehtstehgt
medium	**medium**	mehdeeoom
well-done	**gennemstegt**	gehnermstehgt

Meat *Kød*

beef	**oksekød**	okserkødh
chicken	**kylling**	kewling
duck	**and**	an
ham	**skinke**	skeenger
lamb	**lammekød**	lamerkødh
pork	**svinekød**	sveenerkødh
veal	**kalvekød**	kalverkødh
flæskesteg med svær (flæsgerstigh mehdh svær)	roast pork with crackling, often served with braised red cabbage, gravy and small browned potatoes	
forloren skildpadde (forloarern skeelpadher)	"mock turtle": a traditional dish of meat from a calf's head with meat balls and fish balls	

Vegetables *Grøntsager*

beans	**bønner**	bønerr
cabbage	**kål**	kawl
carrots	**gulerødder**	goolerrødherr
mushrooms	**champignoner**	shampinyong
onions	**løg**	loi
peas	**ærter**	ærderr
potatoes	**kartofler**	kartoflerr
tomatoes	**tomater**	toamaderr

Fruit and dessert *Frugt og nødder*

apple	**et æble**	eht æbler
cherries	**kirsebær**	keerserbær
lemon	**citron**	seetroan
orange	**en appelsin**	aberlseen
pear	**pære**	pærer
plums	**blommer**	blomerr
strawberries	**jordbær**	yoarbær
eis	ēēs	ice-cream
ost	oast	cheese
Weinerbrød	vēēnerbrødh	Danish pastry

bondepige med slør (boanerpēēer mehdh slør)	"veiled country maid": a mixture of rye-bread crumbs, apple sauce, cream and sugar

Drinks *Drikkevarer*

beer	**øl**	øl
(hot) chocolate	**(varm) chokolade**	(varm) shoakoaladher
coffee	**kaffe**	kafer
black	**sort**	soart
with cream	**med fløde**	mehdh flødher
fruit juice	**frugtsaft**	froogtsaft
milk	**mælk**	mælk
mineral water	**mineralvand**	meenehralvan
tea	**te**	tE
with milk/lemon	**med mælk/citron**	mehdh mælk/seetroan
wine	**vin**	vēēn
red/white	**rød/hvid**	rødh/veedh

Complaints–Paying *Klager–Regningen*

This is too...	**Det her er for ...**	dE hehr ehr for
bitter/salty/sweet	**bittert/salt/sødt**	biderdh/salt/søt
That's not what I ordered.	**Det har jeg ikke bestilt.**	dE har yigh igger berstilt
I'd like to pay.	**Jeg vil gerne betale.**	yigh veel gehrner bertāler
I think there's a mistake in this bill.	**Der er vist en fejl i denne regning.**	deh ehr vist ehn fighl ee dehner righning
Can I pay with this credit card?	**Kan jeg betale med dette kreditkort?**	kan yigh bertāler mehdh dehder krehditkort
Is service included?	**Er service inkluderet?**	ehr "service" inkloodērerdh
We enjoyed it, thank you.	**Vi har nydt det.**	vee har newt dE

NUMBERS, see page 15

Travelling around *Rejse omkring*

Plane *Ifly*

Is there a flight to Rønne?	**Er der et fly til Rønne?**	ehr dehr eht flew til **rø**ner
What time should I check in?	**Hvad tid må jeg checke ind?**	vadh teed maw yigh "check"er in
I'd like to ... my reservation.	**Jeg vil gerne ... min bestilling.**	yigh veel **gehr**ner ... meen behs**til**ing
cancel	**annullere**	annool**ē**rer
change	**ændre på**	**æn**drer paw
confirm	**bekræfte**	ber**kræf**der

Train *Tog*

I'd like a ticket to Copenhagen.	**Jeg vil gerne have en billet til København.**	yigh veel **gehr**ner ha ehn bee**lehd** til købern**hown**
single (one-way)	**enkelt**	**ehn**kerlt
return (round trip)	**retur**	reh**toor**
first/second class	**første/anden klasse**	**førs**der/**an**ern **klas**er
How long does the journey (trip) take?	**Hvor længe tager turen?**	vōar **læng**er tar **too**rern
When is the ... train to Århus?	**Hvornår kører det ... tog til Århus?**	vor**nawr kø**rerr deht ... to^{oo} til **awr**hōōs
first/last/next	**første/sidste**	**førs**der/**sees**der
Is this the right train to Aarhus?	**Kører det her tog til Århus?**	**kø**rerr dɛ hehr to^{oo} til **awh**ōōs

Bus *Bus*

Which tram (streetcar) goes to the town centre?	**Hvilken sporvogn kører til centrum?**	**vil**kern spoarvo^{oo}n **kø**rerr til **sen**troom
How much is the fare to ...?	**Hvor meget koster det til ...?**	vōar **migh**ert **kos**derr dɛ til
Will you tell me when to get off?	**Vil De sige til, hvornår jeg skal af?**	veel dee **sēē**er til vor**nawr** yigh skal ah

TELLING THE TIME, see page 14

Taxi *Taxa*

What's the fare to ...?	**Hvad koster det til ...?**	vadh **kos**derr dɛ til
Take me to ...	**Kør mig til ...**	kør migh til
this address	**denne adresse**	**deh**ner ah**dreh**ser
Please stop here.	**Stands her.**	stans hehr
Could you wait for me?	**Kan De vente på mig?**	kan dee **vehn**der paw migh

Car hire (rental) *Biludlejning*

I'd like to hire (rent) a car.	**Jeg vil gerne leje en bil.**	yigh veel **gehr**ner **ligh**er ehn beel
I'd like it for a day/a week.	**Jeg vil gerne have den en enkel dag/en uge.**	yigh veel **gehr**ner ha dehn ehn **ehnk**erl dai/ehn **ōō**er
Where's the nearest filling station?	**Hvor er den nærmeste benzinstation?**	vōar ehr dehn **nær**merster behn**seen**stashon
Give me ... litres of petrol (gasoline).	**... liter benzin.**	... **leed**err ben**seen**
How can I find this place/address?	**Hvordan kan jeg finde frem til dette sted/denne adresse?**	vor**dan** kan yigh **finn**er frehm til **deh**der stehdh/ **deh**ner ah**dreh**ser
I've had a break-down at ...	**Jeg har fået motor-stop ved ...**	yigh har **fāw**erdh **moa**torstop vehdh
Can you send a mechanic?	**Kan De sende en mekaniker?**	kan dee **sehn**ner ehn meh**kan**eekerr
Can you mend this puncture (fix this flat)?	**Kan De reparere denne punktering?**	kan dee reh**parēr**er **deh**ner **poonk**tehring

---

De har kørt forkert.	You're on the wrong road.
Kør ligeud.	Go straight ahead.
Det ligger der til venstre/højre.	It's down there on the left/ right.
overfor/bagved ...	opposite/behind ...
ved siden af/efter ...	next to/after ...
nord/syd/øst/vest	north/south/east/west

NUMBERS, see page 15

Sightseeing *Seværdigheder*

Where's the tourist office?	**Hvor er turistbureauet?**	voār ehr tooreestbewroaert
Is there an English-speaking guide?	**Findes der en engelsktalende guide?**	finners dehr ehn ehngerlsktālernder "guide"
Where is/are the...?	**Hvor er...?**	voār ehr
art gallery	**kunstgalleriet**	koonstgalereēert
botanical gardens	**den botaniske have**	dehn botaneesger hāver
castle	**borgen**	boārgern
city centre	**byens centrum**	bewerns sentroom
church	**kirken**	keērgern
concert hall	**koncertsalen**	konsehrtsālern
market	**torvet**	toārverdh
museum	**museet**	moosseherdh
palace	**slottet**	sloderdh
square	**pladsen/torvet**	plasern/torverdh
tower	**tårnet**	tawrnerdh
town hall	**rådhuset**	rawdhhōōserdh
What are the opening hours?	**Hvornår er der åbent?**	vornawr ehr dehr āwbern
When does it close?	**Hvornår lukkes der?**	vornawr looggers dehr
How much is the entrance fee?	**Hvor meget koster det i entre?**	voār mighert kosderr dɛ ee angtrɛ

Relaxing *Forlystelser*

What's playing at the... Theatre?	**Hvad spiller man på... Teateret?**	vadh speelerr man paw... tɛatrerdh
Are there any seats for tonight?	**Er der flere pladser tilbage til i aften?**	ehr dehr flɛrer plasserr tilbāer til ee afdern
How much are the seats?	**Hvor meget koster billetterne?**	voār mighert kosderr beelehderner
Would you like to go out with me tonight?	**Har du lyst til at gå ud med mig i aften?**	har doo lewst til ah gaw ood mehdh migh ee afdern
Is there a discotheque in town?	**Findes der et diskotek i byen?**	finners dehr eht diskoatēk ee bewern
Would you like to dance?	**Skal vi danse?**	skal vee danser
Thank you, it's been a wonderful evening.	**Tak, det har været en virkelig hyggelig aften.**	tak dɛ har værerdh ehn veerkerlee hewggerlee afdern

TELLING THE TIME, see page 14/DAYS OF THE WEEK, page 15

Shops, stores and services *Butikker og servicevirksomheder*

Where's the nearest...?	Hvor er den/det nærmeste...	voar ehr dehn/deht nærmerster
bakery	bager	bāer
bookshop	boghandel	bo°°hanerl
butcher's	slagter	slagderr
chemist's/drugstore	apotek	apotehk
dentist	tandlæge	tanlæer
department store	stormagasin	stoarmagaseen
grocery	købmand	køman
hairdresser's (ladies/men)	frisør (dame-/herre-)	freesør (damer-/hehrrer-)
newsagent's	bladhandler	bladhhanlerr
post office	posthus	posthoos
supermarket	supermarked	sōōbermarkerdh

General expressions *Almindelige udtryk*

Where's the main shopping area?	Hvor er forretningskvarteret?	voar er forrehtningskvartehrerdh
Do you have any...?	Har De nogen...?	har dee nōaern
Can you show me...?	Kan De vise mig...?	kan dee vēeser migh
this/that	det her/det der	dɛ hehr/dɛ dehr
Don't you have anything...?	Har De ikke noget...?	har dee igger nōaert
cheaper/better larger/smaller	billigere/dyrere større/mindre	beelēeerrer/dēwerrer størrer/mindrer
Can I try it on?	Kan jeg prøve den?	kan yigh prøver dehn
How much is this?	Hvad koster det?	vadh kosder dɛ
Please write it down.	Vær rar og skriv det ned.	vær rar oa skreev dɛ nedh
I don't want to spend more than... kroner.	Jeg vil ikke bruge mere end... kroner.	yigh veel igger brōōer mēhrer ehn ... krōanerr
No, I don't like it.	Det bryder jeg mig ikke om.	dɛ brewdherr yigh migh igger om
I'll take it.	Jeg tager det.	yigh tar dɛ
Do you accept credit cards?	Tager De kreditkort?	tar dee krehditkort
Can you order it for me?	Kan De bestille det til mig?	kan dee berstiler dɛ til migh

black	**sort**	soart
blue	**blå**	blaw
brown	**brun**	broon
green	**grøn**	grøn
orange	**orange**	oarangsher
red	**rød**	rødh
white	**hvid**	veedh
yellow	**gul**	gool
light...	**lyse-**	lewser-
dark...	**mørke-**	mørker-

I want to buy a/an/some...	**Jeg vil gerne have...**	yigh veel **gehr**ner ha
aspirin	**en æske aspirin**	ehn **æsg**er "aspirin"
bottle opener	**oplukker**	op**loog**ger
newspaper	**en avis**	ehn a**vees**
postcard	**et postkort**	eht **post**kort
shampoo	**en shampoo**	ehn "shampoo"
soap	**et stykke sæbe**	eht **stewg**ger **sæ**ber
toothpaste	**en tandpasta**	ehn **tan**pasta
half-kilo of tomatoes	**et halvt kilo tomater**	eht halt **kee**lo to**mad**err
a litre of milk	**en liter mælk**	ehn **lee**derr mælk
I'd like a film for this camera.	**Jeg vil gerne have en film til dette kamera.**	yigh vil **gehr**ner ha ehn film til **dehd**er **ka**merra

Souvenirs *Souvenirer*

antiques	**antikviteter**	anteekveet**ēd**err
ceramics	**keramik**	kehra**mēēk**
furniture	**møbler**	**mø̄**blerr
knitware	**strikvarer**	**streek**vārerr
shag-rug	**et rya-tæppe**	eht **rēw**ataiber

At the bank *I banken*

Where's the nearest currency exchange office/bank?	**Hvor er det nærmeste vekselkontor/bank?**	vōar ehr dɛ **nær**mersterr **vehk**serlkontōar/bank
I want to change some dollars/pounds.	**Jeg ønsker at veksle nogle dollars/pund.**	yigh **øns**gerr at **vehks**ler nōaler "dollars"/poon
I want to cash a traveller's cheque.	**Jeg ønsker at indløse en rejsecheck.**	yigh **øns**gerr at in**lø**ser ehn **righ**ser"cheque"

NUMBERS, see page 15

At the post office *Posthus*

I'd like to send this (by)...	Jeg vil gerne sende det her...	yigh veel **gehr**ner **sehn**er dε hehr
airmail	(med) luftpost	(mehdh) **looft**post
express	expres	**ehks**prehs
A ...-øre stamp, please.	Et ...-øres fri-mærke.	eht ... **ø**rers **free**mærker
What's the postage for a postcard/letter to Los Angeles?	Hvad er portoen for et postkort/brev til Los Angeles?	vadh ehr **porto**aern for eht **post**kort/breh°° til "Los Angeles"
Is there any post (mail) for me?	Er der noget post til mig?	ehr dehr **no**aert post til migh

Telephoning *Telefonering*

Where's the nearest telephone booth?	Hvor er den nær-meste telefonboks?	v**o**ar ehr dehn **nær**merster tehler**foan**boks
I'd like a telephone card.	Jeg vil gerne have et telet.	yigh veel **gehr**ner ha eht **teh**let
Hello. This is...	Hallo. Det er...	hal**loa** dε ehr
I'd like to speak to...	Jeg vil gerne tale med...	yigh veel **gehr**ner **tā**ler mehdh
When will he/she be back?	Hvornår kommer han/hun tilbage?	vor**nawr** k**o**amerr han/hoon til**bā**er

Time and date *Klokken og dato*

It's...	Den er...	dehn ehr
five past one	fem minutter over et	fehm mi**noo**derr o°°er eht
a quarter past three	kvart over tre	kvart o°°er treh
twenty past four	tyve minutter over fire	**tēw**ver mi**noo**derr o°°er **fēē**rer
half past six	halvsyv	**hal**sewv
twenty-five to seven	fem minutter over halvsyv	fehm mi**noo**derr o°°er **hal**sewv
ten to ten	ti minutter i ti	tee mi**noo**derr ee tee
twelve o'clock	tolv	toal
in the morning	om morgenen	om **mō**aernern
in the afternoon	om eftermiddagen	om **ehf**dermiddaern
at night	om natten	om **nad**dern
yesterday/today	i går/i dag	ee gawr/ee dai
tomorrow	i morgen	ee **mō**aern

| spring/summer | **forår/sommer** | forawr/**somerr** |
| autumn/winter | **efterår/vinter** | ehfderawr/**vinderr** |

Sunday	**søndag**	**søn**dai
Monday	**mandag**	**man**dai
Tuesday	**tirsdag**	**teer**sdai
Wednesday	**onsdag**	**oans**dai
Thursday	**torsdag**	**toars**dai
Friday	**fredag**	**freh**dai
Saturday	**lørdag**	**lør**dai
January	**januar**	**yan**ooar
February	**februar**	**fehb**rooar
March	**marts**	marts
April	**april**	a**preel**
May	**maj**	migh
June	**juni**	**yoo**nee
July	**juli**	**yoo**lee
August	**august**	ow**goost**
September	**september**	sehp**tehm**berr
October	**oktober**	ok**toa**berr
November	**november**	noa**vehm**berr
December	**december**	deh**sehm**berr

Numbers *Tal*

0	**nul**	nool
1	**en**	ehn
2	**to**	toa
3	**tre**	treh
4	**fire**	**feer**er
5	**fem**	fehm
6	**seks**	sehks
7	**syv**	sewv
8	**otte**	**oad**er
9	**ni**	nee
10	**ti**	tee
11	**elleve**	**ehl**ver
12	**tolv**	toal
13	**tretten**	**treh**dern
14	**fjorten**	**fyoar**dern
15	**femten**	**fehm**dern
16	**seksten**	**sighs**dern
17	**sytten**	**sew**dern
18	**atten**	**ad**dern
19	**nitten**	**need**dern
20	**tyve**	**tew**ver

21	**enogtyve**	ehnotewver
30	**tredive**	trehdhver
40	**fyrre**	førrer
50	**halvtreds**	haltrehs
60	**tres**	trehs
70	**halvfjerds**	halfyehrs
80	**firs**	feers
90	**halvfems**	halfehms
100/1000	**hundrede/tusind**	hoonrerdher/toosin
first	**første**	førsder
second	**anden/andet**	anern/anerdh
once/twice	**en gang/to gange**	ehn gang/toa ganger
a half	**en halv/et halvt**	ehn hal/eht halt

Emergency *Nødstilfælde*

Call the police	**Tilkald politiet**	tilkal politierdh
Get a doctor	**Tilkald læge**	tilkal læer
Go away	**Gå væk**	gaw vehk
HELP	**HJÆLP**	yehlp
I'm ill	**Jeg er syg**	yigh ehr sew
I'm lost	**Jeg er faret vild**	yigh ehr faarerdh veel
LOOK OUT	**GIV AGT**	giv agt
STOP THIEF	**STOP TYVEN**	stop tewvern
My... has been stolen.	**Min/Mit... er blevet stjålet.**	meen/meet... ehr bleh°°erdh styawlerdh
I've lost my...	**Jeg har tabt...**	yigh har tabt
handbag	**min håndtaske**	meen hawntasger
passport	**mit pas**	meet pas
wallet	**min tegnebog**	meen tighnerbo°°
Where can I find a doctor who speaks English?	**Hvor kan jeg finde en læge, der taler engelsk?**	voar kan yigh finner ehn læer dehr talerr ehngerlsk

Guide to Danish pronunciation *Udtale*

Consonants

Letter	Approximate pronunciation	Symbol	Example	
b, f, l, m, n, v	as in English			
c	1) like **s** in sit	c	**citron**	seetroan
	2) like **k** in kite			
d	1) like **th** in this	dh	**med**	mEdh
	2) as in English	d	**dale**	daler

g	1) as in go	g	**glas**	gals
	2) like **ch** in Scottish loch	y	**sige**	s$\bar{ee}$yer
hv	like **v** in view	v	**hvot**	v$\bar{o}$ar
j, hj	like **y** in yet	y	**ja**	y$\bar{æ}$
k	1) like **g** in go	g	**ikke**	igger
	2) like **k** in kite	k	**kaffe**	kahfer
p	1) like **b** in bit	b	**stoppe**	stobber
	2) like **p** in pill	p	**pude**	p$\bar{oo}$dher
r	pronounced in the back of the throat; otherwise often omitted	r	**rose**	r$\bar{o}$asser
s	always as in see	s	**skål**	skawl
sj	usually like **sh** in sheet	sh	**sjælden**	shehlern
t	1) like **d** in do	d	**lytte**	lewder
	2) like **t** in to (at the end of a word often mute)	t	**torsk**	toarsk

Vowels

a	1) long, like **a** in car	$\bar{a}$	**klare**	kl$\bar{a}$rer
	2) short, like **a** in cart	a	**hat**	hat
e	1) as **e** in the French les	$\bar{E}$	**flere**	fl$\bar{E}$rer
	2) short, like **i** in hit	E	**fedt**	fEt
	3) like **e** in met	eh	**let**	leht
	4) like **a** in above	er	**hjælpe**	yehlper
i	1) long, like **ee** in bee	$\bar{ee}$	**ile**	$\bar{ee}$ler
	2) short, between **a** in plate and **i** in pin	i	**drikke**	drigger
o	1) like the **oa** sound in boat, long or short	$\bar{oa}$	**pol**	p$\bar{oa}$
		oa	**bonde**	boaner
	2) short, like **o** in lot	o	**godt**	god
u	1) long, like **oo** in pool	$\bar{oo}$	**frue**	fr$\bar{oo}$er
	2) short, like **oo** in loot	oo	**nu**	noo
y	put your tongue in the position for the **ee** of bee, but round your lips as for the **oo** of pool, long or short	$\bar{ew}$	**nyde**	n$\bar{ew}$dher
		ew	**lytte**	lewder
æ	1) long, like **ai** in air	$\bar{æ}$	**sæbe**	s$\bar{æ}$ber
	2) short, like **e** in get	eh	**ægte**	ehgter
ø	put your lips together to whistle but make a noise with your voice instead; long or short	$\bar{ø}$	**frøken**	fr$\bar{ø}$gern
		ø	**øl**	øl
å	1) long, like **aw** in saw	$\bar{aw}$	**åben**	$\bar{aw}$bern
	2) short, like **o** in on	aw	**på**	paw

Dutch

Basic expressions *Enkele woorden en uitdrukkingen*

Yes/No.	**Ja/Nee.**	yaa/nay
Please.	**Alstublieft.**	ahlstew**bleeft**
Thank you.	**Dank u.**	dahnk ew
I beg your pardon?	**Wat zegt u?**	√aht zehkht ew

Introductions *Kennismaking*

Good morning.	**Goedemorgen.**	ghooder**mor**ghern
Good afternoon.	**Goedemiddag.**	ghooder**mid**dahkh
Good night.	**Goedenacht.**	ghooder**nahkht**
Hello/Hi.	**Hallo.**	hah**loa**
Good-bye.	**Tot ziens.**	tot seenss
My name is...	**Mijn naam is ...**	maiyn naam iss
Pleased to meet you.	**Prettig kennis te maken.**	preh tikh **keh**niss ter maakern
What's your name?	**Hoe heet u?**	hoo hayt ew
How are you?	**Hoe maakt u het?**	hoo maakt ew heht
Fine thanks.	**Uitstekend, dank u.**	ur^ew**t**staykernt dahnk ew
And you?	**En u?**	ehn ew
Where do you come from?	**Waar komt u vandaan?**	√aar komt ew vahn**daan**
I'm from...	**Ik kom uit ...**	ik kom ur^ew**t**
Australia	**Australië**	oa**straal**eeyer
Great Britain	**Groot-Brittannië**	groat brit**tah**neeyer
Canada	**Canada**	kahnaadaa
United States	**Verenigde Staten**	vehr**ayn**ergder **staa**tern
I'm with my...	**Ik ben met ...**	ik behn neht
wife	**mijn vrouw**	maiyn vro^ow
husband	**mijn man**	maiyn mahn
family	**mijn gezin**	maiyn gher**zin**
boyfriend	**mijn vriend**	maiyn vreent
girlfriend	**mijn vriendin**	maiyn vreen**din**
I'm on a business trip/vacation.	**Ik ben op zaken-reis/met vakantie.**	ik behn op **zaa**kernrayss/ meht vaa**kahn**see

GUIDE TO PRONUNCIATION, see page 31/EMERGENCIES, page 30

Questions *Vragen*

When?	**Wanneer/Hoe laat?**	√ah**nayr**/hoo laat
How?	**Hoe?**	hoo
What?/Why?	**Wat?/Waarom?**	√aht/√a**rom**
Who?	**Wie?**	√ee
Which?	**Welk/Welke?**	√ehlk/√**ehl**ker
Where is/are ...?	**Waar is/zijn ...?**	√aar iss/zaiyn
Where can I find/get ...?	**Waar kan ik ... vinden/krijgen?**	√aar kahn ik ... **vin**dern/**kraiy**ghern
How far?	**Hoever?**	hoo**vehr**
How long?	**Hoelang?**	hoo**lahng**
How much/many?	**Hoeveel?**	hoo**vayl**
Can I have ...?	**Mag ik ... hebben?**	mahk ik ... **heh**bern
Can you help me?	**Kunt u mij helpen?**	kurnt ew maiy **hehl**pern
What does this mean?	**Wat betekent dit?**	√aht ber**tay**kernt dit
I understand.	**Ik begrijp het.**	ik ber**ghraiyp** heht
I don't understand.	**Ik begrijp het niet.**	ik ber**ghraiyp** heht neet
Can you translate this for me?	**Kunt u dit voor mij vertalen?**	kurnt ew dit voar maiy verr**taal**ern
Do you speak English?	**Spreekt u Engels?**	spraykt ew **ehn**gerlss
I don't speak Dutch.	**Ik spreek geen Nederlands.**	ik sprayk ghayn **nay**derr**lahnts**

A few more useful words *Nog een paar nuttige woorden*

better/worse	**beter/slechter**	**bay**terr/**slehkh**terr
big/small	**groot/klein**	ghroat/klaiyn
cheap/expensive	**goedkoop/duur**	ghoot**koap**/dewr
early/late	**vroeg/laat**	vrookh/laat
good/bad	**goed/slecht**	ghoot/slehkht
hot/cold	**warm/koud**	√ahrm/ko^{ow}t
near/far	**dichtbij/ver**	dikht**baiy**/vehr
old/new	**oud/nieuw**	o^{ow}/nee^{oo}
open/shut	**open/dicht**	**oa**pern/dikht
right/wrong	**juist/verkeerd**	yur^{ew}st/verr**kayrt**
vacant/occupied	**vrij/bezet**	vraiy/ber**zeht**

Hotel–Accommodation *Hotel*

I have a reservation.	**Ik heb gereserveerd.**	ik hehp gherr**ray**zehrvayrt
We've reserved 2 rooms.	**Wij hebben 2 kamers gereserveerd.**	√aiy **heh**bern 2 **kaa**merrss gherr**ray**zehrvayrt
Do you have any vacancies?	**Hebt u nog kamers vrij?**	hehpt ew nokh **kaa**merrss vraiy
I'd like a...	**Ik wil graag een ...**	ik √il ghraakh ern
single room	**éénpersoonskamer**	**ayn**pehrsoanskaamerr
double room	**tweepersoons- kamer**	t√**ay**pehrsoanskammerr
with twin beds	**met lits-jumeaux**	meht lee-zhew**moa**
with a double bed	**met een twee- persoonsbed**	meht ern t√**ay**- pehrsoansbeht
with a bath/shower	**met badkamer/ douche**	meht **baht**kaamerr/doosh
We'll be staying...	**Wij blijven ...**	√aiy **blaiy**vern
overnight only	**alleen vannacht**	ah**layn** vahn**nahkht**
a few days	**een paar dagen**	ern paar **daa**ghern
a week	**een week**	ern √ayk
Is there a camp site near here?	**Is hier een kam- peerterrein in de buurt?**	iss heer ern kahm**payr**tehraiyn in der bewrt

Decision *Beslissing*

May I see the room?	**Mag ik de kamer zien?**	mahkh ik der **kaa**merr zeen
That's fine. I'll take it.	**Deze is prima. Die neem ik.**	**day**zer iss **pree**mah. dee naym ik
No. I don't like it.	**Nee. Die bevalt mij niet.**	nay. de ber**vahlt** maiy neet
It's too...	**Het is te ...**	heht iss ter
small	**klein**	klaiyn
noisy	**lawaaierig**	laa√aa**ee**yererrkh
Do you have anything...?	**Hebt u iets ...?**	hehpt ew eets
better/bigger	**beters/groters**	**bay**terrss/**ghroa**terrss
cheaper	**goedkopers**	ghoot**koa**perrss
quieter	**rustigers**	**rurs**tergherrss
May I have my bill, please?	**Mag ik mijn reken- ing, alstublieft?**	mahkh ik maiyn **ra**kerning ahlstew**bleeft**
It's been a very enjoyable stay.	**Het is een erg pret- tig verblijf geweest.**	heht iss ern ehrkh **preh**tikh verr**blaiyf** gher√**ayst**

DAYS OF THE WEEK, see page 29

Nederlands

Eating out *Uit eten*

I'd like to reserve a table for 4.	**Ik wil graag een tafel reserveren voor 4 personen.**	ik √il ghraakh ern **taafer**l rayzehr**vay**rern voar 4 pehr**soa**nern
We'll come at 8.	**Wij komen om 8 uur.**	√aiy **koa**mern om 8 ewr
I'd like...	**Ik wil graag...**	ik √il ghraakh
breakfast/lunch dinner	**ontbijt/koffietafel diner**	ont**bayt**/**kof**feetaaferl dee**nay**
What would you recommend?	**Wat kunt u aanbevelen?**	√aht kurnt ew **aan**bervaylern
Do you have any vegetarian dishes?	**Hebt u vegettarische gerechten**	hehpt ew vayghaytaareeser gher**rehkh**tern

Breakfast *Ontbijt*

May I have some...?	**Mag ik...hebben?**	mahkh ik...**heh**bern
bread	**brood**	broat
butter	**boter**	**boa**terr
cheese	**kaas**	kaass
ham and eggs	**ham en eieren**	hahm ehn **aiy**yerrern
jam	**jam**	zhehm
rolls	**een paar broodjes**	ern paar **broat**yers

Starters *Voorgerechten*

ansjovis	ahn**shoa**viss	anchovies
aspergepunten	ah**spehr**zherpurntern	asparagus tips
bitterballen	**bit**terbahlern	small breaded meat-balls
gevulde eieren	gher**vur**lder **aiy**yerrern	stuffed eggs

Soups *Soepen*

aardappelsoep	**aar**dahperlsoop	potato soup
bruine bonesoep	brur^(ew)ner **boa**nernsoop	thick kidney bean soup
bouillon	boo^(ee)**yon**	clear soup
met groenten	meht **ghroon**tern	with shredded vegetables
erwtensoep (met kluif)	**ehr**ternsoop (meht klur^(ew)f)	thick pea soup (with sausage)
groentesoep (met balletjes)	**ghroon**tersoop (meht **bah**lertyerss)	vegetable soup (with meat balls)
palingsoep	**paa**lingsoop	cream of eel
soep van de dag	soop vahn der dahkh	soup of the day
vissoep	**vis**soop	fish soup

NUMBERS, see page 30

Fish and seafood *Vis, schaal-en schelpdieren*

carp	**karper**	**kahr**perr
cod	**kabeljauw**	kahberlyo°ᵂ
crab	**krab**	krahp
eel	**paling**	**paa**ling
kipper	**bokking**	**bok**king
lobster	**kreeft**	krayft
mussels	**mosselen**	**mos**serlern
scampi	**(kleine) zeekreeft**	(**klay**ner) **zay**krayft

baked/fried	**gebakken**	gher**bah**kern
boiled	**gekookt**	gher**kookt**
grilled	**gegrild**	gher**ghrillt**
roasted	**gebraden**	gher**braa**dern
stewed	**gestoofd**	gher**stoaft**
underdone (rare)	**niet gaar/rood**	neet ghaar/roat
medium	**net gaar gebakken**	neht ghaar gher**bah**kern
well-done	**doorgebakken**	**doar**gher**bah**kern

Meat *Vlees*

I'd like some...	**Ik wil graag ... hebber.**	ik vil ghraakh ...**heh**bern
beef/lamb	**rundvlees/lamvlees**	**rurnt**vlayss/**lahm**svlayss
chicken/duck	**kip/eend**	kip/aynt
pork	**varkensvlees**	**vahr**kernsvlayss
veal	**kalfsvlees**	**kahlfs**vlayss
hete bliksem	hay**ter blik**serm	potato, bacon and apple dish
jachtschotel	**yahkht**skhoaterl	meat casserole
rijsttafel	**raiyst**taaferl	Indonesian rice table
zuurkool	**zewr**koal	sauerkraut

Vegetables *Groenten*

beans	**bonen**	**boa**nern
cabbage	**kool**	koal
carrots	**worteltjes**	**√or**terltyerss
cauliflower	**bloemkool**	**bloom**koal
mushrooms	**champignons**	shahm**pee**ñonss
onions	**uien**	**ur**ᵉᵂyern
peas	**doperwtjes**	**dop**ehrrtyerss
potatoes	**aardappelen**	**aard**ahperlern
tomatoes	**tomaten**	to**aa**tern

Fruit and dessert *Vruchten en nagerechten*

apple	**apple**	ahperl
banana	**banaan**	baanaan
cherries	**kersen**	kehrsern
lemon	**citroen**	seetroon
orange	**sinaasappel**	seenaasahperl
pear	**peer**	payr
strawberries	**aardbeien**	aartbaiyyern
broodschoteltje	**broats**khoaterltyer	bread pudding
flensjes	**flehn**syerss	thin pancakes
Haagse bluf	**haagh**ser blurf	whipped egg white dessert
ijs	aiyss	ice cream
rijstebrijpudding	raiyster**braiy**purding	rice pudding

Drinks *Dranken*

beer	**biertje/pils**	**beert**yer/pilss
(hot) chocolate	**warme chocolade**	√ahrmer shoakoa**laa**dermehlk
	melk	
coffee	**koffie**	**koffee**
a pot	**een potje**	ern **pot**yer
with cream	**met room**	meht roam
fruit juice	**vruchtesap**	vrurkh**ter**sahp
milk	**melk**	mehlk
mineral water	**mineraalwater**	meenerraal√aaterr
tea	**thee**	tay
wine	**wijn**	√aiyn
red/white	**rood/wit**	roat/√it

Complaints and paying *Klachten en de rekening*

This is too...	**Dis is te...**	dit iss ter
bitter/sweet	**bitter/zoet**	**bitt**err/zoot
That's not what I ordered.	**Dit heb ik niet besteld.**	dit hehp ik neet ber**stehlt**
I'd like to pay.	**Ik wil graag betalen.**	ik √il graakh ber**taal**ern
I think there's a mistake in this bill.	**Ik geloof dat er een vergissing is in deze rekening.**	ik gher**loaf** daht ehr ern verr**ghiss**ing iss in **day**zer **ray**kerning
Can I pay with this credit card?	**Kan ik met deze credit card betalen?**	kahn ik meht **day**zer "credit card" ber**taal**ern
We enjoyed it, thank you.	**Wij hebben genoten, dank u.**	√aiy **heh**bern gher**noat**ern dahnk ew

NUMBERS, see page 30

Nederlands

DUTCH

Travelling around *Rondreizen*

Plane *Vliegtuig*

Is there a flight to...?	**Is er een vlucht naar...?**	iss ehr ern vlurkht naar
What time should I check in?	**Hoe laat moet ik inchecken?**	hoo laat moot ik **in**shehkern
I'd like to... my reservation.	**Ik wil graag mijn reservering...**	ik √il ghraakh maiyn rayzehr**vay**ring
cancel	**annuleren**	ahnew**lay**rern
change	**veranderen**	ver**rahn**derrern
confirm	**bevestigen**	ber**veh**sterghern

Train *Trein*

I'd like a ticket to...	**Ik wil graag een naar...**	ik √il ghraakh ern **kaar**tyer naar
single (one-way)	**enkele reis**	**ehn**kerler raiyss
return (roundtrip)	**retour**	rer**toor**
first/second class	**eerste/tweede klas**	**ayr**ster/t√**ay**der klahss
How long does the journey take?	**Hoelahng duurt de rit?**	hoo**lahng** dewrt der rit
When is the... train to...	**Wanneer gaat de... train naar...**	√ah**nayr** ghaat der...trayn naar
first	**eerste**	**ayr**ster
last	**laatste**	**laat**ster
next	**volgende**	**vol**ghernder
Is this the train to...?	**Is dit de trein naar...?**	iss dit der traiyn naar

Bus–Tram (streetcar) *Bus–Tram*

Which tram goes to the town centre?	**Welke tram rijdt naar het stads-centrum?**	**veh**lker trehm raiyt naar heht **stahts**sehntrurm
How much is the fare to...?	**Hoeveel kost het naar...?**	hoo**vayl** kost heht naar
Will you tell me when to get off?	**Wilt u mij zeggen wanneer ik moet uitstappen?**	√ilt ew maiy **zeh**ghern √ah**nayr** ik moot ur**ew**tstahpern

TELLING THE TIME, see page 29

Nederlands

Taxi *Taxi*

Take me to this address.	**Brengt u mij naar dit adresa.**	brehngt ew maiy naar dit aadrehss
Please stop here.	**Wilt u hier stoppen, alstublieft.**	√ilt ew heer **stop**pern ahlstew**bleeft**
Could you wait for me?	**Kunt u op mij wachten, alstublieft?**	kurnt ew op maiy √ahkh**tern** ahlstew**bleeft**

Car hire (rental) *Autoverhuur*

I'd like to hire (rent) a car.	**Ik wil graag een auto huren.**	ik √il ghraakh ern o^ow^toa **hew**rern
I'd like it for...	**Ik wil het graag voor...**	ik √il heht ghraakh voar
a day	**een dag**	ern dahkh
a week	**een week**	ern √ayk
Where's the nearest filling station?	**Waar is het dichtstbijzijnde benzinestation?**	√aar iss heht dikhstbaiy-zaiynder behn**zee**ner stah**syon**
Fill it up, please.	**Vol, alstublieft.**	vol ahlstew**bleeft**
Give me... litres of petrol (gasoline).	**Geeft u mij... liter benzine.**	ghayft ew maiy... **lee**terr behn**zee**ner
How do I get to this place/this address?	**Hoe kom ik naar deze plaats/it adres?**	hoo kom ik naar **day**zer plaats/dit **aa**drehss
I've had a breakdown at...	**Ik sta met autopech bij...**	ik staa meht o^ow^toapehkh baiy
Can you send a mechanic?	**Kunt u een monteur sturen?**	kurnt ew ern montu**rr** **stew**rern
Can you mend this puncture (fix this flat)?	**Kunt u deze lekke band repareren?**	kurnt ew **day**zer **leh**ker bahnt raypaa**ray**rern

---

U bent op de verkeerde weg.	You're on the wrong road.
U moet rechtdoor riden.	Go straight ahead.
Het is daarginds...	It's down there on the...
links/rechts	left/right
tegenover/achter...	opposite/behind...
naast/na...	next to/after...
noord/zuid/oost/west	north/south/east/west

NUMBERS/EMERGENCIES, see page 30

Sightseeing *Sightseeing*

Where's the tourist office?	**Waar is het ver-keersbureau?**	√aar iss heht verr**kayrs**bewroa
Is there an English-speaking guide?	**Is er een Engels-sprekende gids?**	iss ehr ern **ehng**erls-spraykernder ghits
Where is/are …?	**Waar is/zijn …?**	√aar iss/zaiyn
art museum	**het museum voor beeldende kunst**	heht mew**zay**yurm voar **bayl**dernder kurnst
castle	**het kasteel**	heht kah**stayl**
cathedral/church	**de kathedraal/kerk**	der kahter**draal**/kehrk
city centre	**het (stads) centrum**	heht (**stahts**)sehntrurm
museum	**het museum**	heht mew**zay**yurm
What are the opening hours?	**Wat zijn de openingstijden?**	√aht zaiyn der **oa**pernings-taiydern

Relaxing *Ontspanning*

What's playing at the … Theatre?	**Wat wordt er in het … Theater gespeeld?**	√aht √ort ehr in heht … tay**aa**terr gher**spaylt**
Are there any seats for tonight?	**Zijn er nog plaatsen voor vanavond?**	zaiyn ehr nokh **plaat**sern voar vahn**aa**vont
Would you like to go out with me tonight?	**Hebt u zin om vanavond met mij uit te gaan?**	hehpt ew zin om vahn**aa**vont meht maiy ur^{ew}t ter ghaan
Would you like to dance?	**Wilt u dansen?**	√ilt ew **dahn**sern
Thank you, it's been a wonderful evening.	**Dank u, het was een heerlijke avond.**	dahnk ew heht √ahss ern **hayr**lerker **aa**vont

Shops, stores and services *Winkels en diensten*

Where's the nearest …?	**Waar is de/het dichtstbijzinde …?**	√aar iss der/heht dikhtstbaiy**zaiyn**der
bakery	**de bakker**	der **bahk**err
bookshop	**de boekhandel**	der **book**handerl
chemist's/drugstore	**de apotheek**	der ahpoa**tayk**
department store	**het warenhuis**	heht √aarern**hur**^{ew}ss
grocery	**de kruidenier**	der krur^{ew}**der**neer
hairdresser	**de kapper**	der **kah**perr
newsagent	**de krantenkiosk**	der **krahn**ternkeeyosk
post office	**het postkantoor**	heht **post**kahntoar
supermarket	**de supermarkt**	der **sew**perrmahrkt
toilets	**de toiletten**	der t√aa**leh**tern

General expressions *Algemene uitdrukkingen*

Where's the main shopping area?	**Waar is de winkelbuurt?**	√aar iss der √inkerlbewrt
Do you have any...?	**Hebt u...?**	hehpt ew
Don't you have anything...?	**Hebt u niet iets...?**	hehpt ew neet eets
cheaper/better	**goedkopers/beters**	ghoot**koa**perrss/**bay**terrss
larger/smaller	**groters/kleiners**	**ghroa**terrss/**klaiy**nerrss
Can I try it on?	**Kan ik het aanpassen?**	kahn ik heht **aan**pahssern
How much is this?	**Hoeveel Kost dit?**	hoo**vahl** kost dit
No, I don't like it.	**Nee, het bavalt mij niet.**	nay heht ber**vahlt** maiy neet
I'll take it.	**Ik neem dit.**	ik naym dit
Do you accept credit cards?	**Neemt u credit cards aan?**	naymt ew "credit cards" aan

black	**zwart**	z√ahrt
blue	**blauw**	blo^ow
brown	**bruin**	brur^ewn
green	**groen**	ghroon
orange	**oranje**	oarahñer
red	**rood**	roat
white	**wit**	√it
yellow	**geel**	ghayl
light...	**licht...**	likht
dark...	**donker...**	**don**kerr

I want to buy...	**Ik wil graag... kopen.**	ik √il ghraakh... **koa**pern
aspirin	**aspirine**	ahspee**ree**ner
newspaper	**een krant**	ern krahnt
postcard	**een briefkaart**	ern **breef**kaart
shampoo	**shampoo**	**shahm**poa
toothpaste	**tandpasta**	**tahnt**pahstaa
half-kilo of tomatoes	**een pond/halve kilo tomaten**	ern pont/**hahl**ver **kee**loa toa**maa**tern
litre of milk	**een liter melk**	ern **lee**terr mehlk
I'd like a... film for this camera.	**Ik wil graag een... film voor dit toestal.**	ik √il ghraakh ern... film voar dit **too**stehl
black and white	**zwart-wit**	z√ahrt-√it
colour	**kleuren**	**klur**rern

NUMBERS, see page 30

Souvenirs *Souvenirs*

I'd like a/some...	**Ik wil graag...**	ik vil ghraakh
(tulip) bulbs	**(tulpen) bollen**	(turlpern) bollern
china	**porselein**	porserrlaiyn
clogs	**klompen**	klompern
lace	**kant**	kahnt
miniature windmill	**miniatuur molen**	meeneeyaatewr moalern

At the bank *Bank*

Where's the nearest bank/currency exchange office	**Waar is de dichtst-bijzijnde bank/ wisselkantoor?**	vaar iss der dikhtst-baiyzaiynder bahnk/ visserlkahntoar
I want to change some dollars/pounds.	**Ik wil graag dollars/ponden wisselen.**	ik vil ghraakh dollahrss/pondern visserlern
I want to cash a traveller's cheque.	**Ik wil graag een reischeque wisselen.**	ik vil ghraakh ern raiysshehk visserlern

At the post office *Postkantoor*

I'd like to send this by...	**Ik wil dit graag... verzenden.**	ik vil dit ghraakh verrzehndern
airmail	**per luchtpost**	pehr lurkhtpost
express	**per expresse**	pehr ehksprehss
A...-cent stamp, please.	**Een postzegel van... cent, alstublieft.**	ern postzaygherl vahn... sehnt ahlstewbleeft
What's the postage for a letter/postcard to Los Angeles?	**Hoeveel port moet er op ern brief naar Los Angeles?**	hoovayl port moot ehr op een breef naar "los angeles"
Is there any post/ mail for me?	**Is er post voor mij?**	iss ehr post voar maiy

Telephoning *Telefoneren*

Where's the nearest telephone booth?	**Waar is de dichtst-bijzinde telefoon-cel?**	vaar iss der dikhtst-baiyzaiynder taylerfoan-sehl
Hello. This is...	**Hallo. U spreekt met...**	hahloa. ew spraykt meht
I'd like to speak to...	**Ik wil graag... spreken.**	ik vil ghraakh ...spraykern
When will he/she be back?	**Wanneer komt hij/zij terug?**	vahnayr komt haiy/zaiy terrurkh

Days and date *Dagen en datum*

It's...	Het is...	heht iss
five past one	**vijf over een**	vaif **oa**verr ayn
quarter past three	**kwart over drie**	kv/ahrt **oa**verr dree
twenty past four	**tien voor half vijf/**	teen voar hahlf vaiyf/
	twintig over vier	t√interkh **oa**verr veer
half-past six	**half zeven**	hahlf **zay**vern
twenty-five to seven	**vijf over half zeven**	vaiyf **oa**verr hahlf **zay**vern
ten to ten	**tien voor tien**	teen voar teen
noon/midnight	**'s middags/'s**	**smid**dahkhss/**snahkhss**
	nachts	
in the morning	**'s morgens**	**smor**ghernss
in the afternoon	**'s middags**	**smid**dahkhss
in the evening	**'s avonds**	**saa**vontss
during the day	**overdag**	oaverr**dahkh**
at night	**'s nachts**	snahkhts
yesterday	**gisteren**	**ghis**terrern
today	**vandaag**	vahn**daakh**
tomorrow	**morgen**	**mor**ghern
spring/summer	**lente/zomer**	**lehn**ter/**zoa**merr
autumn/winter	**herfst/winter**	**hehrfst/√in**terr

Sunday	**zondag**	**zon**dahkh
Monday	**maandag**	**maan**dahkh
Tuesday	**dinsdag**	**dins**dahkh
Wednesday	**woensdag**	√**oons**dahkh
Thursday	**donderdag**	**don**derrdahkh
Friday	**vrijdag**	**vraiy**dahkh
Saturday	**zaterdag**	**zaa**terrdahkh
January	**abuari**	yahnew√**aari**
February	**februari**	fabrew√**aari**
March	**maart**	maart
April	**april**	ah**pril**
May	**mei**	maiy
June	**juni**	**yew**nee
July	**juli**	**yew**lee
August	**augustus**	oᵒʷ**ghur**sturss
September	**september**	sehp**tehm**berr
October	**oktober**	ok**toa**berr
November	**november**	noa**vehm**berr
December	**december**	day**sehm**berr

NUMBERS, see page 30

Numbers *Getallen*

0	**nul**	nurl
1	**een**	ayn
2	**twee**	t√ay
3	**drie**	dree
4	**vier**	veer
5	**vijf**	vaif
6	**zes**	zehss
7	**zeven**	**zay**vern
8	**acht**	ahkht
9	**negen**	**nay**ghern
10	**tien**	teen
11	**elf**	ehlf
12	**twaalf**	t√aalf
13	**dertien**	**dehr**teen
14	**veertien**	**vayr**teen
15	**vijftien**	**vaiyf**teen
16	**zestien**	**zeh**steen
17	**zeventien**	**zay**vernteen
18	**achttien**	**ahkh**teen
19	**negentien**	**nay**gherteen
20	**twintig**	t√interkh
30	**dertig**	**dehr**terkh
40	**veertig**	**vayr**terkh
50	**vijftig**	**vaiyf**terkh
60	**zestig**	**zeh**sterkh
70	**zeventig**	**zay**vernterkh
80	**tachtig**	**tahkh**terkh
90	**negentig**	**nay**gherterkh
100	**honderd**	**hon**derrt
1,000	**duizend**	**dur**ᵂzernt
first	**eersste**	**ayr**ster
second	**tweede**	t√ayder
once/twice	**eenmaal/tweemaal**	**ayn**maal/t√aymaal
a half	**een helft**	ern hehlft

Emergency *In geval van nood*

Call the police	**Roep de politie**	roop der poa**leet**see
Get a doctor	**Roep een dokter**	roop ern **dokt**err
Go away	**Ga weg**	ghaa √ehkh
HELP	**HELP**	hehlp
I'm ill	**Ik ben ziek**	ik behn zeek
I'm lost	**Ik ben verdwaald**	ik behn verrd√aalt
LOOK OUT	**PAS OP**	pahss op
STOP THIEF	**HOUD DE DIEF**	hoᵒ der deef

TELEPHONING, see page 28

Nederlands

My . . . has been stolen.	**Mijn . . . is gestolen.**	maiyn . . . iss gher**stoa**lern
I've lost my . . .	**Ik heb . . . verloren.**	ik hehp . . . verr**loa**rern
handbag	**mijn handtas**	maiyn **hahn**ttahss
wallet	**mijn portefeuille**	maiyn porter**fur**^{ew}yer
passport	**mijn paspoort**	maiyn **pahs**poort
luggage	**mijn bagage**	maiyn baa**ghaa**zher
Where can I find a doctor who speaks English?	**Waar kan ik een dokter vinen die Engels spreekt?**	√aar kahn ik ern **dok**terr **vin**dern dee **ehng**erlss spraykt

Guide to Dutch pronunciation *Uitspraak*

Consonants

Letter	Approximate pronunciation	Symbol	Example	
f, h, k, l, m, n, p, q, t, u, v, y, z	as in English			
b	as in but; at the end of a word, like p in cup	b p	**ben** **hep**	behn hehp
c	1) like k in keen	k	**inclusief**	inklew**seef**
	2) before e, i, like s in sit	s	**ceintuur**	sehn**tewr**
ch	1) like ch in loch	kh	**nacht**	nahkht
	2) like sh in shut	sh	**cheque**	shehk
d	as in English, but, at the end of a word, like t in hit	d t	**doe** **avond**	doo aa**vont**
g	1) like ch in loch	kh	**deeg**	daykh
	2) like s in pleasure	zh	**genie**	zher**nee**
	3) like a softer voiced version of ch in loch	gh	**groot** **zagen**	ghroat **zaa**ghern
j	1) like y in yes	y	**ja**	yaa
	2) like s in leisure	zh	**jumeaux**	zhew**mo**^{ow}
nj	like ñ in Spanish señor	ñ	**oranje**	oarah**ñ**er
r	always trilled	r	**warm**	√ahrm
sj, stj	like sh in shut	sh	**misje**	maiy**sh**er
th	like t in tea	t	**thee**	tay
tj	like ty in hit you	ty	**katje**	**kah**tyer
v	as in English, but often sounds like f	v	**hoeveel** **van**	hoo**vay** vahn
w	like English v, but with the bottom lip raised	√	**water**	√**aa**terr

Vowels

a	1) when short, between a in cat and u in cut	ah	kat	kaht
	2) when long, like a in cart	aa	vader	vaaderr
e	1) short, like e in bed	eh	bed	beht
	2) long, like a in late	ay	zee	zay
	3) like er in other	er	zitten	zittern
eu	like ur in fur, but pronounced with rounded lips	ur	deur	durr
i	1) short, like i in bit	i	kink	kint
	2) when long (also spelt ie), like ee in bee	ee	zien	zeen
	3) like er in other	er	monnik	monnerk
ij	sometimes, like er in other	er	lelijk	laylerk
o	1) when short, like a very short version of aw in lawn	o	pot	pot
	2) when long, something like oa in road	oa	boot	boat
oe	(long) like oo in moon and well rounded	oo	hoe	hoo
u	1) when short, like ur in hurt, with rounded lips	ur	bus	burss
	2) when long, like u in French sur; say ee, and, without moving your tongue, round your lips	ew	nu	new

Diphthongs

ai	like igh in sigh	igh	ai	igh
ei, ij	between a in late and igh in sigh	aiy	reis	raiyss
			ijs	aiyss
au, ou	like ow in now	o^ow^	koud	ko^ow^t
ieuw	like ee in free, followed by a short oo sound	ee^oo^	nieuw	nee^oo^
ui	like ur in hurt followed by a Dutch u sound, as described in u 2), but shorter	ur^ew^	huis	hur^ew^ss
uw	like the sound described in u 2), followed by a weak oo sound	ew^oo^	duw	dew^oo^

Finnish

Basic expressions *Perusilmaisut*

Yes/No.	**Kyllä/Ei.**	kewllæ/ay^i
Please.	**Olkaa hyvä.**	oalkaa hewvæ
Thank you.	**Kiitos.**	keetoass
I beg your pardon?	**Anteeksi?**	ahntāȳksi

Introductions *Esittely*

Good morning.	**(Hyvää) huomenta.**	(hewvāȳ) h°amayntah
Good afternoon.	**(Hyvää) päivää.**	(hewvāȳ) pæ^įvāȳ
Good night.	**Hyvää yötä.**	hewvāȳ ^ewurtæ
Good-bye.	**Näkemiin.**	nækaymeen
Hello/Hi!	**Hei/Terve!**	hay^i/**tayr**vay
My name is...	**Nimeni on...**	nimmayni oan
What's your name?	**Mikä teidän nimenne on?**	mikkæ tay^idæn nimmaynnay oan
Pleased to meet you.	**Hauska tutustua.**	hah°°skah tootoostooah
How are you?	**Mitä kuuluu?**	mittæ kōōlōō
Very well, thanks. And you?	**Kiitos, hyvää. Entä sinulle?**	keetoass hewvāȳ. ayntæ sinnoollay
Where do you come from?	**Mistä päin tulette?**	mistæ pæ^in toolayttay
I'm from...	**Olen...-sta/...-lta**	oalayn...-stah/...-ltah
Australia	**Australia**	ah°°straaliah
Canada	**Kanada**	kahnahdah
Great Britain	**Iso-Britannia**	isoa-britahnniah
United States	**USA (Yhdysvallat)**	ōōæssaa (ewhdewsvahllaht)
I'm with my...	**Minulla on mukana...**	minnoollah oan mookahnah
wife	**vaimo**	vah^imoa
husband	**aviomies**	ahvioam^iays
family	**perhe**	payrhay
boyfriend	**poikaystävä**	poa^kahewstævæ
girlfriend	**tyttöystävä**	tewtturewstævæ
I'm here on business/ vacation.	**Olen täällä liike/ lomalla.**	oalayn tāȳllæ leekay/ loamahllah

GUIDE TO PRONUNCIATION/EMERGENCIES, see page 47

Questions *Kysymyksiä*

When?/How?	**Milloin?/Kuinka?**	milloa'n/koo'nkah
What?/Why?	**Mitä?/Miksi?**	mittæ/miksi
Who?	**Kuka?**	kookah
Which?	**Mikä?/Kumpi?**	mikkæ/koompi
Where is/are...?	**Missä on/ovat...?**	missæ oan/oavaht
Where can I find/ get...?	**Mistä löydän...?**	mistæ lur^{ew}dæn
How far?	**Kuinka kaukana?**	koo'nkah kah^{oo}kanah
How long (time)?	**Kuinka kauan?**	koo'nkah kah^{oo}ahn
How much/many?	**Kuinka paljon/ monta?**	koo'nkah pahlyoan/ moantah
Can I have...?	**Saanko...?**	saahnkoa
Can you help me?	**Voitteko auttaa minua?**	voa'ttaykoa ah^{oo}ttaa minnooah
What does this/that mean?	**Mitä tämä/tuo tarkoittaa?**	mittæ tæmæ/t^{oo}oa tahrkoa'ttaa
I understand.	**Ymmärrän.**	ewmmærræn
I don't understand.	**En ymmärrä.**	ayn ewmmærræ
Can you translate this for us?	**Voitteko kääntää tämän meille?**	voa'ttaykoa kææntææ tæmæn may'llay
Do you speak English?	**Puhutteko englantia?**	poohoottaykoa aynglahntiah
I don't speak (much) Finnish.	**En puhu (paljon) suomea.**	ayn poohoo (pahlyoan) s^{oo}oamayah

A few more useful words *Muutama hyödyllinen sana lisää*

better/worse	**parempi/huonompi**	pahraympi/h^{oo}oanoampi
big/small	**suuri/pieni**	soori/p'ayni
cheap/expensive	**halpa/kallis**	hahlpah/kahlliss
early/late	**aikainen/myöhäinen**	ah'ka'nayn/m^{ew}urhæ'nayn
good/bad	**hyvä/huono**	hewvæ/h^{oo}oanoa
hot/cold	**kuuma/kylmä**	kōōmah/kewlmæ
near/far	**lähellä/kaukana**	læhayllæ/kah^{oo}kahnah
right/wrong	**oikea/väärä**	oa'kaya/væræ
vacant/occupied	**vapaa/varattu**	vahpaa/vahrahttoo

Hotel—Accommodation *Hotelli*

I have a reservation.	Minulla on varaus.	minnoollah oan vahra°°s
We've reserved 2 rooms.	Olemme varanneet kaksi huonetta.	oalaymmay vahrahnnayt kahksi h°°oanayttah
Do you have any vacancies?	Onko teillä vapaita huoneita?	oankoa tay'llæ vahpah'tah h°°oanay'tah
I'd like a...	Haluaisin...	hahlooah'sin
single room	yhden hengen huoneen	ewhdayn hayngayn h°°oanāyn
double room	kahden hengen huoneen	kahhdayn hayngayn h°°oanāyn
with twin beds	jossa on kaksi vuodetta	yaossah oan kahksi v°°oadayttah
with a double bed	jossa on kaksoisvuode	yaossah oan kahksoa'sv°°oaday
with a bath	jossa on kylpyhuone	yaossah oan kewlpewh°°oanay
with a shower	jossa on suihku	yaossah oan soo'hkoo
We'll be staying...	Viivymme...	veevewmmay
overnight only	vain yhden yön	vah'n ewhdayn ᵉʷurn
a few days	muutamia päiviä	mōōtahmiah pæ'viæ
a week	viikon	veekoan
Is there a camp site near here?	Onko lähellä leirin-täaluetta?	oankoa læhayllæ lay'rintæahlooayttah

Decision *Päätös*

May I see the room?	Saanko nähdä huoneen?	saankoa næhdæ h°°oanāyn
That's fine. I'll take it.	Tämä on hyvä. Otan sen.	tæmæ oan hewvæ. oatahn sayn
No. I don't like it.	Ei. En pidä siitä.	ay' ayn pidæ seettæ
It's too...	Se on liian...	say oan leeahn
dark/small	pimeä/pieni	pimm°ʸæ/p'ayni
Do you have anything...?	Onko teillä mitään...?	oankoa tay'llæ mittæn
better	parempaa	pahraympaa
bigger	suurempaa	sōōraympaa
cheaper	halvempaa	hahlvaympaa
quieter	rauhallisempaa	rah°°hahllissaympaa
May I have my bill?	Saisinko laskuni.	sah'sinkoa lahskooni
It's been a very enjoyable stay.	Olen viihtynyt eri-nomaisesti.	oalayn veehtewnewt ayrinoamah'saysti

NUMBERS, see page 46

Eating out *Ravintolat*

I'd like to reserve a table for 4.	Varaisin pöydän neljälle.	vahrahisin p^wewdæn naylijællay
We'll come at 8.	Tulemme kello 8.	toolaymmay kaylloa kahhdayksahn
I'd like breakfast/ lunch/dinner.	Saisinko aamiaisen/lounas/päivällinen.	sah'sinkoa aamiah'ssayn/ loa°°nahss/pæⁱvællinnayn
What do you recommend?	Mitä suosittelisitte?	mittæ s°°oasittaylissittay
Do you have any vegetarian dishes?	Onko teillä kasvissyöjän annoksia?	oankoa tay'llæ kahsvissew^wyæn ahnnoaksiah

Breakfast *Aamiainen*

I'd like...	Saisinko...	sah'sinkoa
bread/butter	leipää/voita	lay'pææ/voa'tah
cheese	juustoa	y°°stoaah
eggs	munia	mooniah
ham and eggs	kinkkua ja munia	kinkkooah yah mooniah
jam/rolls	hilloa/sämpylöitä	hilloah/sæampewlur'tæ

Starters (Appetizers) *Alkuruokia*

kaviaaria	kahv'aariah	caviar
leikkeleitä	lay'kkaylaytæ	cold meats
lohta	loahtah	salmon
mätiä	mætiæ	roe
parsaa	pahrsaa	asparagus
poronkieltä	poaroank'ayltæ	reindeer tongue
silakoita	sillahkoa'tah	Baltic herring

baked	uunissa paistettu	ōōnissah pah'stayttoo
boiled	keitetty	kay'tayttew
fried/grilled	paistettu/grillattu	pah'stayttoo/grillahttoo
roast	paahdettu	paahdayttoo
stewed	muhennokseksi keitetty	moohaynnoaksayksi kay'tayttew
underdone (rare)	puolikypsä	p°°oalikewpsæ
medium	keski-kypsä	kayski-kewpsæ
well-done	hyvin/kypsäksi paistettu	hewvin/kewpsæksi pah'stayttoo

Meat *Liharuokia*

beef	naudanlihaa	nah°°dahnlihaa
chicken/duck	kana/ankka	kahna/ahnkkah
lamb	lammasta	lahmmahstah
pork	porsaanlihaa	poarsaanlihaa
veal	vasikanlihaa	vahsikkahnlihaa
hirvenliha	hirvaynlihah	elk
karhunpaisti	kahrhoonpah'sti	bear steak
palapaisti	pahlahpah'sti	beef ragout
piparjuuriliha	pippahyōōrilihah	boiled beef with horse-radish sauce
poronkäristys	poaronkæristewss	sautéed reindeer stew
poronliha	poaroanlihah	reindeer meat

Vegetables and salads *Vihanneksia ja salaatteja*

beans	pavut	pahvoot
cabbage	kaali	kaali
carrots	porkkanat	poarkkahnaht
cauliflower	kukkakaali	kookkahkaali
lettuce	lehtisalaatti	layhtisahlaatti
mushrooms	sieni	šayni
onions	sipulit	sippoolit
peas	herneit	hayrnāyt
potatoes	perunat	payroonaht
tomatoes	tomaatit	toamaattit
hapankaalisalaatti	hahpahnkaalisahlaatti	sauerkraut salad
perunalaatikko	payroonahlaatikkoa	potato bake
pinaattiohukaiset	pinnaattioahookah'sayt	spinach pancakes
porkkanaohukaiset	poarkkahnahoa-hookah'sayt	carrot pancakes
rosolli	roasoalli	beetroot salad with salt herring

Fruit and desserts *Hedelmiä ja jälkiruokia*

apple	omena	oamaynah
banana	banaani	bahnaani
cherries	kirsikat	keersikkaht
lemon	sitruuna	sitrōōnah
orange	appelsiini	ahppaylseeni
peach	persikka	payrsikkah
pear	päärynä	pærewnæ
plums	luumut	lōōmoot
strawberries	mansikat	mahnsikkaht

FINNISH

38

jäätelö	yäetaylur	ice-cream
marengit	mahrayngit	meringues
mustikkapiirakka	moostikkahpeerahkkah	bilberry pie
omenapiirakka	oamaynahpeerahkah	apple pie
suklaakakku	sooklaakahkkoo	chocolate cake
vohvelit	voahvaylit	waffles

Drinks Juomia

beer	olut	oaloot
(hot) chocolate	kaakao	kaahkahoa
coffee	kahvi	kahhvi
black	mustana	moostahnah
with milk	maidon kanssa	mah'doan kahnssah
fruit juice	hedelmämehu	haydaylmæmayhoo
milk	maito	mah'to
mineral water	mineraalivesi	minnayraalivaysi
sugar	sokeria	soakayriah
tea	tee	tāy
wine	viini	veeni
red/white	puna/valko	poonah/vahlkoa

Complaints—Bill (check) Valituksia—Lasku

This is too ...	Tämä on liian...	tæmæ oan leeahn
bitter/salty	kitkerää/suolaista	kitkayræ/s°°alah'stah
sweet	makeaa	mahkayaa
That's not what I ordered.	Tämä ei ole sitä, mitä tilasin.	tæmæ ay' oalay sittæ mittæ tillahsin
I'd like to pay.	Haluaisin maksaa.	hahlooah'sin mahksaa
I think there's a mistake in this bill.	Tässä laskussa taitaa olla virhe.	tæssæ lahskoossah tah'taa oallah veerhay
Is everything included?	Sisältyykö siihen kaikki?	sissæltēwkur seehayn kah'kki
Can I pay with this credit card?	Voinko maksaa tällä luottokortilla?	voa'nkoa mahksaa tællæ l°°attoakoartilla
We enjoyed it, thank you.	Kiitos, pidimme siitä kovasti.	keetoass piddimmay seetæ koavahsti

NUMBERS, see page 46

Suomi

Travelling around *Kulkuneuvot*

Plane *Lento*

Is there a flight to Ivalo?	**Onko lentoa Ivaloon?**	oankoa **layn**toah ivvahl**oa**n
What time should I check in?	**Mihin aikaan minun on ilmoit-tauduttava?**	mihin ahⁱkaahn **min**noon oan ilmoaⁱttah^{oo}**doot**tahvah
I'd like to... my reservation.	**Haluaisin... varaukseni.**	hahlooaⁱsiin... **vah**rahooksayn
cancel	**peruuttaa**	pay**roo**ttaa
change	**muuttaa**	**moo**ttaa
confirm	**vahvistaa**	**vahh**vistaa

Train *Juna*

I'd like a ticket to Pori.	**Saisinko lipun Poriin.**	sahⁱsinkoa **lip**poon **poa**reen
single (one-way)	**menolippu**	**may**noalippoon
return (round trip)	**menopaluu**	**may**noapahl**oo**
first/second class	**ensimmäinen/ toinen luokka**	**ayn**simmæⁱnayn/**toa**nayn l^{oo}oakkah
How long does the journey (trip) take?	**Kuinka kauan matka kestää?**	**koo**ⁱnkah kah^{oo}ahn **mah**tkah kayst**æ**
When is the... train to Tampere?	**Milloin Tampe-reelle lähtee... juna?**	**mill**oaⁱn tampayr**ay**llay læht**ay**... **yoo**nah
first	**ensimmäinen**	**ayn**simmæⁱnayn
last/next	**viimeinen/seuraava**	**vee**mayⁱnayn/**say**^{oo}raavah
Is this the right train to Tampere?	**Onko tämä Tampe-reen juna?**	oankoa **tæ**mæ tahm**payr**ayn **yoo**nah

Bus—Tram (streetcar) *Bussi—Raitiovaunu*

Which tram (streetcar) goes to the town centre?	**Mikä raitiovaunu menee kaupungin keskustaan?**	mikkæ rahⁱtioavah^{oo}noo **may**n**ay** kah^{oo}poongin **kays**koostaan
How much is the fare to...?	**Mitä on maksu ...-n/...-lle?**	mittæ oan **mahk**soo...-n/...-llay
Will you tell me when to get off?	**Sanoisitteko, kun minun täytyy nousta pois?**	sahnoaⁱsittaykoa koon minnoon tæ^{ew}t**ew** noa^{oo}stah poais

TELLING THE TIME, see page 45

Taxi *Taksi*

What's the fare to …?	… – Mitä maksaa ajaa sinne?	mittæ **mahk**saa **ah**yaa **sin**nay
Take me to this address.	Viekää minut tähän osoitteeseen.	v'aykæ **min**noot **tæ**hæn **oa**soa'**ttæy**ssæyn
Please stop here.	Pysähtykää tässä.	**pew**ssæhtewkæ **tæ**ssæ
Could you wait for me?	Voitteko odottaa?	**voa**'ttaykoa **oa**doattaa

Car hire (rental) *Auton vuokraus*

I'd like to hire (rent) a car.	Haluaisin vuokrata auton.	**hah**looah'sin v°°**oak**rahtah **ah**°°toan
I'd like it for a day/a week.	Haluaisin sen päiväksi/viikoksi.	hahl°°**ah**'sin sayn **pæ**'**væk**si/**vee**koaksi
Where's the nearest filling station?	Missä on lähin bensiiniasema?	**mis**sæ oan **læ**hin **bayn**seeniahsaymah
Fill it up, please.	Tankki täyteen, kiitos.	**tahnk**ki tæ**ew**tæyn **kee**toass
Give me … litres of petrol (gasoline).	Saanko … litraa bensiiniä.	**saan**koa … **lit**raa **bayn**seeniæ
How do I get to …?	Miten pääsen …-n/…-lle?	**mi**tayn **pææ**sayn …-n/…-llay
I've had a break-down at …	Autoni meni epä-kuntoon …-n koh-dalla.	**a**°°toani **may**ni **ay**pæ**koon**tōan …-n **koah**dahllah
Can you send a mechanic?	Voitteko lähettää korjaajan?	**voa**'ttaykoa **læ**hayttæ **koar**yaayahn
Can you mend this puncture (fix this flat)?	Voitteko korjata tämän renkaan?	**voa**'ttaykoa **koar**yahtah **tæ**mæn **rayn**kaahn

---

Olette väärällä tiellä.	You're on the wrong road.
Ajakaa suoraan eteenpäin.	Go straight ahead.
Se on tuolla vasemmalla/oikealla.	It's down there on the left/right.
Vastapäätä (…-a/…-ta/…-tta)/ …-n takana	opposite/behind …
…-n vieressä/…-n jälkeen	next to/after …
pohjoisessa/etelässä	north/south
idässä/lännessä	east/west

Sightseeing *Kiertoajelu*

Where's the tourist office?	**Missä on matkatoimisto?**	missæ oan...mahtkahtoa'mistoa
Is there an English-speaking guide?	**Onko siellä englantia puhuva opas?**	oankoa s'ayllæ aynglahntiah poohoovah oapahss
Where is/are the...?	**Missä on/ovat...?**	missæ oan/oavaht
botanical gardens	**kasvitieteellinen puutarha**	kahsvit'aytāyllinnayn pōōtahrhah
castle	**linna**	linnah
cathedral	**tuomiokirkko**	t°°amioakeerkkoa
city centre/downtown	**keskusta**	kayskoostah
exhibition	**näyttely**	næ°°ttaylew
harbour	**satama**	sahtahmah
market	**(kauppa)tori**	(kah°°ppah)toari
museum	**museo**	moossayoa
shopping area	**ostoskeskus**	oastoaskayskooss
square	**tori**	toari
tower	**torni**	toarni
zoo	**eläintarha**	aylæ'ntahrhah
What are the opening hours?	**Mitkä ovat aukioloajat?**	mitkæ oavaht ah°°kioaloaahyaht
When does it close?	**Milloin se suljetaan?**	milloa'n say soolyaytaan
How much is the entrance fee?	**Mikä on pääsymaksu?**	mikkæ oan pǣsewmahksoo

Relaxing *Virkistyminen*

What's playing at the... Theatre?	**Mitä... -teatterissa esitetään?**	mittæ... tayahttayrissah ayssittaytǣn
Are there any seats for tonight?	**Onko täksi illaksi paikkoja?**	oankoa tæksi illahksi pah'kkoayah
Would you like to go out with me tonight?	**Lähtisit(te)kö kansani ulos tänä iltana?**	læhtissit(tay)kur kahnssahni ooloass tænæ iltahnah
Is there a discotheque in town?	**Onko tässä kaupungissa diskoa?**	oankoa tæssæ kah°°poongissah diskoaah
Would you like to dance?	**Haluaisitteko tanssia?**	hahlooah'sittaykoa tahnssiah
Thank you, it's been a wonderful evening.	**Kiitos, on ollut ihana ilta.**	keetoass oan oallloot ihhahnah iltah

TELLING THE TIME, see page 45

Shops, stores and services *Myymälät ja palvelut*

Where's the nearest...?	Missä on lähin...?	missæ oan læhin
baker's	leipomo	laypoamoa
bookshop	kirjakauppa	keeryuaka°°uppah
butcher's	lihakauppa	lihahka°°uppah
chemist's/drugstore	apteekki	ahptaykki
dentist	hammaslääkäri	hahmmahslækæri
department store	tavaratalo	tahvahrahtaloa
grocer's	sekatavarakauppa	saykahtahvahrahka°°uppah
hairdresser's/barber's	kampaaja/parturi	kahmpaayah/pahrtoori
market	tori	toari
newsstand	lehtikioski	layhtikioaski
post office	posti	poasti
supermarket	valintamyymälä	vahlintahmēwmælæ

General expressions *Yleisiä ilmauksia*

Where's the main shopping area?	Missä on tärkein ostosalue?	missæ oan tærkay'n oastoasahlooay
Do you have any...?	Onko teillä...-a?	oankoa tay'llæ...-a
Don't you have anything...?	Eikö teillä olisi jotain...?	aykur tay'llæ oalissi yoatah'n
cheaper	halvempaa	hahlvaympaa
better	parempaa	pahraympaa
larger	suurempaa	sōōraympaa
smaller	pienempää	p'aynaympǣ
Can I try it on?	Voinko sovittaa sitä?	voa'nkoa soavittaa sittæ
Where's the fitting room?	Missä on sovituskoppi?	missæ oan soavittooskoappi
How much is this?	Paljonko tämä maksaa?	pahlyoankoa tæmæ mahksaa
Please write it down.	Voisitteko kirjoittaa.	voa'sittayko keeryoattaa
I don't want to spend more than... marks.	En halua maksaa enempää kuin... markkaa.	ayn hahlooah mahksaa aynaympǣ koo'n... mahrkkaa
No, I don't like it.	Ei, en pidä siitä.	ay' ayn piddæ seetæ
I'll take it.	Otan sen.	oatahn sayn
Do you accept credit cards?	Hyväksyttekö luottokortteja?	hewvæksewttaykur l°°oattoakoarttayyah
Can you order it for me?	Voitteko tilata sen minulle?	voa'ttaykoa tillahtah sayn minnoollay

NUMBERS, see page 46

black	mustaa	moostaa
blue	sinistä	sinnistæ
brown	ruskeata	rooskayahtah
green	vihreää	vihrayæ
grey	harmaata	hahrmaahtah
orange	oranssia	oarahnssiah
red	punaista	poonah'stah
white	valkoista	vahlkoa'stah
yellow	keltaista	kayltah'stah
light...	vaalean...	vaalayahn
dark...	tumman...	toommahn

I'd like a/an/ some...	Haluaisin...-n/-a	hahlooah'sin...-n/-a
aspirin	aspiriinia	aahspireeniah
battery	pariston	pahristoan
bottle opener	pullonavaaja	poolloanahvaayah
bread	leipää	lay'pæ
newspaper	sanomalehden	sahnoamahlayhdayn
American/English	amerikkalaisen/	ahmayrikkahlah'sayn/
	englantilaisen	aynglantillah'sen
postcard	postikortin	poastikoartin
shampoo	shampoota	shahmpoatah
soap	saippuaa	sa'ppooaa
sun-tan cream	aurinkovoidetta	ah°°rinkoavoa'dayttah
toothpaste	hammastahnaa	hahmmahstahhnaa
half-kilo of	puoli kiloa	p°°aali killoah
tomatoes	tomaatteja	toamaattayyah
a litre of milk	litran maitoa	litrahn mah'toah
I'd like a film for this camera.	Haluaisin filmin tähän kameraan.	hahlooah'sin filmin tæhæn kahmayraan
black and white	mustavalkoista	moostahvahlkoa'stah
colour	värillistä	værillistæ
I'd like a haircut, please.	Saisinko tukanleik-kuun.	sah'sinkoa tookahnlay'kk°°ōn

Souvenirs *Muistoesineitä*

candles	kyntillät	kewnttilæt
furs	turkikset	toorkiksayt
glass	lasi	lahsi
handicrafts	käsityöt	kæsit^ewurt
reindeer hide	porontalja	poaroantahlyah
table linen	pöytä-ja lautaslii	pur^ewtæ-yah
	nat	lah°°tahsleenaht

At the bank *Pankissa*

Where's the nearest bank/currency exchange office?	**Missä on lähin pankki/valuutan-vaihtopaikka?**	missæ oan **læ**hin **pah**nkki/vah**lōō**tahnvah'h-toapaihkkah
I want to change some dollars/pounds.	**Haluaisin vaihtaa dollareita/puntia.**	hahlooah'sin vah'htaa doallahray'tah/**poon**tiah
I want to cash a traveller's cheque.	**Haluaisin muuttaa matkasekin rahaksi.**	hahlooah'sin **mōōt**taa mahtkahshaykin rahhaahksi
What's the exchange rate?	**Mikä on vaihto-kurssi?**	mikkæ oan vah'h**toakoors**si

At the post office *Posti*

I'd like to send this (by)...	**Lähettäisin tämän...**	læhayttæisin **tæ**mæn
airmail	**lentopostissa**	layntoa**poa**stissah
express	**pikana**	**pik**kahnah
A... penni stamp, please.	**Saisinko... pennin postimerkin.**	sah'sinkoa... paynnin **poa**stimayrkin
What's the postage for a postcard to Los Angeles?	**Mitä maksaa posti-kortti Los Angele-siin?**	mittæ **mahk**saa poastikoartti loas ahn**gay**layseen
Is there any post (mail) for me? My name is...	**Onko minulle pos-tia? Nimeni on...**	oankoa minnoollay **poa**stiah. **nim**mayni oan

Telephoning *Puhelut*

Where's the nearest telephone booth?	**Missä on lähin puhelinkioski?**	missæ oan **læ**hin poohaylink'oaski
May I use your phone?	**Voinko käyttää puhelintanne?**	voa'nnkoa kæ^{ew}ttæ poohaylintahnnay
Hello. This is...	**Hei. Täällä...**	hay' **tæl**læ
I'd like to speak to...	**Onko... tavatta-vissa.**	oankoa... **tah**vahttahvissah
When will he/she be back?	**Milloin hän palaa?**	milloa'n hæn **pah**laa
Will you tell him/her I called?	**Kertoisitteko hänelle, että soitin.**	kayrtoa'sittaykoa **hæn**ayllaay ayttæ soa'tin

NUMBERS, see page 46

Time and date *Päivät ja päivämäärät*

It's...	Se on...	say oan
five past one	**viittä yli yksi**	veettæ ewli ewksi
a quarter past three	**neljännestä/vartin yli kolme**	naylyænnaystæ/**vahr**tin ewli koalmay
twenty past four	**kahtakymmentä yli neljä**	kahhtahkewmmayntæ ewli naylyæ
half past six	**puoli seitsemän**	p°°oali say**t**saymæn
twenty-five to seven	**kahtakym- mentäviittä vaille seitsemän**	kahhtahkewm- mayntæveettæ vah**l**lay say**t**saymæn
a quarter to nine	**viisitoista minuttia vaille yhdeksän**	veesitoa**l**stah minoottiah vah**l**lay ewhhdayksæn
ten to ten	**kymmentä vaille kymmenen**	kewmmayntæ va**l**llay kewmmaynayn
twelve o'clock	**kaksitoista**	kahksitoa**l**stah
in the morning	**aamulla**	aamoollah
in the afternoon/ evening	**päivällä/illalla**	pæ**l**væl læ/illahllah
during the day	**päivällä**	pæ**l**vællæ
at night	**yöllä**	ew**ʷ**llæ
yesterday/today	**eilen/tänään**	ay**l**layn/yæn**ǣ**n
tomorrow	**huomenna**	h°°oamaynnah
spring/summer	**kevät/kesä**	kayvæt/kayssæ
autumn/winter	**syksy/talvi**	sewksew/**tahl**vi

Sunday	**sunnuntai**	soonnoontah**i**
Monday	**maanantai**	maanahntah**i**
Tuesday	**tiistai**	teestah**i**
Wednesday	**keskiviikko**	kayskiveekkoa
Thursday	**torstai**	toarstah**i**
Friday	**perjantai**	payryahntah**i**
Saturday	**lauantai**	lah°°ahntah**i**
January	**tammikuu**	tahmmikk$\overline{oo}$
February	**helmikuu**	haylmik$\overline{oo}$
March	**maaliskuu**	maalissk$\overline{oo}$
April	**huhtikuu**	hoohtikk$\overline{oo}$
May	**toukokuu**	toa°°koak$\overline{oo}$
June	**kesäkuu**	kayssæk$\overline{oo}$
July	**heinäkuu**	hay**i**næk$\overline{oo}$
August	**elokuu**	ayloak$\overline{oo}$
September	**syyskuu**	s$\overline{ew}$sk$\overline{oo}$
October	**lokakuu**	loakahk$\overline{oo}$
November	**marraskuu**	mahrrahsk$\overline{oo}$
December	**joulukuu**	yoa°°look$\overline{oo}$

NUMBERS, see page 46

Numbers *Luvut*

0	**nolla**	noallah
1	**yksi**	ewksi
2	**kaksi**	kahksi
3	**kolme**	koalmay
4	**neljä**	naylyæ
5	**viisi**	veessi
6	**kuusi**	kōōssi
7	**seitsemän**	say'tsaymæn
8	**kahdeksan**	kahhdayksahn
9	**yhdeksän**	ewhdayksæn
10	**kymmenen**	kewmmaynayn
11	**yksitoista**	ewksitoa'stah
12	**kaksitoista**	kahksitoa'stah
13	**kolmetoista**	koalmaytoa'stah
14	**neljätoista**	naylyætoa'stah
15	**viisitoista**	veessitoa'stah
16	**kuusitoista**	kōōssitoa'stah
17	**seitsemäntoista**	say'tsaymæntoa'stah
18	**kahdeksantoista**	kahhdayksahntoa'stah
19	**yhdeksäntoista**	ewhdayksæntoa'stah
20	**kaksikymmentä**	kahksikewmmayntæ
21	**kaksikym-mentäyksi**	kahksikewmmayntæewksi
30	**kolmekymmentä**	koalmaykewmmayntæ
40	**neljäkymmentä**	naylyækewmmayntæ
50	**viisikymmentä**	veessikewmmayntæ
60	**kuusikymmentä**	kōōssikewmmayntæ
70	**seitsemänkym-mentä**	say'tsaymænkewm-mayntæ
80	**kahdeksankym-mentä**	kahhdayksahnkewm-mayntæ
90	**yhdeksänkym-mentä**	ewhdayksænkewm-mayntæ
100	**sata**	sahtah
1000	**tuhat**	toohaht
1,000,000	**miljoona**	milyōānah
1,000,000,000	**miljardi**	milyahrdi
first	**ensimmäinen**	aynsimmæinayn
second	**toinen**	toa'nayn
third	**kolmas**	koalmahss
once	**kerran**	kayrrahn
twice	**kahdesti**	kahhdaysti
a half	**puolikas**	p°°oalikkahs
a quarter	**neljäsosa**	naylyæsoassah
a third	**kolmasosa**	koalmahsoassaa

TELEPHONING, see page 44

Emergency *Hätätilanne*

Call the police	**Kutsukaa poliisi**	koot**s**ookaa po**a**leessi
Get a doctor	**Hakekaa lääkäri**	hahkaykaa læ̈kæri
Go away	**Menkää tiehenne**	maynkæ̈ t'aynaynnay
HELP	**APUA**	ahpooah
I'm ill	**Olen sairas**	oalayn sah'rahs
I'm lost	**Olen eksynyt**	oalayn ayksewnewt
Leave me alone	**Jättäkää minut rauhaan**	yættækæ̈ minnoot rah°°haan
LOOK OUT	**VAROKAA**	vahroakaa
STOP THIEF	**OTTAKAA VARAS KIINNI**	oattahkaa vahrahs keenni
My... has been stolen.	**...-ni on varastettu**	-ni oan vahrahstayttoo
I've lost my...	**Olen kadottanut...-ni.**	oalayn kahdoattahnoot...-ni
handbag	**käsilaukku**	kæssilah°°kkooni
passport	**passi**	pahssi
wallet	**lompakko**	loampahkkoa
Where can I finid a doctor who speaks English?	**Mistä loytyisi lääkäri, joka puhuu englantia?**	mistæ lur⁰ᵂtew'si læ̈kæri yoakah poohōō aynglahntiah

Guide to Finnish pronunciation *Ääntäminen*

Consonants

Letter	Approximate pronunciation	Symbol	Example	
k, m, n, t, v	as in English			
d	as in ready, but sometimes very weak	d	**taide**	tah'day
g	in words of Finnish origin, only found after n; ng is pronounced as in singer	ng	**sangen**	sahngayn
h	as in hot, whatever its position in the word	h	**lahti**	lahhti
j	like y in you	y	**ja**	yah
l	as in let	l	**talo**	tahloa
r	always rolled	r	**raha**	rahhah

TELEPHONING, see page 44

s	always as in set (never as in present)	s/ss	**sillä** **kiitos**	**sillæ** **keetoass**

To make doubly sure that the Finnish **s** receives its correct pronunciation as **s** in English **set**, and not as a **z** sound in **present**, **ss** is often used in our phonetic transcriptions. Similarly, a double consonant is sometimes employed after **i** to ensure this is pronounced like **i** in **pin**, and not like **i** in **kite**. In these cases you can quickly check with the Finnish spelling whether you should pronounce a single or a double consonant.

Vowels

a	like **a** in **car**; short or long	ah aa	**matala** **iltaa**	**mah**tahlah **il**taa
e	like **a** in **late**; but a pure vowel, not a diphthong; short or long	ay	**kolme** **teevati**	**koal**may **tāy**vati
i	like **i** in **pin** (short) or **ee** in **see** (long); ir + consonant like **i** in **pin** (short)	i ee eer	**takki** **siitä** **kirkko**	**tah**kki seetæ **keer**koa
o	a sound between **aw** in **law** and **oa** in **coat**; short or long	oa ōa	**olla** **kookas**	**oa**llah **kōa**kahss
u	like **oo** in **pool**; short or long	oo ōō	**hupsu** **uuni**	**hoop**soo **ōō**ni
y	like **u** in French **sur** or **ü** in German **über**; say **ee** as in **see**, and round your lips while still trying to pronounce **ee**; it can be short or long	ew ēw	**yksi** **syy**	**ew**ksi sēw
ä	like **a** in **hat**; short or long	æ ǣ	**äkkiä** **hyvää**	**æk**kiæ **hew**vǣ
ö	like **ur** in **fur**, but without any **r** sound, and with the lips rounded; short or long	ur ūr	**tyttö** **likööri**	**tew**ttur **lik**kūrri

Dipthongs

In Finnish, dipthongs occur only in the first syllable of a word, except those ending in **-i**, where they can occur anywhere. They should be pronounced as a combination of the two vowel sounds. The phonetic transcription indicates which vowel should be pronounced louder.

French

Basic expressions *Expressions courantes*

Yes/No.	**Oui/Non.**	wee/nawng
Please.	**S'il vous plaît.**	seel voo pleh
Thank you.	**Merci.**	mehrsee
I beg your pardon?	**Pardon?**	pahrdawng

Introductions *Présentations*

Good morning.	**Bonjour.**	bawngzhoor
Good afternoon.	**Bonjour.**	bawngzhoor
Good night.	**Bonne nuit.**	bon nwee
Good-bye.	**Au revoir.**	oa rervwahr
My name is...	**Je m'appelle...**	zher mahpehl
Pleased to meet you.	**Enchanté(e).**	ahngshahngtay
What's your name?	**Comment vous appelez-vous?**	kommahng voo zahperlay voo
How are you?	**Comment allez-vous?**	kommahng tahlay voo
Fine thanks.	**Très bien, merci.**	treh byang mehrsee
And you?	**Et vous?**	ay voo
Where do you come from?	**D'où êtes-vous?**	doo eht voo
I'm from...	**Je viens...**	zher vyang
Australia	**de l'Australie**	der loastrahlee
Canada	**du Canada**	dew kahnahdah
Great Britain	**de la Grande-Bretagne**	der lah grahngd brertañ
United States	**des Etats-Unis**	day zaytah zewnee
I'm with my...	**Je suis avec...**	zher swee ahvehk
wife	**ma femme**	mah fahm
husband	**mon mari**	mawng mahree
family	**ma famille**	mah fahmeey
boyfriend	**mon ami**	mawng nahmee
girlfriend	**mon amie**	mawng nahmee
I'm here on business.	**Je suis en voyage d'affaires.**	zher swee zahng vwahyahzh dahfehr
I'm here on holiday (vacation).	**Je suis en vacances.**	zher swee zahng vahkahngss

GUIDE TO PRONUNCIATION, see page 63/EMERGENCIES, page 62

Questions *Questions*

When?	**Quand?**	kahng
How?	**Comment?**	kommahng
What?/Why?	**Quoi?/Pourquoi?**	kwah/poorkwah
Who?	**Qui?**	kee
Which?	**Lequel/Laquelle?**	lerkehl/lahkehl
Where is...?	**Où est/Où se trouve...?**	oo eh/oo ser troov
Where are...?	**Où sont/Où se trouvent...?**	oo sawng/oo ser troov
Where can I find/ get...?	**Où puis-je trouver...?**	oo pweezh troovay
How far?	**A quelle distance?**	ah kehl deestahngss
How long?	**Combien de temps?**	kawngbyang der tahng
How much/many?	**Combien?**	kawngbyang
Can I have...?	**Puis-je avoir...?**	pweezh ahvwahr
Can you help me?	**Pouvez-vous m'aider?**	poovay voo mehday
What does this/that mean?	**Que veut dire ceci/ cela?**	ker vur deer serssee/ serlah
I understand.	**Je comprends.**	zher kawngprahng
I don't understand.	**Je ne comprends pas.**	zher ner kangprahng pah
Can you translate this for me?	**Pouvez-vous me traduire ceci?**	poovay voo mer trahdweer serssee
Do you speak English?	**Parlez-vous anglais?**	pahrlay voo ahnggleh
I don't speak (much) French.	**Je ne parle pas (bien) français.**	zher ner pahrl pah (byang) frahngsseh

A few more useful words *Autres mots utiles*

better/worse	**meilleur/pire**	mehyurr/peer
big/small	**grand/petit**	grahng/pertee
cheap/expensive	**bon marché/cher**	bawng mahrshay/sherhr
early/late	**tôt/tard**	toa/tahr
good/bad	**bon/mauvais**	bawng/moaveh
hot/cold	**chaud/froid**	shoa/frwah
near/far	**près/loin**	preh/lwang
old/new	**ancien/nouveau**	ahngssyang/noovoa
right/wrong	**juste/faux**	zhewst/foa
vacant/occupied	**libre/occupé**	leebr/okkewpay

Hotel–Accommodation *Hôtel*

I have a reservation.	**J'ai fait réserver.**	zhay feh rayzehrvay
We've reserved 2 rooms.	**Nous avons réservé deux chambres.**	noo zahvawng rayzehrvay dur shahngbr
Do you have any vacancies?	**Avez-vous de chambres disponibles?**	ahvay voo day shahngbr deesponeebl
I'd like a... room	**Je voudrais une chambre...**	zher voodreh ewn shahngbr
single	**pour une personne**	poor ewn pehrson
double room	**pour deux personnes**	poor dur pehrson
with twin beds	**avec des lits jumeaux**	ahvehk day lee zhewmoa
with a double bed	**avec un grand lit**	ahvehk ang grahng lee
with a bath/shower	**avec salle de bains/douche**	ahvehk sahl der bang/doosh
We'll be staying...	**Nous resterons...**	noo rehsterrawng
overnight only	**juste cette nuit**	zhewst seht nwee
a few days	**quelques jours**	kehlker zhoor
a week	**une semaine**	ewn sermehn
Is there a camp site near here?	**Y a-t-il un camping près d'ici?**	ee ahteel ang kahngpeeng preh deessee

Decision *Décision*

May I see the room?	**Puis-je voir la chambre?**	pweezh vwahr lah shahngbr
That's fine. I'll take it.	**D'accord. Je la prends.**	dahkor. zher lah prahng
No. I don't like it.	**Non, elle ne me plaît pas.**	nawng ehl ner mer pleh pah
Do you have anything...?	**Avez-vous quelque chose...?**	ahvay voo kehlker shoaz
bigger	**de plus grand**	der plew grahng
cheaper	**de meilleur marché**	de mehyurr mahrshay
quieter	**de plus tranquille**	der plew trahngkeel
May I have my bill, please?	**Puis-je avoir ma note, s'il vous plaît?**	pweezh ahvwahr mah not seel voo pleh
It's been a very enjoyable stay.	**Le séjour a été très agréable.**	ler sayzhoor ah aytay treh zahgrayahbl

NUMBERS, see page 62

Eating out *Restaurant*

I'd like to reserve a table for 4.	**Je voudrais réserver une table pour 4 personnes.**	zher voodreh rayzehrvay ewn tahbl poor 4 pehrson
We'll come at 8.	**Nous viendrons à 8 heures.**	noo vyangdrawng ah 8 urr
I'd like...	**Je voudrais...**	zher voodreh
breakfast	**le petit déjeuner**	ler pertee dayzhurnay
lunch	**le déjeuner**	ler dayzhurnay
dinner	**le dîner**	ler deenay
What do you recommend?	**Que me recommandez-vous?**	ker mer rerkommahngday voo
Do you have any vegetarian dishes?	**Avez-vous des plats végétariens?**	ahvay voo day plah vayzhaytahryang

Breakfast *Petit déjeuner*

May I have some...	**Pourrais-je avoir...?**	poorehzh ahvwahr
bread	**du pain**	dew pang
butter	**du beurre**	dew burr
cheese	**du fromage**	dew fromahzh
ham and eggs	**des œufs au jambon**	day zur oa zhahngbawng
jam	**de la confiture**	der lah kawngfeetewr
rolls	**des petit pains**	da pertee pang

Starters *Hors-d'œuvre*

assiette anglaise	ahssyeht ahngglehz	assorted cold cuts
bouchée à la reine	boohsay ah lah rehn	pastry shell filled with sweetbreads
œufs à la diable	ur ah lah dyahbl	devilled eggs
pâté	pahtay	liver purée blended with other meats

Soups *Potages et soupes*

bisque	beesk	seafood chowder
consommé	kawngssommay	consommé
crème	krehm	cream
d'asperges	dahspehrzh	of asparagus
potage	potahzh	soup
au cresson	oa krehssawng	watercress
julienne	zhewlyehn	shredded vegetables
soupe à l'oignon	soop ah lonyawng	French onion soup

NUMBERS, see page 62

Fish and seafood *Poissons et fruits de mer*

cod	**morue**	morew
crab	**crabe**	krahb
frog's legs	**cuissses de grenouilles**	kweess der grernooy
mussels	**moules**	mool
oysters	**huîtres**	weetr
salmon	**saumon**	soamawng
snails	**escargots**	ehskahrgoa

baked	**au four**	oa foor
boiled	**bouilli**	booyee
fried	**frit**	free
grilled	**grillé**	greeyay
roast	**rôti**	roatee
stewed	**à l'étouffée**	ah laytoofay
underdone (rare)	**saignant**	sehñahng
medium	**à point**	ah pwang
well-done	**bien cuit**	byang kwee

Meat *Viande*

I'd like some...	**Je voudrais...**	zher voodreh
beef	**du boeuf**	dew burf
chicken/duck	**du poulet/canard**	dew pooleh/kahnahr
lamb	**de l'agneau**	der lahñoa
pork/veal	**du porc/veau**	dew por/voa
boeuf bourguignon	burf boorgeeñawng	rich beef stew with red burgundy wine
carbon(n)ade flamande	kahrbonnahd flahmahngd	beef slices with onions braised in beer
coq au vin	kok oa vang	chicken stewed in red wine

Vegetables *Légumes*

beans (French green)	**haricots verts**	ahreekoa vehr
carrots	**carottes**	kahrot
mushrooms	**champignons**	sshahngpeeñawng
onions	**oignons**	oñawng
peas	**petits pois**	pertee pwah
potatoes	**pommes (de terre)**	pom (der tehr)
truffles	**truffes**	trewf

Fruit and dessert *Fruits et desserts*

| apple | **pomme** | pom |
| cherries | **cerises** | serreez |

lemon	**citron**	seetrawng
orange	**orange**	orahngzh
pear	**poire**	pwahr
plums	**prunes**	prewn
strawberries	**fraises**	frehz
crêpe suzette	krehp sewzeht	thin pancakes in orange juice
gâteau au chocolat	gahtoa oa shokolah	chocolate cake
glace aux fraises/à la vanille	glahss oa frehz/ah lah vahneey	strawberry/vanilla ice-cream
tarte aux pommes	tahrt oa pom	apple tart (pie)

Drinks *Boissons*

beer	**une bière**	ewn byehr
(hot) chocolate	**un chocolat (chaud)**	ang shokolah (shoa)
coffee	**un café**	ang kahfay
black	**noir**	nwahr
with cream	**crème**	krehm
fruit juice	**un jus de fruits**	ang zhew der frwee
milk	**un lait**	ang leh
mineral water	**de l'eau minérale**	der loa meenayrahl
tea	**un thé**	ang tay
wine	**de vin**	der vang
red/white	**rouge/blanc**	roozh/blahng
a bottle	**une bouteille**	ewn bootehy
a glass	**un verre**	ang vehr

Complaints and paying *Réclamations et l'addition*

This is too...	**C'est trop...**	seh troa
bitter/sweet	**amer/sucré**	ahmehr/sewkray
salty	**salé**	sahlay
That's not what I ordered.	**Ce n'est pas ce que j'ai commandé.**	ser neh pah ser ker zhay kommahngday
I'd like to pay.	**L'addition, s'il vous plaît.**	lahdeessyawng seel voo pleh
I think there's a mistake in this bill.	**Je crois qu'il y a une erreur dans l'addition.**	zher krwah keel ee ah ewn ehrurr dahng lahdeessyawng
Can I pay with this credit card?	**Puis-je payer avec cette carte de crédit?**	pweez pehyay ahvehk seht kahrt der kraydee
We enjoyed it, thank you.	**C'était très bon, merci.**	sayteh treh bawng mehrsee

NUMBERS, see page 62

Travelling around *Excursions*

Plane *Avion*

Is there a flight to...?	**Y a-t-il un vol pour...?**	ee ahteel ang vol poor
What time should I check in?	**A quelle heure est l'enregistrement?**	ah kehl urr eh lahng-rerzheestrermahng
I'd like to... my reservation.	**Je voudrais... ma réservation.**	zher voodreh... mah rayzehrvahssyawng
cancel	**annuler**	ahnnewlay
change	**changer**	shahnzhay
confirm	**confirmer**	kawngfeermay

Train *Train*

I'd like a ticket to...	**Je voudrais un billet pour...**	zher voodreh ang beeyeh poor
single (one-way)	**aller**	ahlay
return (round trip)	**aller-retour**	ahlay rertoor
first/second class	**première/deuxième classe**	prermyehr/durzyehm klahss
How long does the journey (trip) take?	**Combien de temps dure le trajet?**	kawnbyang der tahng dewr ler trahzheh
When is the... train to...?	**Quand part le... train pour...?**	kahng pahr ler... trang poor
first	**premier**	prermyay
next	**prochain**	proshang
last	**dernier**	dehrnyay
Is this the train to...?	**C'est bien le train pour..., n'est-ce pas?**	seh byang ler trang poor ... nehss pah

Bus–Tram (streetcar) *Bus–Tram*

Which tram goes to the town centre?	**Quel bus va au centre-ville?**	kehl boos vah oh sahngtr veel
How much is the fare to...?	**Quel est le prix du trajet jusqu'à...?**	kehl eh ler pree dew trahzheh zhewskah
Will you tell me when to get off?	**Pourriez-vous me dire quand je dois descendre?**	pooryay voo mer deer kahng zher dwah dehssahngdr

TELLING THE TIME, see page 61

Taxi *Taxi*

How much is the fare to...?	Quel est le tarif pour...?	kehl eh ler tahreef poor
Take me to this address.	Conduisez-moi à cette adresse.	kawngdweezay mwah ah seht ahdrehss
Please stop here.	Arrêtez-vous ici, s'il vous plaît.	ahrehtay voo eessee seel voo pleh
Could you wait for me?	Pourriez-vous m'attendre?	pooray voo mahtahngdr

Car hire (rental) *Location de voitures*

I'd like to hire (rent) a car.	Je voudrais une voiture.	zher voodreh looay ewn vwahtewr
I'd like it for...	Je l'utiliserai...	zher lewteeleezerray
a day	un jour	ang zhoor
a week	une semaine	ewn sermehn
Where's the nearest filling station?	Où est la station-service la plus proche?	oo eh lah sstahssyawng sehrveess lah plew prosh
Full tank, please.	Le plein, s'il vous plaît.	ler plang seel voo pleh
Give me... litres of petrol (gasoline).	Donnez-moi... litres d'essence.	donnay mwah... leetr dehssahngss
How do I get to...?	Comment-puis-je aller à...?	kommahng pweezh ahlay ah
I've had a break-down at...	Je suis tombé en panne à...	zher swee tawngbay ahng pahn ah
Can you send a mechanic?	Pouvez-vous envoyer un mécan-icien?	poovay voo ahngvwahyay ang maykahneessyyang
Can you mend this puncture (fix this flat)?	Pourriez-vous réparer ce pneu?	pooryay voo raypahray ser pnur

---

Vous êtes sur la mauvaise route.	You're on the wrong road.
Allez tout droit.	Go straight ahead.
C'est là-bas à...	It's down there on the...
gauche/droite	left/right
à côté de/au-delà de...	next to/after...
nord/sud/est/ouest	north/south/east/west

EMERGENCIES, see page 62

Sightseeing *Visites touristiques*

Is there an English-speaking guide?	**Y a-t-il un guide qui parle anglais?**	ee ahteel ang geed kee pahrl ahnggleh
Where is...?	**Où se trouve...?**	oo ser troov
Where are...?	**Où se trouvent...?**	oo ser troov
botanical garden	**le jardin botanique**	ler zhahrdang bottahneek
castle	**le château**	ler shahtoa
cathedral	**la cathédrale**	lah kahtaydrahl
church	**l'église**	laygleez
city centre	**le centre (de la ville)**	ler sahngtr (der lah veel)
exhibition	**l'exposition**	lehxpozeessyawng
harbour	**le port**	ler por
market	**le marché**	ler mahrshay
museum	**le musée**	ler mewzay
shopping area	**le quartier commerçant**	ler kahrtyay kommehrssahng
square	**la place**	lah plahss
tower	**la tour**	lah toor
When does it open?	**A partir de quelle heure est-ce ouvert?**	ah pahrteer der kehl urr ehss oovehr
When does it close?	**Quelle est l'heure de fermeture?**	kehl eh lurr der fermertewr
How much is the entrance fee?	**Combien coûte l'entrée?**	kawngbyang koot lahngtray

Relaxing *Divertissements*

What's playing at the... Theatre?	**Que joue-t-on au théâtre...?**	ker zhootawng oa tayahtr
Are there any seats? for tonight?	**Y a-t-il des place pour ce soir?**	ee ahteel day plahss poor ser swahr
How much are the seats?	**Combien coûtent les places?**	kawngbyang koot lay plahss
Would you like to go out with me tonight?	**Voulez-vous sortir avec moi ce soir?**	voolay voo sorteer ahvehk mwah ser swahr
Is there a disco-theque in town?	**Y a-t-il une disco-thèque en ville?**	ee ahteel ewn deeskotehk ahng veel
Would you like to dance?	**Voulez-vous danser?**	voolay voo dahngssay
Thank you, it's been a wonderful evening.	**Merci, j'ai passé une merveilleusse soirée.**	mehrsee zhay pahssay ewn mehrvehyurz swahray

DAYS OF THE WEEK, see page 61/NUMBERS, see page 62

Shops, stores and services *Magasins et services*

Where's the nearest...?	**Où est... le/la plus proche?**	oo eh... ler/lah plew prosh
bakery	**la boulangerie**	lah boolahngzherree
bookshop	**la librairie**	lah leebrehree
butcher's	**la boucherie**	lah boosherree
chemist/drugstore	**la pharmacie**	lah fahrmahssee
dentist	**le dentiste**	ler dahngteest
department store	**le grand magasin**	ler grahng mahgahzang
grocery	**l'épicerie**	laypeesserree
hairdresser	**le coiffeur**	ler kwahfurr
newsagent	**le marchand de journaux**	ler mahrshahng de zhoornoa
post office	**le bureau de poste**	ler bewroa de post
supermarket	**le supermarché**	ler sewpehrmahrshay
toilets	**les toilettes**	lay twahleht

General expressions *Expressions générales*

Do you have any...?	**Avez-vous...?**	ahvay voo
Can I show me this/that?	**Pouvez-vous me montrer ceci/cela?**	poovay voo mer mawngtray sersee/serlah
Haven't you any-thing...?	**N'auriez-vous pas quelque chose de...?**	noarayay voo pah kehlker shoaz der
cheaper	**meilleur marché**	mahyurr mahrshay
better	**mieux**	myur
larger	**plus grand**	plew grahng
smaller	**plus petit**	plew pertee
Can I try it on?	**Puis-je l'essayer?**	pweezh lehssehyay
How much is this?	**Combien coûte ceci?**	kawngbyang koot serssee
Please write it down.	**Pourriez-vous l'écrire, s'il vous plaît.**	pooryay voo laykreer seel voo pleh
I don't want to spend more than... francs.	**Je ne veux pas dépenser plus de ... francs.**	zher ner vur pah daypahngssay plew der ...frahng
No, I don't like it.	**Non, cela ne me plaît pas.**	nawng serlah ner mer pleh pah
I'll take it.	**Je le prends.**	zher ler prahng
Do you accept credit-cards?	**Acceptez-vous les cartes de crédit?**	ahksehptay voo lay kahrt der kraydee

NUMBERS, see page 62

black	**noir**	nwahr
blue	**bleu**	blur
brown	**brun**	brang
green	**vert**	vehr
orange	**orange**	orahngzh
red	**rouge**	roozh
yellow	**jaune**	zhoan
white	**blanc**	blahng
light...	**... clair**	klehr
dark...	**... foncé**	fawngssay

I want to buy a/an/ some...	**Je voudrais acheter...**	zher voodreh ahshertay
aspirin	**de l'aspirine**	der lahspeereen
bottle-opener	**un ouvre-bouteilles**	ahng noovr bootehy
bread	**du pain**	dew pang
newspaper American/English	**un journal américain/ anglais**	ang zhoornahl amayreekang/ahnggleh
postcard	**une carte postale**	ewn kahrt postahl
shampoo	**du shampooing**	dew shahngpwang
soap	**du savon**	dew sahvawng
sun-tan cream	**de l'huile solaire**	der lweel solehr
toothpaste	**du dentifrice**	dew dahngteefreess
a half kilo of tomatoes	**un demi-kilo/une livre de tomates**	ang dermee keeloa/ewn leevr der tomaht
a litre of milk	**un litre de lait**	ang leetr der leh
I'd like a film for this camera.	**Je voudrais un film pour cet appareil.**	zher voodreh ang feelm poor seht ahpahrehy
black and white	**en noir et blanc**	ang nwahr ay blahng
colour	**en couleurs**	ang koolurr
I'd like a hair-cut, please.	**Un coup de cheveaux, s'il vous plaît.**	ewn koop de shervur seel voo pleh

Souvenirs *Souvenirs*

chocolate	**le chocolat**	ler shocolat
cuckoo clock	**le coucou**	ler kookoo
crystal	**le cristal**	ler kreestahl
lace	**les dentelles**	lay dahngtehl
perfume	**le parfum**	le pahrfang
tapestry	**la tapisserie**	lah tahpeesserree
women's top fashion	**la haute couture**	lah oat kootewr

At the bank *A la banque*

Where's the nearest bank/currency exchange office?	**Où est la banque/ bureau de change la plus proche?**	oo eh lah bahngk/ bewroa der shahngzh lah plew prosh
I want to change some dollars/pounds.	**Je voudrais changer des dollars/ livres.**	zher voodreh shahngzhay day dollahr/leevr
What's the exchange rate?	**Quel est le cours du change?**	kehl eh ler koor dew shahngzh
I want to cash a traveller's cheque.	**Je désire toucher ce chèque de voyage.**	zher dayzeer tooshay ser shehk der vwahyahzh

At the post office *A la poste*

I want to send this by...	**Je voudrais envoyer ceci...**	zher voodreh ahngvwahyay sersee
airmail	**par avion**	pahr ahvyawng
express	**par exprès**	pahr ehxprehss
I want... ...-centime stamps.	**Je voudrais...timbres à... centimes.**	zher voodreh... tangbr ah... sahngteem
What's the postage for a postcard/letter to United States?	**Quel est le tarif d'une carte postale/lettre pour les Etats-Unis?**	kehl eh ler tahreef dewn kahrt postahl/lettre poor lay zaytah zewnee
Is there any post/mail for me? My name is...	**Y a-t-il du courrier pour moi? Je m'appelle...**	ee ahteel dew kooryay poor mwah. zher mahpehl

Telephoning *Pour téléphoner*

Where is the nearest telephone?	**Où se trouve le téléphone le plus proche?**	oo ser troov ler taylayfon ler plew prosh
May I use your phone?	**Puis-je utiliser votre téléphone?**	pweezh ewteeleezay votr taylayfon
Hello. This is...	**Allo. C'est...**	ahloa. seh
I'd like to speak to...	**Je désire parler à...**	zher dayzeer pahrlay ah
When will he/she be back?	**Quand sera-t-il/elle de retour?**	kahng serrah teel/tehl der rertoor
Will you tell him/her I called?	**Veuillez lui dire que j'ai appelé.**	vuryay lwee deer ker zhay ahperlay

Time and date *L'heure et date*

It's…	Il est…	eel eh
five past one	une heure cinq	ewn urr sangk
quarter past three	trois heures un quart	trwah zuur ang kahr
twenty past four	quatre heures vingt	kahtr urr vang
half past six	six heures et demie	see zurr ay dermee
twenty-five to seven	sept heures moins vingt-cinq	seht urr mwang vangt sangk
ten to ten	dix heures moins dix	dee zurr mwang deess
noon/midnight	midi/minuit	meedee/meenwee
in the morning	du matin	dew mahtang
in the afternoon	de l'après-midi	der lahpreh meedee
in the evening	du soir	dew swahr
during the day	pendant la journée	pahngdahng lah zhoornay
at night	la nuit	lah nwee
yesterday	hier	yehr
today	aujourd'hui	oazhoorwee
tomorrow	demain	dermang
spring/summer	le printemps/l'été	le prangtahng/laytay
autumn/winter	l'automne/l'hiver	loaton/leevehr

Sunday	dimanche	deemahngsh
Monday	lundi	langdee
Tuesday	mardi	mahrdee
Wednesday	mercredi	mehrkrerdee
Thursday	jeudi	zhurdee
Friday	vendredi	vahngdredee
Saturday	samedi	sahmdee
January	janvier	zhahngvyay
February	février	fayvreeyay
March	mars	mahrs
April	avril	ahvreel
May	mai	may
June	juin	zhwang
July	juillet	zhweeyeh
August	août	oot
September	septembre	sehptahngbr
October	octobre	oktobr
November	novembre	novahngbr
December	décembre	dayssahngbr

NUMBERS, see page 62

Numbers *Nombres*

0	**zéro**	zayroa
1	**un, une**	ang ewn
2	**deux**	dur
3	**trois**	trwah
4	**quatre**	kahtr
5	**cinq**	sangk
6	**six**	seess
7	**sept**	seht
8	**huit**	weet
9	**neuf**	nurf
10	**dix**	deess
11	**onze**	owngz
12	**douze**	dooz
13	**treize**	trehz
14	**quatorze**	kahtorz
15	**quinze**	kangz
16	**seize**	sehz
17	**dix-sept**	deess seht
18	**dix-huit**	deez weet
19	**dix-neuf**	deez nurf
20	**vingt**	vang
21	**vingt et un**	vang tay ang
30	**trente**	trahngt
40	**quarante**	kahrahngt
50	**cinquante**	sangkahngt
60	**soixante**	swahssahngt
70	**soixante-dix**	swahssahngt deess
80	**quatre-vingt**	kahtrer vang
90	**quatre-vingt-dix**	kahtrer vang deess
100	**cent**	sahng
1000	**mille**	meel
first	**premier (1er)**	prermyay
second	**deuxième (2e)**	durzyehm
once/twice	**une fois/deux fois**	ewn fwah/dur fwah
a half	**une moitié**	ewn mwahtyay

Emergency *Urgences*

Call the police	**Appelez la police**	ahperlay lah poleess
Get a doctor	**Appelez un méde-cin**	ahperlay ang maydssang
Go away	**Allez-vous-en**	ahlay voo zahng
HELP	**AU SECOURS**	oa serkoor
I'm ill	**Je suis malade**	zher swee mahlahd

TELEPHONING, see page 60

I'm lost	**Je me suis perdu(e)**	zher mer swee pehrdew
Leave me alone	**Laissez-moi tran-quille**	lehssay mwah trahngkeel
LOOK OUT	**ATTENTION**	ahtahngssyawng
STOP THIEF	**AU VOLEUR**	oa volurr
My ... has been stolen.	**On m'a volé ...**	awng mah volay
I've lost my ...	**J'ai perdu ...**	zhay pehrdew
handbag	**mon sac à main**	mawng sahk ah mang
wallet	**mon portefeuille**	mawng portfury
passport	**mon passeport**	mawng pahsspor
luggage	**mes bagages**	may bahgahzh
Where can I find a doctor who speaks English?	**Où puis-je trouver un mèdecin qui parle anglais?**	oo pweezh troovay ang maydssang kee pahrl ahnggleh

Guide to French pronunciation *Prononciation*

Consonants

Letter	Approximate pronunciation	Symbol	Example	
b, c, d, f, k, l, m, n, p, s, t, v, x, z	as in English			
ch	like **sh** in **sh**ut	sh	**ch**ercher	shershay
ç	like **s** in **s**it	s	**ç**a	sah
g	1) before **e, i, y,** like **s** in pleasure	zh	man**g**er	mahngzhay
	2) before **a, o, u,** like **g** in **g**o	g	**g**arçon	gahrsawng
gn	like **ni** in onion	ñ	li**gn**e	leeñ
h	always silent		**h**omme	om
j	like **s** in pleasure	zh	**j**amais	zhahmeh
qu	like **k** in **k**ill	k	**qu**i	kee
r	rolled in the back of the mouth	r	**r**ouge	roozh
w	usually like **v** in **v**oice	v	**w**agon	vahgawng

FRENCH

Vowels

a, à, â	between the a in hat and the a in father	ah	mari	mahree
é, er, ez	like a in late	ay	été	aytay
è, ê, e	like e in get	eh	même	mehm
e	sometimes like er in other (quite short)	er	je	zher
i	like ee in meet	ee	il	eel
o	generally like o in hot	o	donner	donner
	but sometimes as in wrote	oa	rose	roaz
ô	like o in wrote	oa	Rhône	roan
u	no equivalent in English. Round your lips and try to say ee	ew	cru	krew

Sounds spelt with two or more letters

ai, ay, ey	can be pronounced as a in late	ay	j'ai	zhay
aient, ais	like e in get	eh	chaîne	shehn
ait, aï, ei	like e in get	eh	peine	pehn
eu, eû, œu	like ur in fur, but with lips rounded, not spread	ur*	peu	pur
oi, oy	like w followed by the a in hat	wah	moi	mwah
ou, oû	like oo in look	oo	nouveau	noovoa
ui	approximately like wee in between	wee	traduire	trahdweer

Nasal sounds

am, an, em, en	something like arn in tarnish	ahng	tante	tahngt
ien	like yan in yank	yang	bien	byang
im, in, aim, ain, eim, ein	like ang in rang	ang	instant	angstahng
om, on	like ong in song	awng	maison	mayzawng
um, un	like ang in rang	ang	brun	brang

---

*The r should not be pronounced when reading this transcription.

Français

German

Basic expressions *Die ersten Worte*

Yes/No.	**Ja/Nein.**	yaa/nighn
Please.	**Bitte.**	**bitt**er
Thank you.	**Danke.**	**dahn**ker
I beg your pardon?	**Wie bitte?**	vee **bitt**er

Introductions *Vorstellen*

Good morning.	**Guten Morgen.**	**goo**tern **mor**gern
Good afternoon.	**Guten Tag.**	**goo**tern taag
Good night.	**Guten Abend.**	**goo**tern **aa**bernt
Good-bye.	**Auf Wiedersehen.**	owf **vee**derrzayern
My name is...	**Ich heiße...**	ikh **high**sser
Pleased to meet you.	**Sehr erfreut.**	zayr ehr**froyt**
What's your name?	**Wie heißen Sie?**	vee **high**ssern zee
How are you?	**Wie geht es Ihnen?**	vee gayt ehss **ee**nern
Fine thanks.	**Danke, gut.**	**dahn**ker goot
And you?	**Und Ihnen?**	unt **ee**nern
Where do you come from?	**Woher kommen Sie?**	voa**hayr kom**mern zee
I'm from...	**Ich bin aus...**	ikh bin owss
Australia	**Australien**	ow**straa**liern
Canada	**Kanada**	**kah**nahdah
Great Britain	**Großbritannien**	**groas**brittahniern
United States	**den Vereinigten Staaten**	dayn fehr**righ**nigtern **shtaa**tern
I'm with my...	**Ich bin mit... hier.**	ikh bin mit... heer
wife	**meiner Frau**	**migh**nerr frow
husband	**meinem Mann**	**migh**nerm mahn
family	**meiner Familie**	**migh**nerr fah**mee**lier
boyfriend	**meinem Freund**	**migh**nerm froynt
girlfriend	**meiner Freundin**	**migh**nerr **froyn**din
I'm on my own.	**Ich bin allein hier.**	ikh bin ah**lign** heer
I'm here on business/ vacation.	**Ich bin geschäftlich/auf Urlaub hier.**	ikh bin ger**shehft**likh/ owf **oor**lowp heer

GUIDE TO PRONUNCIATION, see page 79/EMERGENCIES, page 78

Questions *Fragen*

When?	**Wann?**	vahn
How?	**Wie?**	vee
What?/Why?	**Was?/Warum?**	vahss/vah**rum**
Who?	**Wer?**	vayr
Which?	**Welcher/Welche/ Welches?**	**vehl**kherr/**vehl**kher/ vehl**kherss**
Where is/are...?	**Wo ist/sind...?**	voa ist/zint
Where can I find/ get...?	**Wo finde/ bekomme ich...?**	voa **fin**der/ber**kom**mer ikh
How far?	**Wie weit?**	vee vight
How long?	**Wie lange?**	vee **lahn**ger
How much?	**Wieviel?**	vee**feel**
How many?	**Wie viele?**	vee **feel**er
Can I have...?	**Kann ich... haben?**	kahn ikh... **haa**bern
Can you help me?	**Können Sie mir helfen?**	**kur**nern zee meer **hehl**fern
What does that mean?	**Was bedeutet das?**	vahss ber**doy**tert dahss
I understand.	**Ich verstehe.**	ikh fer**shtay**er
I don't understand.	**Ich verstehe nicht.**	ikh fer**shtay**er nikht
Can you translate this for me?	**Könnten Sie mir das übersetzen?**	**kurn**tern zee meer dahss ewber**zeht**sern
Do you speak English?	**Sprechen Sie Englisch?**	**shpreh**khern see **ehng**lish
I don't speak much German.	**Ich spreche kaum Deutsch.**	ikh **shpreh**kher kowm doych

A few more useful words *Weitere nützliche Wörter*

better/worse	**besser/schlechter**	**behs**serr/**shlehkh**terr
big/small	**groß/klein**	groass/klighn
cheap/expensive	**billig/teuer**	**bil**likh/**toy**err
early/late	**früh/spät**	frew/shpait
good/bad	**gut/schlecht**	goot/shlehkht
hot/cold	**heiß/kalt**	highss/kahlt
near/far	**nah/weit**	naa/vight
old/new	**alt/neu**	ahlt/noy
right/wrong	**richtig//falsch**	**rikh**tikh/fahlsh
vacant/occupied	**frei/besetzt**	frigh/ber**zehtst**

Hotel—Accommodation *Hotel*

I have a reservation.	**Ich habe reservieren lassen.**	ikh **haa**ber rehzerr**vee**rern **lahs**sern
We've reserved 2 rooms.	**Wir haben zwei Zimmer reservieren lassen.**	veer **haa**bern tsvigh **tsim**merr rehzerr**vee**rern **lahs**sern
Do you have any vacancies?	**Haben Sie noch freie Zimmer?**	**haa**bern zee nokh **frigh**er **tsim**mer
I'd like a...	**Ich hätte gern ein...**	ikh **heh**ter gehrn ighn
single room	**Einzelzimmer**	**ighn**tserltsimmerr
double room	**Doppelzimmer**	**dopp**erltsimmerr
with twin beds	**mit zwei Einzelbetten**	mit tsvigh **ighn**tserlbehtern
with a double bed	**mit einem Doppelbett**	mit **igh**nerm **dopp**erlbeht
with a bath/shower	**mit Bad/Dusche**	mit baat/**du**sher
We'll be staying...	**Wir bleiben...**	veer **bligh**bern
overnight only	**nur eine Nacht**	noor **igh**ner nakht
a few days	**einige Tage**	**igh**nigger **taa**ger
a week	**eine Woche**	**igh**ner **vokh**er
Is there a camp site near here?	**Gibt es hier in der Nähe einen Campingplatz?**	gipt ehss heer in derr **nai**er **igh**nern **kehm**pingplahts

Decision *Entscheidung*

May I see the room?	**Kann ich das Zimmer sehen?**	kahn ikh dahss **tsim**mer **zay**ern
That's fine. I'll take it.	**Gut, ich nehme es.**	goot ikh **nay**mer ehss
No. I don't like it.	**Nein, es gefällt mir nicht.**	nighn ehss ger**fehlt** meer nikht
It's too...	**Es ist zu...**	ehss ist tsu
dark/small	**dunkel/klein**	**dun**kerl/**klighn**
Do you have anything...?	**Haben Sie etwas...?**	**haa**bern see **eht**vahss
better/bigger	**Besseres/Größeres**	**behss**errerss/**grurss**errerss
cheaper	**Billigeres**	**bill**iggerrerss
quieter	**Ruhigeres**	**roo**iggerrerss
May I have my bill, please?	**Kann ich bitte die Rechnung haben?**	kahn ikh **bit**ter dee **rehkh**nung **haa**bern
It's been a very enjoyable stay.	**Es war ein sehr angenehmer Aufenthalt.**	ehss vaar ighn zayr **ahn**gernaymerr **owf**ehnthahlt

NUMBERS, see page 78

Eating out *Gaststätten*

I'd like to reserve a table for 4.	Ich möchte einen Tisch für 4 Personen reservieren lassen.	ikh murkhter ighnern tish fewr 4 pehrzoanern rehzehrveerern lahssern
We'll come at 8.	Wir kommen um 8 Uhr.	veer kommern um 8 oor
I'd like...	Ich hätte gern...	ikh hehter gehrn
breakfast	das Frühstück	dahss frewshtewk
lunch	das Mittagessen	dahss mittahgehssern
dinner	das Abendessen	dahss aaberntehssern
What do you recommend?	Was würden Sie mir empfehlen?	vahss vewrdern zee meer ehmpfaylern
Do you have any vegetarian dishes?	Haben Sie vegetarische Gerichte?	haabern zee vehgehtaarisher gerrikhter

Breakfast *Frühstück*

May I have some...	Kann ich... haben?	kahn ikh... haabern
bread	Brot	broat
butter	Butter	butterr
cheese	Käse	kaizer
ham and eggs	Spiegeleier mit Schinken	shpeegerligherr mit shinkern
jam	Marmelade	mahrmehlaader
rolls	Brötchen	brurtkhern

Starters *Vorspeisen*

Appetithäppchen	ahpehteethehpkhern	canapés
Bismarckhering	bismahrkhayring	soused herring with onion
Hoppel-Poppel	hopperl-popperl	scrambled eggs with sausage or bacon
Käsehäppchen	kaizerhehpkhern	cheese sticks
Russische Eier	russisher igherr	boiled eggs with mayonnaise

Soups *Suppen*

Bauernsuppe	bowernzupper	cabbage and frankfurter soup
Fischsuppe	fishzuppper	fish soup
Hühnerbrühe	hewnerrbrewer	chicken broth
Labskaus	laapskowss	thick stew
Linsensuppe	linzernzupper	lentil soup
Schildkrötensuppe	shiltkrurternzupper	turtle soup

NUMBERS, see page 78

Deutsch

Fish and seafood *Fissch und Meeresfrüchte*

cod	**Kabeljau**	**kaa**berlow
lobster	**Hummer**	**hum**merr
mussels	**Muscheln**	**mush**erln
oysters	**Austern**	**ow**sterrn
plaice	**Scholle**	**shol**ler
shrimp	**Garnelen**	gah**rnay**lern

baked	**gebacken**	ger**bahk**ern
boiled	**gekocht**	ger**kokht**
fried	**gebraten**	ger**braa**tern
grilled	**gegrillt**	ger**grilt**
roasted	**gebraten**	ger**braa**tern
stewed	**gedämpft**	ger**dehmpft**
underdone (rare)	**blutig**	**bloo**tikh
medium	**mittel**	**mitt**erl
well-done	**gut durchgebraten**	goot **doorch**ger**braa**tern

Meat *Fleisch*

I'd like some...	**Ich hätte gern...**	ikh **heh**ter gehrn
beef	**Rindfleisch**	**rint**flighsh
chicken/duck	**Huhn/Ente**	hoon/**ehn**ter
lamb	**Lammfleisch**	**lahm**flighsh
pork	**Schweinefleisch**	**shvigh**nerflighsh
veal	**Kalbfleisch**	**kahlp**flighsh

Bauernschmaus
(**bow**ernshmowsr)
saurkraut, bacon, sausage, dumplings and potatoes

Kohlroulade
(**koal**roolaader)
cabbage leaves stuffed with minced meat

Würste	**voor**ster	sausages
Bierwurst	**beer**voorst	smoked pork/beef
Bratwurst	**braat**voorst	fried pork
Weißwurst	**vighs**voorst	veal and bacon

Vegetables *Gemüse*

beans	**Bohnen**	**boa**nern
cabbage	**Kohl**	koal
carrots	**Karotten**	kah**rott**ern
mushrooms	**Pilze**	**pilt**ser
onions	**Zwiebeln**	**tsvee**berln
peas	**Erbsen**	**ehrp**sern
potatoes	**Kartoffeln**	kah**rtoff**erln
tomatoes	**Tomaten**	tom**maa**tern

Fruit and dessert *Obst und Nachtisch*

apple	**Apfel**	**ah**pferl
cherries	**Kirschen**	**keers**hern
lemon	**Zitrone**	tsi**troa**ner
orange	**Aprikosen**	ahprek**koa**zern
pear	**Birne**	**beer**ner
strawberries	**Erdbeeren**	**ehrt**bayrern
-eis, -glace	-ighss -**glah**sser	ice-cream
Schwarzwälder- **kirschtorte**	**schvarts**vehlderr-**keersh** torter	Black Forest gateau

Apfelstrudel (**ah**pferlshtrooderl)	pastry filled with apple, nuts, raisins and jam
Hefekranz (**hay**ferkrahnts)	ring shaped cake with almonds or candied fruit

Drinks *Getränke*

I'd like ...	**Ich hätte gern ...**	ikh **heh**ter gehrn
beer	**ein Bier**	ighn beer
(hot) chocolate	**eine (heiße)** **Schokolade**	**igh**ner (**high**sser) shokko**laa**der
coffee	**einen Kaffee**	**igh**nern kah**fay**
with cream	**mit Sahne**	mit **zaa**ner
fruit juice	**einen Fruchtsaft**	**igh**nern **frukht**zahft
(glass of) milk	**(ein Glas) Milch**	(ighn glaass) milkh
mineral water	**ein Mineralwasser**	ighn minner**raal**vahsserr
red/white wine	**Rotwein/Weißwein**	**roat**vighn/**vighs**vighn
tea	**einen Tee**	**igh**nern tay

Complaints and paying *Reklamationen und die Rechnung*

This is too ...	**Das ist zu ...**	dahss ist tsu
bitter/sweet	**bitter/süß**	**bi**tter/zewss
salty	**salzig**	**zahl**tsikh
That's not what I ordered.	**Das habe ich nicht bestellt.**	dahss **haa**ber ikh nikht ber**stehlt**
I'd like to pay.	**Ich möchte zahlen.**	ikh **murkh**ter **tsaa**lern
I think there's a mistake in this bill.	**Ich glaube, Sie haben sich verrech-net.**	ikh **glow**ber zee **haa**bern zikh fehr**rehkh**nert
Can I pay with this credit card?	**Kann ich mit dieser Kreditkarte bezah-len?**	kahn ikh mit **dee**zer krayditkahrter bert**saa**lern
That was a very good meal.	**Das Essen war sehr gut.**	dahss **eh**ssern vaar zayr goot

NUMBERS, see page 78

Travelling around *Reisen im Lande*

Plane *Flugzeug*

Is there a flight to...?	**Gibt es einen Flug nach...?**	gipt ehss ** igh**nern floog naakh
What time should I check in?	**Wann muß ich einchecken?**	vahn muss ikh **ighn**shehkern
I'd like to... my reservation.	**Ich möchte meine Reservierung...**	ikh **murkh**ter **migh**ner rehzer**vee**rung
cancel	**annullieren**	ahnu**llee**rern
change	**umbuchen**	**um**bookhern
confirm	**bestätigen**	ber**shtait**iggern

Train *Eisenbahn*

I'd like a ticket to...	**Ich möchte eine Fahrkarte nach...**	ikh **murkh**ter **igh**ner **faar**kahrter naakh
single (one-way)	**einfach**	**ighn**fahkh
return (round trip)	**hin und zurück**	hin unt stoo**rewk**
first/second class	**erste/zweite Klasse**	**ehr**ster/**tsvigh**ter **klah**sser
How long does the journey (trip) take?	**Wie lange dauert die Fahrt?**	vee **lahn**ger **dow**errt dee faart
When is the... train to ..?	**Wann fährt der... Zug nach...?**	vahn fairt derr... tsoog naakh
first/next	**erste/nächste**	**ehr**ster/**naikh**ster
last	**letzte**	**leht**ster
Is this the right train to...?	**Ist das der Zug nach...?**	ist dahss derr tsoog naakh

Bus–Tram (streetcar) *Bus–Straßenbahn*

Which tram goes to the town centre?	**Welche Straßenbahn fährt ins Stadtzentrum?**	**vehl**kher **shtraa**ssern-baan fairt ins **shtaht**tsehntrum
How much is the fare to...?	**Was kostet es nach...?**	vahss **ko**stert ehss naakh
Will you tell me when to get off?	**Könne Sie mir bitte sagen, wann ich aussteigen muß?**	**kur**nern zee meer **bit**ter **zaa**gern vahn ikh **ows**shtighgern muss

Taxi *Taxi*

What's the fare to...?	**Was kostet es bis...?**	vahs **ko**stert ehss biss

TELLING THE TIME, see page 77

Take me to this address.	**Bringen Sie mich zu dieser Adresse.**	bringern zee mikh tsoo deezer ahdrehsser
Please stop here.	**Halten Sie hier, bitte.**	hahltern zee heer bitter
Will you wait for me?	**Würden Sie bitte auf mich warten?**	vewrdern zee bitter owf mikh vahrtern

Car hire (rental) *Autoverleih*

I'd like to hire (rent) a car.	**Ich möchte ein Auto mieten.**	ikh murkhter ighn owto meetern
I'd like it for a a day/a week.	**Ich möchte es für einen Tag/eine Woche.**	ikh murkhter ehss fewr ighnern taag/ighner vokher
Where's the nearest filling station?	**Wo ist die nächste Tankstelle?**	voa ist dee naikhster tahnkshtehler
Fill it up, please.	**Volltanken, bitte.**	voltahnkern bitter
Give me... litres of petrol (gasoline).	**Geben Sie mir... Liter Benzin.**	gaybern zee mir... leeterr behntseen
Where can I find this address/place?	**Wie komme ich zu dieser Adresse/ diesem Ort?**	vee kommer ikh tsoo deezerr ahdrehsser/ deezerm ort
I've had a breakdown.	**Ich habe eine Panne.**	ikh haaber ighner pahner
Can you send a mechanic?	**Können Sie einen Mechaniker schicken?**	kurnern zee ighnern mehkhahnikkerr shikkern
Can you mend this puncture (fix this flat)?	**Können Sie diesen Reifen flicken?**	kurnern zee deezern righfern flikkern

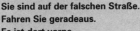

Sie sind auf der falschen Straße.	You're on the wrong road.
Fahren Sie geradeaus.	Go straight ahead.
Es ist dort vorne ...	It's down there on the...
links/rechts	left/right
neben/nach...	next to/after...
Nord/Süd/Ost/West	north/south/east/west

EMERGENCIES, see page 78

Sightseeing *Besichtigungen*

Is there an English-speaking guide?	**Gibt es einen englischsprechenden Fremden-führer?**	gipt ehss **igh**nern **ehng**lishshprehkkherndern **frehm**dernfewrerr
Where is/are the...?	**Wo ist/Wo sind...?**	voa ist/voa zint
art gallery	**die Kunstgalerie**	derr **kunst**gahlehree
cathedral	**die Kathedrale/der Dom**	dee kahtehdr**aa**ler/derr doam
church	**die Kirche**	dee **keer**kher
city centre/downtown	**die Innenstadt**	dee **innern**shtaht
exhibition	**die Ausstellung**	dee **owss**htehlung
market	**der Markt**	derr mahrkt
museum	**das Museum**	dahss mu**zay**um
shopping area	**das Geschäfts-viertel**	dahss ger**shehfts**feerterl
square	**der Platz**	derr plahts
tower	**der Turm**	der toorm
zoo	**der Zoo**	derr tsoa
What are the opening hours?	**Welches sind die Öffnungszeiten?**	**vehl**kherss zint dee **urfnungstsightern**
When does it close?	**Wann schließt es?**	vahn shleest ehss
How much is the entrance fee?	**Was kostet der Eintritt?**	vahss **ko**stert derr **ighn**trit

Relaxing *Unterhaltung*

What's playing at the... Theatre?	**Was wird im ... Theater gegeben?**	vahss veert im ... tayaaterr ger**gay**bern
Are there any tickets for tonight?	**Gibt es noch Karten für heute abend?**	gipt ehss nokh **kah**rtern fewr **hoy**ter **aa**bernt
How much are the tickets?	**Wie teuer sind die Karten?**	vee **toy**err zint dee **kah**rtern
Would you like to go out with me tonight?	**Möchten Sie heute abend mit mir ausgehen?**	**murkh**tern zee **hoy**ter **aa**bernt mit meer **ows**gayern
Is there a discoteque in town?	**Gibt es hier eine Diskothek?**	gipt ehss heer **igh**ner diskot**tayk**
Would you like to dance?	**Möchten Sie tanzen?**	**murkh**tern zee **tahn**tsern
Thank you, it's been a wonderful evening.	**Danke, es war ein wunderbarer Abend.**	**dahn**ker ehss vaar ighn **voon**derrbaarerr **aa**bernt

TELLING THE TIME, see page 77

Shops, stores and services *Geschäfte, Läden usw.*

Where's the nearest...?	Wo is der/die/das nächste...?	voa ist derr/dee/dahss naikhster
bakery	die Bäckerei	dee behkerrigh
bookshop	die Buchhandlung	dee bukhhahndlung
butcher's	die Fleischerei/ Metzgerei	dee flighsherrigh/ mehtsgerrigh
chemist's/drugstore	die Apotheke	dee ahpottayker
dentist	der Zahnarzt	derr tsaanahrtst
department store	das Warenhaus	dahss vaarernhowss
grocery	das Lebensmittel- geschäft	dahss laybernsmitterl- gershehft
hairdresser (ladies/ men)	der Damenfriseur/ Herrenfriseur	derr daamernfrizurr/ hehrernfrizurr
newsagent	der Zeitungs- händler	derr tsightungshehndlerr
post office	das Postamt	dahss postahmt
souvenir shop	der Andenkenladen	derr ahndehnkernlaadern
supermarket	der Supermarkt	derr zooperrmahrkt
toilets	die Toilette	dee toahlehter

General expressions *Allgemeine Redewendungen*

Where's the main shopping area?	Wo ist das Geschäftsviertel?	voa ist dahss gershehftsfeerterl
Do you have any...?	Haben Sie...?	haabern zee
Can you show me...?	Können Sie mir... zeigen?	kurnern zee meer... tsighgern
that/those	das da/die dort	dahss daa/dee dort
Haven't you anything...?	Haben Sie nichts...?	haabern zee nikhts
cheaper/better	Billigeres/Besseres	billiggerrerss/behsserrerss
larger/smaller	Größeres/Kleineres	grursserrerss/klighnerrerss
Can I try it on?	Kann ich es anprobieren?	kahn ikh ehss ahnprobbeerern
How much is this?	Wieviel kostet das?	veefeel kostert dahss
Please write it down.	Schreiben Sie es bitte auf.	shrighbern zee ehss bitter owf
I don't want to spend more than... marks.	Ich möchte nicht mehr als... Mark ausgeben.	ikh murkhter nikht mayr ahlss... mahrk owsgaybern
No, I don't like it.	Nein, das gefällt mir nicht.	nighn dahss gerfehlt meer nikht
I'll take it.	Ich nehme es.	ikh naymer ehss

NUMBERS, see page 78

Do you accept credit cards?	**Nehmen Sie Kreditkarten?**	naymern zee krayditkahrtern

black	**schwarz**	shvahrts
blue	**blau**	blow
brown	**braun**	brown
green	**grün**	grewn
orange	**orange**	orr**rahng**zher
red	**rot**	roat
yellow	**gelb**	gehlp
white	**weiß**	vighss
light...	**hell...**	hehl
dark...	**dunkel...**	**d**unkerl

I'd like a/an/some ...	**Ich hätte gern ...**	ikh **heh**ter gehrn
aspirin	**Aspirin**	ahspi**reen**
battery	**eine Batterie**	**igh**ner bahter**ree**
newspaper	**eine Zeitung**	**igh**ner **tsigh**tung
American	**amerikanische**	ahmehrik**kaa**nisher
English	**englische**	**ehng**lisher
postcard	**eine Postkarte**	**igh**ner **post**kahrter
shampoo	**ein Haarwasch-mittel**	ighn **haar**vahshmitterl
soap	**eine Seife**	**igh**ner **zigh**fer
sun-tan cream	**Sonnencreme**	**zon**nernkraym
toothpaste	**Zahnpasta**	**tsaan**pahstah
half-kilo of tomatoes	**ein halbes Kilo Tomaten**	ighn **hahl**bers **kee**lo tom**maa**tern
litre of milk	**einen Liter Milch**	**igh**nern **lee**terr milkh
I'd like a ... film for this camera.	**Ich hätte gern einen Film für diese Kamera.**	ikh **heh**ter gehrn **igh**nern film fewr **dee**zer kah**meh**raa
black and white	**Schwarzweißfilm**	shvahrts**vighs**film
colour	**Farbfilm**	**fahrp**film
I'd like a hair-cut, please.	**Haare schneiden, bitte.**	**haa**rer **shnigh**dern **bit**ter

Souvenirs *Andenken*

I'd like a/an/some ...	**Ich hätte gern ...**	ikh **heh**ter gehrn
beer stein	**der Bierkrug**	derr **beer**kroog
chocolate	**die Schokolade**	dee shok**kol**laader
leather goods	**die Lederwaren**	dee **lay**derrvaarern
ski equipment	**dei Skiausrüstung**	dee **shee**owsrewstung
wood carving	**die Holzschnitz-arbeit**	dee **holts**shnitsahrbight

At the bank *Bank*

Where's the nearest bank/currency exchange office?	**Wo ist die nächste Bank/Wechsel-stube?**	voa ist dee **naikh**ster bahnk/**vehk**serlshtoober
I want to change some dollars/pounds.	**Ich möchte Dollar/Pfund wechseln.**	ikh **murkh**ter **doll**ahr/pfunt **vehk**serln
What's the exchange rate?	**Wie ist der Wechselkurs?**	vee ist derr **vehk**serlkoorss
I want to cash a traveller's cheque.	**Ich möchte einen Reisescheck ein-lösen.**	ikh **murkh**ter **igh**nern **righ**zershehk **igh**nlurzern

At the post office *Post*

I'd like to send this by...	**Ich möchte dies... senden.**	ikh **murkh**ter deess... **zehn**dern
airmail	**per Luftpost**	pehr **luft**post
express	**per Expreß**	pehr ehk**sprehss**
A...-pfennig stamp please.	**Eine Briefmarke zu ... Pfennig, bitte.**	**igh**ner **breef**maarker tsoo ... **pfehn**nikh **bit**ter
What's the postage for a letter/postcard to Los Angeles?	**Was kostet ein Brief/eine Post-karte nach Los Angeles?**	vahss **kost**et ighn breef/**igh**ner **post**kaarter naakh los **ehnd**zehrlerss
Is there any post/mail for me?	**Ist Post für mich da?**	ist post few mikh daa

Telephoning *Telefonieren*

Where's the nearest telephone booth?	**Wo ist die nächste Telefonzelle?**	voa ist dee **naikh**ster taylay**foan**tsehler
May I use your phone?	**Darf ich Ihr Telefon benutzen?**	dahrf ikh eer taylay**foan** ber**nut**sern
Hello. This is... speaking.	**Hallo. Hier spricht...**	**hahl**oa. heer shprikht
I'd like to speak to...	**Ich möchte... sprechen.**	ikh **murkh**ter... **shprehkh**ern
When will he/she be back?	**Wann ist er/sie zurück?**	vahn ist err/zee tsoo**rewk**
Will you tell him/her that I called?	**Würden Sie ihm/ihr sagen, daß ich angerufen habe?**	**vewr**dern zee eem/eer **zaa**gern dahss ikh **ahn**gerroofern **haa**ber

Days and date *Tage und Datum*

It's...	**Es ist...**	ehss ist
five past one	**fünf nach eins**	fewnf nakh ighns
quarter past three	**viertel nach drei**	feerterl nahkh drigh
twenty past four	**zwanzig nach vier**	tsvahntsikh nahkh feer
half-past six	**halb sieben**	hahlp zeebern
twenty-five to seven	**fünf nach halb sieben**	fewnf nakh hahlp zeebern
ten to ten	**zehn vor zehn**	tsayn foar tsayn
noon/midnight	**Mittag/Mitternacht**	mittaag/mitterrnahkht
in the morning	**morgens**	morgerns
in the afternoon	**nachmittags**	nahkhmittaags
in the evening	**abends**	aaberns
during the day	**tagsüber**	taagsewberr
at night	**nachts**	nahkhts
yesterday	**gestern**	gehsterrn
today	**heute**	hoyter
tomorrow	**morgen**	morgern
spring	**der Frühling**	derr frewling
summer	**der Sommer**	derr zommerr
autumn	**der Harbst**	derr hehrpst
winter	**der Winter**	derr vinterr

Sunday	**Sonntag**	zontaag
Monday	**Montag**	moantaag
Tuesday	**Dienstag**	deenstaag
Wednesday	**Mittwoch**	mitvokh
Thursday	**Donnerstag**	donnerrstaag
Friday	**Freitag**	frightaag
Saturday	**Samstag/Sonnabend**	zahmstaag/zonnaabernt
January	**Januar**	yahnuarr
February	**Februar**	faybruaar
March	**März**	mehrts
April	**April**	ahpril
May	**Mai**	migh
June	**Juni**	yooni
July	**Juli**	yooli
August	**August**	owgust
September	**September**	sehptehmberr
October	**Oktober**	oktoaberr
November	**November**	novvehmberr
December	**Dezember**	daytsehmberr

NUMBERS, see page 78

Numbers *Zahlen*

0	**null**	nul
1	**eins**	ighns
2	**zwei**	tsvigh
3	**drei**	drigh
4	**vier**	feer
5	**fünf**	fewnf
6	**sechs**	zehks
7	**sieben**	**zee**bern
8	**acht**	ahkht
9	**neun**	noyn
10	**zehn**	tsayn
11	**elf**	ehlf
12	**zwölf**	tsvurlf
13	**dreizehn**	**drigh**tsayn
14	**vierzehn**	**feer**tsayn
15	**fünfzehn**	**fewnf**tsayn
16	**sechzehn**	**zehkht**tsayn
17	**siebzehn**	**zeep**tsayn
18	**achtzehn**	**ahkht**sayn
19	**neunzehn**	**noynt**sayn
20	**zwanzig**	**tsvahnt**sikh
30	**dreißig**	**drighs**sikh
40	**vierzig**	**feert**sikh
50	**fünfzig**	**fewnft**sikh
60	**sechzig**	**zehkht**sikh
70	**siebzig**	**zeept**sikh
80	**achtzig**	**ahkht**sikh
90	**neunzig**	**noynt**sikh
100	**(ein)hundert**	(ighn)**hund**errt
1,000	**(ein)tausend**	(ighn)**tow**zernt
first/second	**erste/zweite**	**ehr**ster/**tsvigh**ter
once/twice	**einmal/dreimal**	**ighn**mal/**tsvigh**maal
a half	**eine Hälfte**	**igh**ner **hehl**fter

Emergency *Notfall*

Call the police	**Rufen sie die Polizei**	**roo**fern zee dee pollit**sigh**
Get a doctor	**Holen Sie einen Arzt**	**hoa**lern zee **igh**nern ahrtst
Go away	**Gehen Sie weg**	**gay**ern zee vehk
HELP	**HILFE**	**hil**fer
I'm ill	**Ich bin krank**	ikh bin krahnk
I'm lost	**Ich habe mich verirrt**	ikh **haa**ber mikh feh**reert**
STOP THIEF	**HALTET DEN DIEB**	**hahl**tert dayn deep

TELEPHONING, see page 76

My ... has been stolen.	Mein(e) ... ist mir gestohlen worden.	mighn(er) ... ist meer gershtoalern voardern
I've lost my ...	Ich habe meine ... verloren.	ikh haaber mighner ... fehrloarern
handbag	Handtasche	hahnttahsher
wallet	Brieftasche	breeftahsher
passport	Paß	pahss
luggage	Gepäck	gerpehk
Where is there a doctor who speaks English?	Wo gibt es einen Arzt, der Englisch spricht?	voa gipt ehss ighnern ahrtst derr ehnglish shprikht

Guide to German pronunciation *Aussprache*

Consonants

Letter	Approximate pronunciation	Symbol	Example	
f, h, k, l, m, n, p, t, x	as in English			
b	1) at the end of a word like p in up	p	ab	ahp
	2) as in English	b	bis	biss
c	1) before e, i, ö and ä, like ts in hits	ts	Celsius	tsehlziuss
	2) like c in cat	k	Café	kahfay
ch	1) like ch in Scottish loch, otherwise more like h in huge	kh	doch	dokh
	2) sometimes like k in kit	k	Wachs	vahks
d	1) at the end of a word like t in eat	t	Rad	raat
	2) elsewhere, like d in do	d	durstig	doorstikh
g	1) always hard as in go but at the end of a word like ck in tack	g	gehen	gayern
		k	weg	vehk
	2) when preceded by i at the end of a word like ch in Scottish loch	kh	billig	billikh
j	like y in yes			
qu	like k followed by v as in vat	kv	Quark	kvark
r	generally rolled in the back of the mouth	r	warum	vahrum

s	1) like z in zoo	z	sie	zee
	2) like sh in shut	sh	spät	shpait
	3) like s in sit	s/ss	es ist	ehss ist
ß	always like s in sit	s/ss	heiß	highss
sch	like sh in shut	sh	schnell	shnehl
tsch	like ch in chip	ch	deutsch	doych
tz	like ts in hits	ts	Platz	plahts
v	1) like f in for	f	vier	feer
	2) like v in vice	v	Vase	vaazer
w	like v in vice	v	wie	vee
z	like ts in hits	ts	zeigen	tsighgern

Vowels

a	1) short like u in cut	ah	lassen	lahssern
	2) long like a in car	aa	Abend	aabernt
ä	1) short like e in let	eh	Lärm	lehrm
	2) long like ai in hair	ai	spät	shpait
e	1) short like e in let	eh	sprechen	shprehkhern
	2) long like a in late, but pronounced without moving tongue or lips	ay	geben	gaybern
	3) unstressed, like er in other	er*	bitte	bitter
i	1) short like i in hit	i	billig	billikh
	2) long like ee in meet	ee	ihm	eem
ie	like ee in bee	ee	hier	heer
o	1) short like o in got	o	voll	fol
	2) long like o in note, but pronounced without moving tongue or lips	oa	ohne	oaner
ö	like ur in fur	ur*	können	kurnern
u	1) short like oo in foot	u	Nuß	nuss
	2) long like oo in moon	oo	gut	goot
ü	like French u in une; round your lips and try to say ea as in mean	ew	über	ewber
y	like German ü	ew	typisch	tewpish

Diphthongs

ai, ay, ei, ey	like igh in high	igh	mein	mighn
au	like ow in now	ow	auf	owf
äu, eu	like oy in boy	oy	new	noy

The r should not be pronounced when reading this transcription.

Deutsch

Greek

Basic expressions *Μερικές βασικές εκφράσεις*

Yes/No.	Ναι/Οχι.	neh/**okhee**
Please.	Παρακαλώ.	pahrahkah**lo**
Thank you.	Ευχαριστώ.	ehfkhahree**sto**
Sorry!	Συγγνώμη!	seengh**no**mmee

Introductions *Συστάσεις*

Good morning.	Καλημέρα.	kahlee**meh**rah
Good afternoon.	Καλησπέρα.	kahlee**speh**rah
Good night.	Καληνύχτα.	kahlee**neek**tah
Good-bye.	Αντίο.	ahn**dee**o
My name is...	Λέγομαι...	**leh**ghommeh
Pleased to meet you.	Χαίρομαι που σας γνωρίζω!	**kheh**rommeh poo sahss ghnor**ree**zo
What's your name?	Πώς λέγεστε;	poss **leh**yehsteh
How are you?	Πώς είστε;	poss **ee**steh
Fine thanks. And you?	Πολύ καλά, ευχαριστώ. Εσείς;	pol**lee** kah**lah** ehfkhahree**sto**. eh**seess**
Where do you come from?	Από πού είστε;	ah**po** poo **ee**steh
I'm from...	Είμαι από το/την...	**ee**meh ah**po** to/teen
Australia	Αυστραλία	ahfstrah**lee**ah
Canada	Καναδά	kahnah**dhah**
Great Britain	Μεγάλη Βρετανία	meh**ghah**lee vrahtah**nee**ah
United States	Ηνωμένες Πολιτείες	eenom**meh**nehss polleeteeehss
I'm with my...	Είμαι με... μου.	**ee**meh meh... moo
wife	την γυναίκα	teen yee**neh**kah
husband	τον άνδρα	tonn **ahn**drah
family	την οικογένεια	teen eeko**yeh**neeah
boyfriend/girlfriend	τον φίλο/την φίλη	tonn **fee**lo/teen **fee**lee
I'm here on vacation.	Είμαι εδώ για διακοπές.	**ee**meh eh**dho** yeeah dheeahko**ppehss**
I'm here on business.	Είμαι εδώ για δουλειά.	**ee**meh eh**dho** yeeah dhoolee**ah**

GUIDE TO PRONUNCIATION/EMERGENCIES, see page 95

Αγγλικά

Questions *Ερωτήσεις*

When?	Πότε;	**pot**teh
How?	Πώς;	poss
What?/Why?	Τί;/Γιατί;	tee/yeeah**tee**
Who?/Which?	Ποιός;	pee**oss**
Where is/are...?	Πού είναι...;	poo **ee**neh
Where can I find/ get...?	Πού μπορώ να βρω/αγοράσω...;	poo bo**rro** nah vro/ agho**rass**o
How far?	Πόσο μακρυά;	**poss**o mahkree**ah**
How long?	Πόση ώρα;	**poss**i ora
How much/many?	Πόσο/Πόσα;	**poss**o/**poss**ah
May I?	Μπορώ...;	bo**rro**
Can I have...?	Μπορώ να έχω...;	bo**rro** nah **ehk**ho
Can you help me?	Μπορείτε να με βοηθήσετε;	bo**ree**teh nah meh voee**thee**sehteh
What does this mean?	Τι σημαίνει αυτό;	tee see**meh**nee ah**fto**
I understand.	Καταλαβαίνω.	kahtahlah**veh**no
I don't understand.	Δεν καταλαβαίνω.	dhehn kahtahlah**veh**no
Can you translate this for me?	Μπορείτε να μου το μεταφράσετε;	bo**ree**teh nah moo to mehtah**frah**ssehteh
Do you speak English?	Μιλάτε Αγγλικά;	mee**lah**teh ahngglee**kah**
I don't speak (much) Greek.	Δεν μιλώ (καλά) Ελληνικά.	dhehn mee**lo** (kah**lah**) ehleenee**kah**

A few more useful words *Περισσότερες χρήσιμες λέξεις*

better/worse	καλύτερος/ χειρότερος	kah**lee**tehross/ khee**rot**tehross
big/small	μεγάλος/μικρός	meh**ghah**loss/mee**kross**
cheap/expensive	φθηνός/ακριβός	ftee**noss**/ahkree**voss**
early/late	νωρίς/αργά	nor**reess**/ahr**ghah**
good/bad	καλός/κακός	kah**loss**/kah**koss**
hot/cold	ζεστός/κρύος	zah**stoss**/**kree**oss
old/new	παλιός/καινούργιος	pahlee**oss**/kehn**oor**yeeoss
right/wrong	σωστός/λάθος	so**stoss**/**lah**thoss
vacant/occupied	ελεύθερος/ κατειλημμένος	ehl**ehf**thehross/ kahteelee**meh**noss

Hotel—Accommodation   Ξενοδοχείο

I have a reservation.	Έχω κάνει κράτηση.	ehkho kahnee krahteessee
We've reserved two rooms.	Έχουμε κλείσει δύο δωμάτια.	ehkhommeh kleessee dheeo dhommahtteeah
Do you have any vacancies?	Υπάρχουν άδεια δωμάτια;	eepahrkoon ahdheeah dhommahtteeah
I'd like a... room.	Θα ήθελα ένα... δωμάτιο.	thah eethehlah ehnah... dhommahtteeo
single/double	μονό/διπλό	monno/dheeplo
with twin beds	με δύο κρεββάτια	meh dheeo krehvahtteeah
with a double bed	με διπλό κρεββάτι	meh dheeplo krevahtee
with a bath/shower	με μπάνιο/ντους	meh bahneeo/dooss
We'll be staying...	Θα μείνουμε...	thah meenoomeh
overnight only	μόνο μια νύχτα	monno meeah neektah
a few days	λίγες μέρες	leeyehss mehrehss
a week	μια εβδομάδα	meeah ehvdhommahdhah
Is there a campsite near here?	Υπάρχει μέρος για κάμπινγκ εδώ κοντά;	eepahrkhee mehross yeeah "camping" ehdho kondah

Decision   Απόφαση

May I see the room?	Μπορώ να δω το δωμάτιο;	borro nah dho to dhommahtteeo
That's fine. I'll take it.	Είναι εντάξει. Θα το πάρω.	eeneh ehndahksee. thah to pahro
No. I don't like it.	Όχι. Δεν μου αρέσει.	okhee. dhehn moo ahrehssee
It's too...	Είναι πολύ...	eeneh pollee
dark/small	σκοτεινό/μικρό	skotteeno/meekro
It's too noisy.	Έχει πολύ θόρυβο.	ehkhee pollee thorreevo
Do you have anything...?	Έχετε κάτι..;	ehkhehteh kahtee
better	καλύτερο	kahleetehro
bigger	μεγαλύτερο	mehghahleetehro
cheaper	φθηνότερο	fteenottehro
quieter	πιο ήσυχο	peeo eesseekho
May I have my bill, please?	Μπορώ να έχω τον λογαριασμό, παρακαλώ;	borro nah ehkho tonn loghahreeahzmo pahrahkahlo
It's been a very enjoyable stay.	Η διαμονή ήταν πολύ ευχάριστη.	ee dheeahmonnee eetahn pollee ehfkhahreestee

Eating out *Εστιατόριο–Φαγητά*

I'd like to reserve a table for four.	**Θα ήθελα να κλείσω ένα τραπέζι για 4.**	thah eethehlah nah kleesso ehnah trahpehzee yeeah 4
We'll come at 8.	**Θα έλθουμε στις 8.**	thah ehlthoomeh steess 8
I'd like...	**Θα ήθελα...**	thah eethehlah
breakfast	**πρωινό**	proyehno
lunch	**μεσημεριανό**	mehseemehreeahno
dinner	**δείπνο**	dheepno
What do you recommend?	**Τι μας συστήνετε;**	tee mahss seesteenehteh
Do you have any vegetarian dishes?	**Έχετε πιάτα για χορτοφάγους;**	ehkhehteh peeahtah yeeah khortofahghooss

Breakfast *Πρωινό*

May I have some...	**Μπορώ να έχω...;**	borro nah ehkho
bread	**λίγο ψωμί**	leegho psommee
butter	**λίγο βούτυρο**	leegho vooteero
cereal	**δημητριακά**	dheemeetreeahkah
ham and eggs	**αυγά με ζαμπόν**	ahvghah meh zahmbonn
jam	**μαρμελάδα**	mahrmehlahdhah
rolls	**λίγα ψωμάκια**	leegah psommahkeeah

Starters (Appetizers) *Ορεκτικά*

αγγινάρες	ahnggeenahgrehss	artichokes
ελιές (γεμιστές)	ehleeehss (yehmeestehss)	(stuffed) olives
ντολμαδάκια	dolmahdhakeeah	stuffed vine leaves
ταραμοσαλάτα	tahrahmossahlahtah	fish roe paté
τυροπιττάκια	teeroppeetahkeeah	cheese filled pastries

Fish and seafood *Ψάρι και θαλασσινά*

crab	**καβούρι**	kahvooree
mullet	**κέφαλος**	kehfahlos
prawns (shrimps)	**γαρίδες**	ghahreedhehss
sardines	**σαρδέλλα**	sahrdhehlah
swordfish	**ξιφίας**	kseefeeahss
trout	**πέστροφα**	pehstroffah
tuna	**τόννος**	tonnos
χταπόδι κρασάτο	khtahpodhee krahssahto	octopus in wine sauce

NUMBERS, see page 94

baked	του φούρνου	too **foor**noo
boiled	βραστό	vrah**sto**
fried	τηγανητό	teeghahnee**to**
grilled	της σχάρας	teess **skhah**rahss
roast	ψητό	psee**to**
underdone (rare)	λίγο ψμένο	leegho psee**meh**no
medium	μέτρια ψημένο	**meh**treeah psee**meh**no
well-done	καλοψημένο	kahlopsee**meh**no

Meat Κρέας

I'd like some...	Θα ήθελα...	thah **ee**thehlah
bacon	μπέικον	**bee**konn
beef	βοδινό	vodhee**no**
chicken	κοτόπουλο	ko**tto**poollo
duck	πάπια	**pah**peeah
ham	ζαμπόν	zahm**bonn**
lamb	αρνί	ahr**nee**
pork	χοιρινό	kheereeno
veal	μοσχάρι	mos**khah**ree

παπουτσάκια (pahpoot**sah**keeah)	baked vegetable marrow (zucchini) stuffed with rice and/or meat, onions and white sauce
σουβλάκι (soo**vlah**kee)	chunks of meat marinated in olive oil and lemon juice, and grilled on a skewer
λαγός στιφάδο (lah**ghoss** stee**fah**dho)	hare cooked with spring onions, wine or tomatoes

Vegetables Λαχανικά

beans (green)	φασόλια	fahs**so**lleeah
carrots	καρότα	kah**rot**tah
mushrooms	μανιτάρια	mahnee**tah**reah
onions	κρεμμύδια	kreh**mee**dheeah
peas	μπιζέλια	beezehleeah
potatoes	πατάτες	pah**tah**tehss
spinach	σπανάκι	spah**nah**kee
tomatoes	ντομάτες	dom**mah**tehss

μουσακάς χωρίς κρέας (moossah**kahss** khor**ees** kreh**ahss**)	vegetarian moussaka made of aubergines, tomatoes, onions and cheese, with a béchamel sauce
χωριάτικη σαλάτα (khorree**ah**teekee sah**lah**tah)	salad made of olives, tomatoes, onions, cucumber, green pepper and feta (goat cheese)

Fruits and dessert *Φρούτα και Επιδόρπια*

apples	μήλα	**meela**
banana	μπανάνα	**bah**nahnah
cherries	κεράσια	keh**rah**ssah
lemon	λεμόνι	leh**mon**nee
orange	πορτοκάλι	porto**kkah**lee
pear	αχλάδι	ahkh**lah**dhee
strawberries	φράουλες	**frah**oolah
λουκούμι	lookoomee	Turkish delight
μηλόπιτα	meeloppeetah	apple pie
παγωτό	pahghotto	ice cream
πάστα	pahstah	tart
ρυζόγαλο	reezoghahlo	rice pudding

Drinks *Ποτάν*

beer	μπύρα	**beer**ah
(hot) chocolate	μια (ζεστή) σοκολάτα	**mee**ah (zeh**stee**) sokko**llah**tah
coffee	έναν καφέ	**eh**nah kah**feh**
black	σκέτο	**skeh**to
with milk	με γάλα	meh **ghah**lah
fruit juice	ένα χυμό φρούτων	**eh**nah kheemo **froo**tonn
milk	ένα γάλα	**eh**nah **ghah**lah
mineral water	ένα μεταλλικό νερό	**eh**nah mehtahleeko nahro
tea	ένα τσάι	**eh**nah **tsah**ee
wine	κρασί	krah**ssee**
red/white	κόκκινο/άσπρο	**kokk**eeno/**ahs**pro

Complaints and paying *Παράπονα – λογαριασμός*

This is too... bitter/sweet/salty	Αυτό είναι πολύ... πικρό/αλμυρό/ γλυκό	ahfto **ee**neh pollee peekro/ahlmeero/ ghleeko
That's not what I ordered.	Δεν είναι αυτό που παράγγειλα.	dhehn **ee**neh ahfto poo pahrahnggeelah
I'd like to pay.	Θα ήθελα να πληρώσω.	thah **ee**thehlah nah pleerosso
I think there's a mistake in this bill.	Νομίζω έχει γίνει λάθος στον λογαριασμό.	nommeezo **ekh**ee yeenee **lah**thoss stonn loghahreeahzmo
Can I pay with this credit card?	Μπορώ να πληρώσω με αυτή την πιστ- ωτική κάρτα;	borro nah pleerosso meh ahftee teen peestoteekee **kahr**tah
We enjoyed it, thank you.	Το απολαύσαμε, ευχαριστούμε.	to ahpo**llahf**sahmeh ehfkhahree**stoo**meh

Travelling around Ταξιδεύοντας

Plane Αεροπλάνο

Is there a flight to Athens?	Υπάρχει πτήση για την Αθήνα;	eepahrkhee pteessee yeeah teen ahtheenah
What time should I check in?	Τι ώρα πρέπει να είμαι στο αεροδρόμιο;	tee orrah prehpee nah eemeh sto ahehrodhrommeeo
I'd like to... my reservation.	Θα ήθελα να... την κράτησή μου.	thah eethehlah nah... teen krahteessee moo
cancel	ακυρώσω	ahkeerosso
change	αλλάξω	ahlahkso
confirm	επιβεβαιώσω	ehpeevehvehosso

Train Τραίνο

I'd like a ticket to Patras.	Θα ήθελα ένα εισιτήριο για Πάτρα.	thah eethehlah ehnah eesseeteereeo yeeah pahtrah
single (one-way)	απλό	ahplo
return (roundtrip)	με επιστροφή	meh ehpeestroffee
first/second class	πρώτη/δεύτερη θέση	prottee/dhehftehree thehssee
How long does the journey (trip) take?	Πόση ώρα διαρκεί το ταξίδι;	possee orrah dheeahrkee to tahkseedhee
When is the... train to Patras?	Πότε είναι το... τραίνο για την Πάτρα;	potteh eeneh to... trehno yeeah teen pahtrah
first/next/last	πρώτο/τελευταίο/ επόμενο	protto/tehlehfteho/ ehpommehno
Is this the right train to Tripolis?	Είναι αυτό το τραίνο για Τρίπολη;	eeneh ahfto to trehno yeeah treepollee

Bus Λεωφορείο

Which bus goes to the town centre?	Ποιό λεωφορείο πηγαίνει στο κέντρο της πόλης;	peeo lehofforreeo peeyehnee sto kehndro teess polleess
How much is the fare to...?	Πόσο κάνει το εισιτήριο για...;	posso kahnee to esseeteereeo yeeah
Will you tell me when to get off?	Θα μου πείτε πότε να κατέβω;	thah moo peeteh potteh nah kahtehvo

TELLING THE TIME, see page 93/NUMBERS, see page 94

Taxi *Ταξί*

How much is the fare to...?	Ποιά είναι η τιμή για...;	peeah eeneh ee teemee yeeah
Take me to this address.	Πηγαίνω σε αυτή τη διεύθυνση.	peeyehneh seh ahftee tee dheeehftheensee
Please stop here.	Παρακαλώ σταματήστε εδώ.	pahrahkahlo stahmahteesteh ehdho

Car hire (rental) *Ενοικίαση αυτοκινήτων*

I'd like to hire (rent) a car.	Θα ήθελα να νοικιάσω ένα αυτοκίνητο.	thah eethehlah nah neekeeahsso ehnah ahftokkeeneeto
I'd like it for...	Θα το ήθελα για...	thah to eethehlah yeeah
a day/week	μια μέρα/βδομάδα	meeah mehrah/ vdhommahdhah
Where's the nearest filling station?	Πού είναι το κοντινότερο πρατήριο βενζίνης;	poo eeneh to kondeenottehro prahteereeo vehnzeeneess
Full tank, please.	Γεμίστε το, παρακαλώ.	yehmeezmah pahrahkahlo
Give me... litres of petrol (gasoline).	Θα ήθελα... λίτρα βενζίνη.	thah eethehlah... leetrah vehnzeenee
How do I get to...?	Πώς μπορώ να πάω στο..;	poss borro nah paho sto
I've broken down at...	Έπαθα βλάβη στο...	ehpahthah vlahvee sto
Can you send a mechanic?	Μπορείτε να στείλετε έναν μηχανικό;	borreeteh nah steelehteh ehnan meekhahneeko
Can you mend this puncture (fix this flat)?	Το λάστιχο έχει τρυπήσει. Μπορείτε να το φτιάξετε;	to lahsteekho ehkhee treepeessee. borreeteh nah to dheeorthossehteh

---

Έχετε πάρει λάθος δρόμο.	You're on the wrong road.
Να πάτε ίσια.	Go straight ahead.
Είναι εκεί κάτω...	It's down there on the...
αριστερά/δεξιά	left/right
δίπλα σε/μετά...	next to/after...
βόρεια/νότια/ανατολικά/δυτικά	north/south/east/west

Αγγλικά

NUMBERS, see page 94

Sightseeing Αξιοθέατα

Where's the tourist office?	Πού είναι το γραφείο τουρισμού;	poo **ee**neh to ghrah**fee**o tooree**zmoo**
Is there an English-speaking guide?	Υπάρχει ξεναγός που να μιλάει Αγγλικά;	ee**pahr**khee ksehnah-**ghoss** poo nah mee**lah**ee ahng**glee**kah
Where is/are...?	Πού είναι...;	poo **ee**neh
art gallery	η γκαλερί (τέχνης)	ee gahleh**ree** (**tehkh**neess)
botanical garden	ο βοτανικός κήπος	o vottahnee**koss** kee**poss**
cathedral	η μητρόπολη	ee meet**rop**pollee
church	η εκκλησία	ee ehklee**see**ah
city centre/downtown	το κέντρο της πόλης	to **kehn**dro teess **poll**eess
exhibition	η έκθεση	ee **ehk**thehssee
harbour	το λιμάνι	to lee**mah**nee
market	η αγορά	ee ahgho**rrah**
museum	το μουσείο	to moo**ssee**o
square	η πλατεία	ee plah**tee**ah
temple	ο ναός	o nah**oss**
tower	ο πύργος	o **peer**ghoss
zoo	ο ζωολογικός κήπος	o zo-olloyee**koss** kee**poss**
What are the opening hours?	Ποιές είναι οι ώρες λειτουργίας;	pee**ehss ee**neh ee **orr**ehss leetoor**yee**ahss
When does it close?	Πότε κλείνει;	**pott**eh **klee**nee
How much is the entrance fee?	Πόσο κοστίζει η είσοδος;	**poss**o kos**tee**zee ee **ee**ssodhoss

Relaxing Ξεκούραση

What's playing at the... Theatre?	Τι παίζουν στο Θέατρο...;	tee **peh**zoon sto **theh**ahtro
Are there any seats for tonight?	Υπάρχουν θέσεις για απόψε;	ee**pahr**khoon **thehss**seess yee**ah** ah**pop**seh
How much are the seats?	Πόσο κοστίζει η είσοδος;	**poss**o kos**tee**zee ee **ee**ssodhoss
Would you like to go out with me tonight?	Θα θέλατε να βγούμε έξω μαζί απόψε;	thah **theh**lahteh nah **vghoo**meh **ehk**so mah**zee** ah**pop**seh
Is there a disco-theque in town?	Υπάρχει ντισκοτέκ στην πόλη;	ee**pahr**khee dheesko**theek** steen **poll**ee
Would you like to dance?	Θα θέλατε να χορέψουμε;	thah **theh**lahteh nah khor**rehp**soomeh
Thank you, it's been a wonderful evening.	Ευχαριστώ, ήταν μια υπέροχη βραδυά.	ehfkhahree**sto ee**tahn meeah ee**peh**rokhee vrah**dhee**ah

DAYS OF THE WEEK, see page 93

Shops, stores and services *Μαγαζιά και εξυπηρέτηση*

Where's the nearest...?	Πού είναι ο κοντινό-τερο...;	poo **ee**neh to kondee-**not**tehro
bakery	το αρτοποιείο (ο φούρνος)	to ahrtoppeee**ee**o (o **foor**noss)
bookshop/store	το βιβλιοπωλείο	to veevleeoppoll**ee**o
butcher's	το κρεοπωλείο	to krehoppoll**ee**o
chemist/drugstore	το φαρμακείο	to fahrmah**kee**o
dentist	ο οδοντίατρος	o odhon**dee**ahtross
department store	το πολυκατάστημα	to poleekah**tah**steemah
grocery	το παντοπωλείο	to pahndoppoll**ee**o
hairdresser (ladies/men)	το κομμωτήριο/ κουρείο	to kommotteer**ee**o/ koor**ee**o
news-stand	το περίπτερο	to peh**reep**tehro
post office	το ταχυδρομείο	to tahkheedhrom**mee**o
supermarket	σουπερμάρκετ	"supermarket"
toilets/restrooms	οι τουαλέττες	ee tooah**leh**tehss

General expressions *Γενικές εκφράσεις*

Where's the main shopping area?	Πού είναι το εμπορικό κέντρο;	poo **ee**neh to ehm**bor**eeko **kehn**dro
Do you have any...?	Έχετε μερικά...;	**eh**khehteh mehree**kah**
Can you show me this/that?	Μπορείτε να μου δείξετε αυτό/εκείνο;	borr**ee**teh nah moo **dhee**ksehteh ahf**to**/eh**kee**no
Haven't you any-thing...?	Δεν έχετε τίποτε...;	dhehn **eh**khehteh **tee**poteh
cheaper/better	φθηνότερο/καλύτερο	ftee**not**tehro/kah**lee**tehro
larger	μεγαλύτερο	mehghah**lee**tehro
smaller	μικρότερο	mee**krot**tehro
Can I try it on?	Μπορώ να το δοκιμάσω;	borro nah to dhokkee**mah**sso
How much is this?	Πόσο κάνει αυτό;	**poss**o **kah**nee ahf**to**
Please write it down.	Γράψτε το, παρακαλώ.	**ghrahps**teh to pahrahkah**lo**
I don't want to spend more than... drachmas.	Δεν θέλω να ξοδέψω περισσό-τερα από... δραχμές.	dhehn **thehl**o nah kso-**dheh**pso pehree**sso**ttehrah ahpo ... dhrahkh**mehss**
No, I don't like it.	Όχι, δεν μου αρέσει.	okhee dhehn moo ah**rehss**ee
I'll take it.	Θα το πάρω.	thah to **pah**ro
Do you accept credit cards?	Δέχεστε πιστωτικές κάρτες;	**dheh**khehsteh peestottee-**kehss** kahr**tehss**

NUMBERS, see page 94

black	μαύρο	**mahv**ro
blue	μπλε	bleh
brown	καφέ	kah**feh**
green	πράσινο	**prahs**seeno
orange	πορτοκαλί	portokkah**lee**
red	κόκκινο	**ko**kkeeno
white	άσπρο	**ahs**pro
yellow	κίτρινο	**kee**treeno
light...	ανοιχτό...	ahneekh**to**
dark...	σκούρο...	**skoo**ro

I want to buy a/an/ some...	Θέλω να αγοράσω...	**the**hlo nah ahghorr**rrah**zo
aspirin	ασπιρίνες	ahspeer**ee**nehss
newspaper	μια εφημερίδα	meeah ehfeemehr**ree**dhah
American	Αμερικανική	ahmehreekahnee**kee**
English	Αγγλική	ahnggleek**ee**
postcard	μια καρτ-ποστάλ	meeah kahrt po**stahl**
shampoo	ένα σαμπουάν	**eh**nah sahm**boo**ahn
soap	ένα σαπούνι	**eh**nah sah**poo**nee
sun-tan cream	μια κρέμα για τον ήλιο	meeah **kreh**mah yeeah tonn **ee**leeo
toothpaste	μια οδοντόπαστα	meeah odhon**do**pahstah
a half kilo of tomatoes	μισό κιλό τομάτες	mee**sso** kee**lo** dom**mah**tehss
a litre of milk	ένα λίτρο γάλα	**eh**nah **lee**tro **ghah**lah
I'd like a film for this camera.	Θα ήθελα ένα φιλμ γι' αυτή τη μηχανή.	thah **ee**thehla **eh**nah feelm yeeah**ftee** tee meekhah**nee**
black and white	ασπρόμαυρο	ahs**prom**mahvro
colour	έγχρωμο	**ehng**khrommo
I'd like a hair-cut, please.	Θέλω να με κουρψετε, παρακαλώ.	**the**hlo nah meh kooreh-**pseh**teh pahrahkah**lo**

Souvenirs Σουβενίρ (Ενθύμια)

ceramics	κεραμικά	kehrahmee**kah**
embroidery	κέντημα	**kehn**deemah
hand-knotted carpet	κιλίμι	kee**lee**mee
icon	εικόνα	ee**kon**nah
olive oil	ελαιόλαδο	ehleh**ol**lahdho
pottery	είδη αγγειο-πλαστικής	**ee**dhee ahnggeeoplah-stee**keess**
woollen rug	φλοκάτη	flo**kah**tee

At the bank Τράπεζα

Where's the nearest currency exchange office?	Πού είναι το κοντινότερο γραφείο συναλλάγματος;	poo **ee**neh to kondee**no**ttehro ghrah**fee**o seenah**lahgh**mahtoss
Where's the nearest bank?	Πού είναι η κοντινότερη τράπεζα;	poo **ee**neh ee kondee**no**ttehree **trah**pehzah
I want to change some dollars/pounds.	Θέλω ν' αλλάξω μερικά δολάρια/λίρες.	**the**hlo nah**lah**kso mahree**kah** dho**llahr**reah/**lee**rehs
I want to cash a traveller's cheque.	Θέλω να εξαργυρώσω ένα τράβελερς τσεκ.	**the**hlo nah ehksahryee-**ro**sso **eh**nah "traveller's" tshehk

At the post office Ταχυδρομείο

I want to send this by...	Θέλω να στείλω αυτό...	**the**hlo nah **stee**lo ahf**to**...
air mail	αεροπορικώς	ahehropporree**koss**
express	εξπρές	"express"
A... drachma stamp, please.	Γραμματόσημα των ... δραχμών, παρακαλώ.	ghrahmah**tos**seeman tonn... dhrah**khmonn** pahrahkah**lo**
What's the postage for a letter to the United States?	Πόσο κοστίζει ένα γράμμα για Ηνωμένες Πολιτείες;	**po**sso kost**ee**zee **eh**nah **ghrah**mah yee**ah** eeno-**mmeh**nehss polleet**ee**ehss
Is there any post/mail for me?	Υπάρχουν γράμματα για μένα;	ee**pahr**khoon **grah**mmahtah yee**ah meh**nah

Telephoning Τηλεφωνώντας

Where is the nearest telephone booth?	Πού είναι ο κοντινότερος τηλεφωνικός θάλαμος;	pee **ee**neh o kondee**no**tehross teelehfonnee**koss thah**lahmoss
May I use your phone?	Μπορώ να χρησιμοποιήσω το τηλέφωνό σας;	bo**rro** nah khreessee-mopp**ee**esso to teeleh**fonno** sahss
Hello. This is... speaking.	Γειά σας. Είμαι ο/η...	yeeah**ssahss**. **ee**meh o/ee...
I'd like to speak to...	Θα ήθελα να μιλήσω με...	thah **ee**thehlah nah mee**lee**sso meh
When will he/she be back?	Πότε θα επιστρέψει;	**po**tteh thah ehpee-**streh**psee

Time and date *Ώρα και Ημερομηνία*

It's...	Είναι...	eeneh
five past one	μία και πέντε	**mee**ah keh **pehn**deh
quarter past three	τρεις και τέταρτο	**treess** keh **teht**ahrto
twenty past four	τέσσερις και είκοσι	**tehss**sehreess keh **ee**kossee
half past six	έξι και μισή	**ehk**see keh mee**ssee**
twenty-five to seven	επτά παρά εικοσιπέντε	ehp**tah** pahrah eekossee**pehn**deh
ten to ten	δέκα παρά δέκα	**dheh**kah pahrah **dheh**kah
twelve o'clock	δώδεκα	**dho**dhehkah
in the morning/ afternoon/evening	το πρωί/απόγευμα/ βράδυ	to pro**ee**/ahp**oy**ehvmah/ **vrah**dhee
during the day	στη διάρκεια της ημέρας	stee dhee**ahr**keeah teess **meh**rahss
at night	τη νύχτα	tee **neek**tah
yesterday	χθές	kht**hehss**
today	σήμερα	**see**mehrah
tomorrow	αύριο	**ahv**reeo
spring/summer	άνοιξη/καλοκαίρι	**ah**neeksee/kahlo**kkeh**ree
autumn (fall)	φθινόπωρο	ftheen**op**porro
winter	χειμώνας	kheem**on**nahss

Sunday	**Κυριακή**	keereeah**kee**
Monday	**Δευτέρα**	dhehf**teh**rah
Tuesday	**Τρίτη**	**tree**tee
Wednesday	**Τετάρτη**	teht**ahr**tee
Thursday	**Πέμπτη**	**pehmp**tee
Friday	**Παρασκευή**	pahrahskeh**vee**
Saturday	**Σάββατο**	**sah**vahto
January	**Ιανουάριος**	eeahnoo**ah**reeoss
February	**Φεβρουάριος**	fehvroo**ah**reeoss
March	**Μάρτιος**	**mahr**teeoss
April	**Απρίλιος**	ah**pree**leeoss
May	**Μάιος**	**mah**eeoss
June	**Ιούνιος**	ee**oo**neeoss
July	**Ιούλιος**	ee**oo**leeoss
August	**Αύγουστος**	**ahv**ghoostoss
September	**Σεπτέμβριος**	sehpt**ehm**vreeoss
October	**Οκτώβριος**	okt**ov**reeoss
November	**Νοέμβριος**	noehm**v**reeoss
December	**Δεκέμβριος**	dhehk**ehm**vreeoss

NUMBERS, see page 94

Numbers *Αριθμο ι*

0	μηδέν	**mee**dhehn
1	ένα	**eh**nah
2	δύο	**dhee**o
3	τρία	**tree**ah
4	τέσσερα	**teh**ssehrah
5	πέντε	**pehn**deh
6	έξι	**ehk**see
7	επτά	ehp**tah**
8	οκτώ	ok**to**
9	εννιά	ehnee**ah**
10	δέκα	**dheh**kah
11	έντεκα	**ehn**dehkah
12	δώδεκα	**dho**dhehkah
13	δεκατρία	dhehkah**tree**ah
14	δεκατέσσερα	dhehkah**teh**ssehrah
15	δεκαπέντε	dhehkah**pehn**deh
16	δεκαέξι	dhehkah**ehk**see
17	δεκαεπτά	dhehkahehp**tah**
18	δεκαοκτώ	dhehkahok**to**
19	δεκαεννιά	dhehkahehnee**ah**
20	είκοσι	**ee**kossee
21	είκοσι ένα	**ee**kossee **eh**nah
30	τριάντα	tree**ahn**dah
40	σαράντα	sah**rahn**dah
50	πενήντα	peh**neen**dah
60	εξήντα	ehk**seen**dah
70	εβδομήντα	ehvdho**mmeen**dah
80	ογδόντα	ogh**dhon**dah
90	ενενήντα	ehneh**neen**dah
100	εκατό	ehkah**to**
1,000	χίλια	**kheel**eeah
100,000	εκατό χιλιάδες	ehkah**to** kheelee**ah**dehss
1,000,000	ένα εκατομμύριο	**eh**nah ehkahtom**mee**reeo
first	πρώτος	**pro**ttoss
second	δεύτερος	**dhehf**tehross
third	τρίτος	**tree**toss
once	μια φορά	**mee**ah for**rah**
twice	δύο φορές	**dhee**o for**rehss**
a half	μισό	mee**sso**
a quarter	ένα τέταρτο	**eh**nah **teh**tahrto
a third	ένα τρίτο	**eh**nah **tree**to

Emergency *Έκτακτες–Ανάγκες*

Call the police!	Καλέστε την αστυνομία	kahlehsteh teen ahsteenomeeah
Get a doctor	Καλέστε ένα γιατρό	kahlehsteh ehnah yeeahtro
Go away	Απομακρυνθείτε	ahpomahkreentheeteh
HELP	ΒΟΗΘΕΙΑ	voeetheeah
I'm ill	Είμαι άρρωστος (-η)	eemeh ahrostoss (-ee)
I'm lost	Έχω χαθεί	eehkho khahthee
Leave me alone	Αφήστε με ήσυχο (-η)	ahfeesteh meh eesseekho (-ee)
LOOK OUT	ΠΡΟΣΟΧΗ	prossokhee
STOP THIEF	ΣΤΑΜΑΤΗΣΤΕ ΤΟΝ ΚΛΕΦΤΗ	stahmahteesteh tonn klehftee
My ... has been stolen.	Εκλάπη το... μου.	ehklahpee to ... moo
I've lost my...	Έχασα... μου.	ehkhahssah ... moo
handbag	την τσάντα	teen tsahndah
passport	το διαβατήριο	to dheeahvahteereeo
wallet	το πορτοφόλι	to portoffollee
Where can I find a doctor who speaks English?	Πού μπορώ να βρω ένα γιατρό να μιλά Αγγλικά;	poo borro nah vro ehnah eeahtro nah meelahee ahnggleekah

Guide to Greek pronunciation *Προφορά*

Vowels

Letter	Approximate pronunciation	Symbol	Example	
α	like the vowel in car, but pronounced further forward in the mouth	ah	άρομα	ahrommah
ε	like e in sell	eh	μέρα	mehrah
η, ι, υ	like ee in meet	ee	κύριος	keereeoss
ο, ω	like o in got	o	παρακαλώ	pahrahkahlo

TELEPHONING, see page 92

Consonants

β	like **v** in vine	v	βιβλίο	vee**vlee**o
γ	1) a voiced version of the **ch** sound in Scottish loch	gh	μεγάλος	meh**ghah**loss
	2) like **y** in yet	y	γεμάτος	yeh**mah**toss
δ	like **th** in this	dh	δεν	dhehn
ζ	like **z** in zoo	z	ζεστός	zeh**stoss**
θ	like **th** in thing	th	θα	thah
κ	like **k** in kit	k	καλός	kah**loss**
λ	like **l** in lemon	l	λάθος	**lah**thoss
μ	like **m** in man	m	μέσα	**meh**ssah
ν	like **n** in new	n	νέος	**neh**oss
ξ	like **x** in six	ks	έξω	**ehk**so
π	like **p** in pot	p	προς	pross
ϱ	like **r** in red	r	πριν	preen
σ, ς	1) like **z** in zoo	z	κόσμος	**koz**moss
	2) like **s** in see	s/ss	Πόσσο στο	**posso** sto
τ	like **t** in tea	t	τότε	**tot**teh
6	like **f** in five	f	φέρτε	**fehr**teh
χ	like **ch** in Scottish loch	kh	άσχημος	**ahs**khee-moss
ψ	like **ps** in dropsy	ps	διψώ	dheep**so**

Groups of letters

αι	like **e** in get	eh	είναι	**ee**neh
ει, οι	like **ee** in see	ee	ρείτε	**pee**teh
ου	like **oo** in root	oo	μου	moo
αυ	1) like **uff** in puff	ahf	αυτό	ahf**to**
	2) similar to **ave** in have	ahv	αυγό	ahv**gho**
ευ	1) like **ef** in left	ehf	ευχή	ehf**khee**
	2) like **ev** in level	ehv	ευμενής	ehvmeh**neess**
γγ	like **ng** in linger	ngg	Αγγλία	ahng**glee**ah
γκ	1) like **g** in go	g	γκαμήλα	gah**meelah**
	2) like **ng** in linger	ngg	άγκυρα	**ahng**geerah
γξ	like **nks** in links	ngks	φάλαγξ	fah**lahngks**
γχ	like **ng** followed by the **ch** of Scottish loch	ngkh	μελαγχολία	mehlahng-**kholleeah**
μπ	1) like **b** in beer	b	μπορείτε	bor**reeteh**
	2) like **mb** in lumber	mb	Όλυμπος	**olleem**boss
ντ	1) like **d** in dear	d	ντομάτα	dom**mahtah**
	2) like **nd** in under	nd	κένσρο	**kehn**dro
τ	like **ds** in seeds	dz	τζάκι	**dzah**kee

Italian

Basic expressions *Espressioni correnti*

Yes/No.	**Sì/No.**	see/no
Please.	**Per favore.**	pair fah**voa**ray
Thank you.	**Grazie.**	**graat**seeay
I beg your pardon?	**Prego?**	**pray**goa

Introductions *Presentazioni*

Good morning.	**Buon giorno.**	bwon **joar**noa
Good afternoon.	**Buon giorno.**	bwon **joar**noa
Good night.	**Buona notte.**	**bwo**nah **not**tay
Good-bye.	**Arrivederci.**	ahrreevay**dair**chee
So long.	**Ciao!**	**chaa**oa
My name is...	**Mi chiamo ...**	mee kee**aa**moa
Pleased to meet you.	**Piacere.**	peeah**chay**ray
What's your name?	**Come si chiama?**	**koa**may see kee**aa**mah
How are you?	**Come sta?**	**koa**may stah
Fine thanks. And you?	**Bene grazie. E lei?**	**bai**nay **graat**seeay. ay **la**iee
Where do you come from?	**Da dove viene?**	dah **doa**vay vee**ay**nay
I'm from...	**Sono ...**	**soa**noa
Australia	**di l'Australia**	dee low**straa**leeah
Canada	**di Canada**	dee **kah**nah**dah**
Great Britain	**di Gran Bretagna**	dee grahn bray**taa**ñah
United States	**degli Stati Uniti**	**day**lee **staa**tee oo**nee**tee
I'm with my...	**Sono con ...**	**soa**noa kon
wife	**mia moglie**	**mee**ah **moa**lyay
husband	**mio marito**	**mee**oa mah**ree**toa
family	**la mia famiglia**	lah **mee**ah fah**mee**lyah
boyfriend	**il mio ragazzo**	eel **mee**oa rah**gaht**tsoa
girlfriend	**la mia ragazza**	lah **mee**ah rah**gaht**tsah
I'm here on business/ on vacation.	**Sono qui per affari/ in vacanza.**	**soa**noa **kooee** pair ahf**faa**ree/een vah**kahn**tsah

GUIDE TO PRONUNCIATION/EMERGENCIES, see page 111

Questions *Domande*

When?	**Quando?**	kwahndoa
How?	**Come?**	koamay
What?	**Che cosa/Che?**	kay kawsah/kay
Why?	**Perchè?**	pehrkay
Who?/Which?	**Chi?/Quale?**	kee/kwaalay
Where is...?	**Dov'è/Dove si trova...?**	doavai/doavay see trawvah
Where are...?	**Dove sono/Dove si trovano...?**	doavay soanoa/doavay see trawvahnoa
Where can I find/get...?	**Dove posso trovare...?**	doavay possoa trovaaray
How far?	**Quanto dista?**	kwahntoa deestah
How long?	**Quanto tempo?**	kwahntoa tehmpoa
How much/many?	**Quanto/Quanti?**	kwahntoa/kwahntee
Can I have...?	**Posso avere...?**	possoa ahvayray
Can you help me?	**Può aiutarmi?**	pwo aheeootaarmee
What does this mean?	**Che cosa significa questo?**	kay kawsah seeñeefeekah kooaystoa
I understand.	**Capisco.**	kahpeeskoa
I don't understand.	**Non capisco.**	noan kahpeeskoa
Can you translate this for me?	**Può tradurmi questo?**	pwo trahdoormee kooaystoa
Do you speak English?	**Parla inglese?**	pahrlah eengglaysay
I don't speak (much) Italian.	**Non parlo (bene) l'italiano.**	noan pahrloa (bainay) leetahleeaanoa

A few more useful words *Qualche altra parola utile*

better/worse	**migliore/peggiore**	meelyoaray/paydjoaray
big/small	**grande/piccolo**	grahnday/peekkoaloa
cheap/expensive	**buon mercato/caro**	bwawn mayrkahtoa/kaaroa
early/late	**presto/tardi**	prehstoa/tahrdee
good/bad	**buono/cattivo**	bwawnoa/kahtteevoa
hot/cold	**caldo/freddo**	kahldoa/frayddoa
near/far	**vicino/lontano**	veecheenoa/lontaanoa
old/new	**vecchio/nuovo**	vehkkeeoa/nwawvoa
right/wrong	**giusto/sbagliato**	joostoa/zbahlyaatoa
vacant/occupied	**libero/occupato**	leebayroa/okkoopaatoa

Italiano

Hotel–Accommodation *Albergo*

I have a reservation.	**Ho fatto una prenotazione.**	oa **fah**ttoa **oo**nah praynoatahtseeoo**anay**
We've reserved 2 rooms.	**Abbiamo prenotato due camere.**	ahb**bee**aamoa praynoatah-toa **doo**ay **kaa**mayray
Do you have any vacancies?	**Avete camere libere?**	ah**vay**tay **kaa**mayray **lee**bayray
I'd like a…room…	**Vorrei una camera…**	vor**raiee oo**nah **kaa**marah
single	**singola**	**seeng**goalah
double	**doppia**	**doapp**eeah
with twin beds	**con due letti**	kon **doo**ay **leh**ttee
with a double bed	**con un letto matrimoniale**	kon oon **leh**ttoa matreemoanee**aa**lay
with a bath/shower	**con bagno/doccia**	kon **baa**ñoa/**dot**chah
We'll be staying…	**Resteremo…**	raystay**ray**moa
overnight only	**una notte**	**oo**nah **not**tay
a few days	**qualche giorno**	**kwahl**kay **joar**noa
a week	**un settimana**	**oo**nah saytteem**aa**nah
Is there a camp site near here?	**C'è un campeggio qui vicino?**	chai oon kahm**payd**joa **koo**ee veecheenoa

Decision *Decisione*

May I see the room?	**Posso vedere la camera?**	**poss**oa vay**day**ray lah **kaa**mayrah
That's fine. I'll take it.	**Va bene, la prendo.**	vah **bai**nay lah **prehn**doa
No. I don't like it.	**No, non mi piace.**	noa noan mee pee**ah**chay
It's too…	**È troppo…**	ai **trop**poa
dark/small	**buia/piccola**	**boo**eeah/**peek**koalah
noisy	**rumorosa**	roomoar**oa**zah
Do you have anything…?	**Ha qualcosa…?**	ah kwahl**kaw**sah
better	**migliore**	meel**yoa**ray
bigger	**più grande**	pee**oo grahn**day
cheaper	**meno caro**	**mai**noa **kaa**roa
quieter	**più tranquillo**	pee**oo** trahng**kooeel**loa
May I have my bill, please?	**Posso avere il conto, per favore?**	**poss**oa ah**vay**ray eel **koan**toa pair fah**voa**ray
It's been a very enjoyable stay.	**È stato un soggiorno molto piacevole.**	ai **staa**toa oon soad**joar**noa **moal**toa peeh**chay**voalay

NUMBERS, see page 110

Eating out *Ristorante*

I'd like to reserve a table for 4.	**Vorrei riservare un tavolo per 4.**	vorraiee reesehrvaaray oon taavoala pair 4
We'll come at 8.	**Verremo alle 8.**	vayrraymoa ahllay 8
I'd like...	**Vorrei...**	vorraiee
breakfast	**la colazione**	lah kolahtseeoanay
lunch	**il pranzo**	eel prahndzoa
dinner	**la cena**	lah chaynah
What do you recommend?	**Cosa consiglia?**	kawsah akonseelyah
Do you have any vegetarian dishes?	**Avete dei piatti vegetariani?**	ahvaytay daiee peeahtte vajyaytahreeaanee

Breakfast *Colazione*

May I have some...	**Posso avere...**	possoa ahvayray
bread	**del pane**	dayl paanay
butter	**del burro**	dayl boorroa
cheese	**del formaggio**	dayl foarmahdjoa
ham and eggs	**uova e prosciutto**	wawvah ay proashoottoa
jam	**della marmellata**	dayllah mahrmayllaatah
rolls	**dei panini**	daiee pahneenee

Appetizers *Antipasti*

carciofini sottolio	kahrchofeenee soattolyoa	artichoke hearts in olive oil
frutti di mare	froottee ee maaray	mixed seafood
insalata di pollo	eensahlaatah dee poalloa	chicken salad
sardine all'olio	sahrdeenay ahllolyoa	sardines in oil

Pasta and sauces *Pasta e salse*

agnolotti (ahñoalottee)	round parcels filled with meat, vegetables and cheese
amatriciana (ahmahtreechaanah)	sauce of tomatoes, red peppers, bacon, onion garlic and wine
cappelletti (kahppayllayttee)	small ravioli filled with meat, herbs, ham and cheese
carrettiera (kahrraytteeayrah)	sauce of tuna, mushrooms, tomato purée and pepper
puttanesca (poottahnayskah)	sauce of capers, olives, parsley, garlic, olive oil and black pepper

ITALIAN

Fish and seafood *Pesci e frutti di mare*

carp	**carpa**	kahrpah
cod	**merluzzo**	mayrloottsoa
crab	**granchi**	grahngkee
lobster	**aragosta**	ahrahgoastah
mussels	**cozze**	koatsay
oysters	**ostriche**	ostreekay
scallops	**arselle**	ahrsehllay
swordfish	**pesce spada**	payshay spaadah

Meat *Carne*

I'd like some…	**Vorrei…**	vorraiee
beef	**del manzo**	dayl **mahn**dzoa
chicken	**del pollo**	dayl **poal**loa
lamb	**dell'agnello**	dayl**lah**ñehlloa
pork	**del maiale**	dayl maaeeaalay
veal	**del vitello**	dal veetehlloa
abbacchio	ahb**bahk**keeoa	roast lamb with anchovies
pollo alla diavola	**poal**loa ah**llah** deeaavoalah	highly spiced grilled chicken
spezzatino	spaytsah**teen**oa	meat or poultry stew

baked	**al forno**	ahl **for**noa
boiled	**lesso**	**lays**soa
fried/roast	**fritto/arrosto**	**freet**toa/ahr**roas**toa
grilled	**ai ferri**	ahee **fehr**ree
stewed	**in umido**	een **oo**meedoa
underdone (rare)	**al sangue**	ahl **sahng**gooay
medium	**a puntino**	al poon**teen**oa
well-done	**ben cotto**	bain **kot**toa

Vegetables *Verdure*

beans (French)	**fagiolini**	fahjoa**leen**ee
cabbage	**cavolo**	**kaa**voaloa
carrots	**carote**	kah**raw**tay
mushrooms	**funghi**	**foong**gee
onions	**cipolle**	chee**pol**lay
peas	**piselli**	pee**sehl**lee
potatoes	**patate**	pay**taa**tay
tomatoes	**pomodoro**	poamoa**da**wroa

Italiano

Fruit and dessert *Frutta e dolce*

apple	**mela**	maylah
cherries	**ciliege**	cheeleeayjay
lemon	**limone**	leemoanay
orange	**arancia**	ahrahnchah
pear	**pera**	payrah
plums	**susina**	soozeenah
strawberries	**fragole**	fraagoalay
budino	boodeenoa	pudding
gelato	jaylaatoa	ice-cream
zabaglione	dzahbahlyoanay	eggyolks, sugar and Marsala wine

Drinks *Bevande*

I'd like...	**Vorrei...**	vorraiee
beer	**una birra**	oonah beerrah
(hot) chocolate	**un cioccolato**	oon choakkoalaatoa
coffee	**un caffè**	oon kahffai
with cream	**con panna**	kon pahnnah
fruit juice	**un succo di frutta**	oon sookkoa dee froottah
milk	**del latte**	dayl lahttay
mineral water	**dell'acqua minerale**	dayyllahkkwah meenayraalay
tea	**un tè**	oon tai
wine	**di vino**	dee veenoa
a bottle	**una bottiglia**	oonah botteelyah
a glass	**un bicchiere**	oon beekkeeairay
red/white	**rosso/bianco**	roassoa/beeahngkoa

Complaints and paying *Reclami e il conto*

This is too bitter/sweet.	**Questo è troppo amaro/dolce.**	kooaystoa ai troppoa ahmaaroa/doalchay
That's not what I ordered.	**Non è ciò che avevo ordinato.**	noan ai cho kay ahvayvoa oarkeenaatoa
I'd like to pay.	**Vorrei pagare.**	vorraiee pahgaaray
I think there's a mistake in this bill.	**Penso che abbiate fatto un errore nel conto.**	pehnsoa kay ahbbeeaatay fahttoa oon ayrroaray nayl koantoa
Can I pay with this credit card?	**Posso pagare con questa carta di credito?**	possoa pahgaaray kon kooaystah kahrtah dee kraydeetoa
We enjoyed it, thank you.	**Ci è piaciuto, grazie.**	chee ai peeahchootoa graatseeay

NUMBERS, see page 110

Italiano

Travelling around *Escursioni*

Plane *Aereo*

Is there a flight to...?	C'è un volo per...	chai oon **voa**loa pair
What time should I check in?	A che ora devo presentarmi?	ah kay **oa**rah **day**voa prayzehn**taar**mee
I'd like to... my reservation.	Vorrei... la mia prenotazione.	vor**raie**... lah **mee**ah praynoatahtseeo**a**nay
cancel	annullare	ahnnool**laa**ray
change	cambiare	kahmbee**aa**ray
confirm	confermare	koanfayr**maa**ray

Train *Treno*

I'd like a ticket to...	Desidero un biglietto per...	day**zee**dayroa oon bee**lyay**ttoa pair
single (one-way)	andata	ahn**daa**tah
return (round trip)	andata e ritorno	ahn**daa**tah ay ree**tor**noa
first/second class	prima/secondo classe	**pree**mah/say**koan**dah **klahs**say
How long does the journey (trip) take?	Quanto tempo dura il percorso?	**kwahn**toa **tehm**poa **doo**rah eel payr**kor**soa
When is the... train to...?	Quando parte... treno per...?	**kwahn**doa **pahr**tay... **tray**noa pair
first	il primo	eel **pree**moa
next	il prossimo	eel **pros**seemoa
last	l'ultimo	**lool**teemoa
Is this the right train to...?	È il treno guisto per...?	ai eel **tray**noa **joos**toa pair

Bus–Tram (streetcar) *Autobus –Tram*

Which bus do I take for the Colosseum?	Quale autobus devo prendere per andare al Colosseo?	**kwaa**lay owtoa**booss day**voa **prehn**dayray pair ahn**daa**ray ahl koaloass**aio**a
How much is the fare to...?	Quanto costa il biglietto per...?	**kwahn**toa **kos**tah eel bee**lyay**ttoa pair
Will you tell me when to get off?	Può dirmi quando devo scendere?	pwo **deer**mee **kwahn**doa **day**voa **shayn**dayray

Taxi *Taxi*

What's the fare to...?	Qual è il prezzo della corsa fino a...?	kwahl ai eel **preht**tsoa **dayl**lah **kors**sah **fee**noa ah

TELLING THE TIME, see page 109

Take me to this address.	**Mi conduca a questo indirizzo.**	mee koan**doo**kah ah kooay**stoa** eendee**reet**tsoa
Please stop here.	**Per favore, si fermi qui.**	pair fah**voa**ray see **fayr**mee koo**ee**
Could you wait for me?	**Può aspettarmi?**	pwo ahspeht**taar**mee

Car hire (rental) *Autonoleggio*

I'd like to hire (rent) a car.	**Vorrei noleggiare una macchina.**	vor**raiee** noalayd**jaaray oo**nah **mahk**keenah
I'd like it for...	**La vorrei per...**	lah vor**raiee** pair
a day	**un giorno**	oon **joar**noa
a week	**una settimana**	**oo**nah sayttee**maa**nah
Where's the nearest filling station?	**Dov'è la stazione di rifornimento più vicina?**	doa**vai** lah stahtsee**oo**nay dee reeforne**mayn**toa pee**oo** vee**chee**nah
Fill it up, please.	**Il pieno, per favore.**	eel pee**ai**noa pair fah**voa**ray
Give me... litres of petrol (gasoline).	**Mi dia... litri di benzina.**	mee **dee**ah... **lee**tree dee bayn**dzee**nah
How do I get to...?	**Come si va a...?**	**koa**may see vah ah
I've had a breakdown at...	**Ho avuto un guasto a...**	oa ah**voo**too oon **gwaa**stoa ah
Can you send a mechanic?	**Può mandare un meccanico?**	pwo mahn**daa**ray oon mayk**kaa**neekoa
Can you mend this puncture (fix this flat)?	**Può riparare questa foratura?**	pwo reepah**raa**ray kooay**stah** forah**too**rah

---

Lei è sulla strada sbagliata.	You're on the wrong road.
Vada diritto.	Go straight ahead.
È laggiù a...	It's down there on the...
sinistra/destra	left/right
di fronte/dietro...	opposite/behind...
accanto a/dopo...	next to/after...
nord/sud/est/ovest	north/south/east/west

NUMBERS, see page 110

Sightseeing *Visite turistiche*

Where's the tourist office?	Dov'è l'ufficio turistico?	doavai looffeechoa tooreesteekoa
Is there an English-speaking guide?	C'è una guida che parla inglese?	chai oonah gooeedahkay pahrlah eengglaysay
Where is...?	Dove si trova...?	doavay see trawvah
Where are...?	Dove si trovano...?	doavay see trawvahnoa
abbey	l'abbazia	lahbbahtseeah
castle	il castello	eel kahstehlloa
cathedral	la cattedrale	lah kahttaydraalay
church	la chiesa	lah keeayzah
city centre	il centro città	eel chayntroa cheettah
exhibition	l'esposizione	layspozeetseeoanay
harbour	il porto	eel portoa
market	il mercato	eel mayrkaatoa
museum	il museo	eel moozaioa
shopping area	la zona dei negozi	lah dzonah daiee naygotsee
square	la piazza	lah peeahtsah
tower	la torre	lah toarray
When does it open?	Quando apre?	kwahndoa aapray
When does it close?	Quando chuide?	kwahndoa keeoooday
How much is the entrance fee?	Quanto costa l'entrata?	kwahntoa kostah layntraatah

Relaxing *Divertimenti*

What's playing at the... Theatre?	Che spettacolo c'è al teatro...?	kay spayttaakoaloa chai ahl tayaatroa
Are there any seats for tonight?	Ci sono posti per questa sera?	chee soanoa postee pair kooaysstah sayrah
How much are the seats?	Quanto costano i posti?	kwahntoa kostahnoa ee postee
Would you like to go out with me tonight?	Uscirebbe con me stasera?	oosheerehbbay kon mai stahsayrah
Is there a disco-theque in town?	C'è una discoteca in città?	chai oonah deeskoataykah een cheettah
Would you like to dance?	Vuole ballare?	vwolay bahllaaray
Thank you, it's been a wonderful evening.	Grazie, è stata una magnifica serata.	graatseeay ai staatah oonah mahñeefeekah sayraatah

TELLING THE TIME, see page 109

Shops, stores and services *Negozi e servizi*

Where's the nearest...?	Dove si trova... più vicino(a)?	doavay see trawvah... peeeoo veecheenoa(ah)
bakery	la panetteria	lah pahnehttayreeah
bookshop	la libreria	lah leebrayreeah
butcher's	la macelleria	lah mahchayllayreeah
chemist/drugstore	la farmacia	lah fahrmahacheeah
delicatessen	la salumeria	lah sahloomayreeah
department store	il grande magazzino	eel grahnday mahgahdzeenoa
grocery	il megozio di alimentari	eel maygotseeoa dee ahleemayntaaree
hairdresser	il parrucchiere	eel pahrrookkeeayray
newsagent	il giornalaio	eel joarnahlaaeeoa
post office	l'ufficio postale	looffeechoa poastaalay
supermarket	il supermercato	eel soopairmayrkaatoa
toilets	i gabinetti	ee gahbeenayttee

General expressions *Espressioni generali*

Where's the main shopping area?	Dov'è la zona principle dei negozi?	doavai lah dzoanah preencheepaalay daieenaygotsee
Do you have any...?	Ha dei...?	ah daiee
Can you show me this/that?	Mi può mostrare questo/quello?	mee pwo moastraaray kooaystoa/kooaylloa
Haven't you anything...?	Non ha qualcosa...?	noan ah kwahlkawsah
cheaper	meno caro	maynoa kaaroa
better	migliore	meelyoaray
larger/smaller	più grande	peeoo grahnday
Can I try it on?	Posso provarlo?	possoa provahrloa
How much is this?	Quanto costa questo?	kwahntoa kostah kooaystoa
Please write it down.	Per favore, me lo scriva.	pair fahvoaray may loa skreevah
I don't want to spend more than... lire.	Non voglio spendere più di... lire.	noan volyoa spehndayray peeoo dee... leeray
No, I don't like it.	No, non mi piace.	noa noan mee peeaachay
I'll take it.	Lo prendo.	loa prayndoa
Do you accept credit-cards?	Accettate carte di credito?	ahtchehttaatay kahrtay dee kraydeetoa
Can you order it for me?	Può ordinarmelo?	pwo oardeenaarmayloa

NUMBERS, see page 110

black	nero	nayroa
blue	blu	bloo
brown	marrone	mahrroanay
green	verde	vayrday
grey	grigio	greejoa
orange	arancio	ahrahnchoa
red	rosso	roassoa
yellow	giallo	jahlloa
white	bianco	beeahngkoa
light...	... chiaro	keeaaroa
dark...	... scuro	skooroa

I'd like a/an/some...	Desidero...	dayzeedayroa
aspirin	delle aspirine	dayllay ahspeereenay
bottle-opener	un apribottiglia	oon ahpreebotteelyah
bread	del pane	dayl paanay
newspaper	un giornale	oon joarnaalay
postcard	una cartolina	oonah kahrtoaleenah
shampoo	dello shampoo	daylloa shahmpoa
soap	una saponetta	oonah sahpoanayttah
sun-tan cream	una crema solare	oonah kraimah soalaaray
toothpaste	un dentifricio	oon daynteefreechoa
a half kilo of tomatoes	mezzo chillo di pomodori	mehdzoa keeloa dee pomodawree
a litre of milk	un litro di latte	oon leetroa dee lahttay
I'd like a film for this camera.	Vorrei una pellicola per questa macchina fotografica.	vorraiee oonah pehlleekoalah pair kooaystah mahkkeenah foatoagraafeekah
black and white	in bianco e nero	een beeahngkoa ay nayroa
colour	a colori	ah koaloaree
I'd like a hair-cut, please.	Voglio il taglio dei capelli, per favore.	volyoa eel taalyoa daiee kahpehllee pair fahvoaray

Souvenirs *Oggetti ricordo*

antiques	l'antichità	lahteekeetah
chocolate	il cioccolato	eel choakkoalaatoa
flask of Chianti	il fiasco di Chianti	eel feeaaskoa dee keeahntee
leather work	la pelletteria	lah paylleyttayreeah
porcelain	la porcellana	lah poarchallaanah
silk	la seta	lah saitah

At the bank *In banca*

Where's the nearest bank/currency exchange office?	Dov'è la banca/ l'ufficio cambio più vicina?	doavai lah bahngkah looffeechoa kahmbeeoa peeoo veecheenah
I want to change some dollars/pounds.	Desidero cambiare dei dollari/delle sterline.	dayzeedayroa kahmbeeaa-ray daiee dollahree/dayllay stayrleenay
What's the exchange rate?	Qual è il corso del cambio?	kwahl ai ee koarsoa dayl kahmbeeoa
I want to cash a traveller's cheque.	Voglio incassare un traveller's cheque	voloa eengkahssaaray oon "traveller's cheque"

At the post office *Ufficio postale*

I want to send this by...	Desidero inviare questo per...	dayzeedayroa eenveeaaray kooaystoa pair
airmail	via aerea	veeah ahayrayah
express	espresso	aysprehssoa
I want... ...-lire stamps.	Vorrei... franco-bolli da... lire.	vorraiee... frahngkoa-boallee dah... leeray
What's the postage for a postcard/letter to United States?	Qual è l'affranca-tura per una cartolina/lettera per gli Stati Uniti?	kwahl ai lahffrahngkahtoo-rah pair oonah kahrtoa-leenah/lehttayrah pair lyee staatee ooneetee
Is there any post/mail for me?	C'è dela posta per me?	chai dayllah postah pair may?

Telephoning *Per telefonare*

Where is the nearest telephone booth?	Dov'è la cabina te-lefonica più vicina?	doavai lah kahbeenah tay-layfoneekah peeoo veecheenah
I'd like a telephone token.	Vorrei un gettone (telefonico).	vorraiee oon jayttoanay (taylayfoneekoa)
May I use your phone?	Posso usare i suo tekefono?	possoa oozaaray eel soooa taylayfoanoa
Hello. This is... speaking.	Pronto. Qui parla...	prontoa. kooee pahrlah
I'd like to speak to...	Vorrei parlare a...	vorraiee pahrlaaray
When will he/she be back?	Qundo ritornerà?	kwahndoa reetoarnehrah

Time and date *Ore e data*

It's...	Sono le...	soanoa lay...
ten past two	due e dieci	dooay ay deeaichee
quarter past three	tre e un quarto	tray ay oon kwahrtoa
twenty past four	quattro e venti	kwahttroa ay vayntee
half past six	sei e mezza	sehee ay mehddzah
twenty-five to eight	sette e trenta- cinque	sehttay ay trayntahcheengkooay
ten to ten	dieci meno dieci	deeaichee mainoa deeaichee
noon/midnight	mezzogiorno/ mezzanotte	mehdzoajoarnoa/ mehdzahnottay
in the morning	del mattino	dayl mahtteenoa
in the afternoon	del pomeriggio	dayl poamayreedjoa
in the evening	della sera	dayllah sayrah
during the day	durante il giorno	doorahntay eel joarnoa
at night	la nottee	lah nottay
yesterday/today	ieri/oggi	eeairee/odjee
tomorrow	domani	doamaanee
spring	la primavera	lah preemahvayrah
summer	l'estate	laystaatay
autumn	l'autonno	lowtoonnoa
winter	l'inverno	leenvehrnoa

Sunday	domenica	doamayneekah
Monday	lunedì	loonaydee
Tuesday	martedì	mahrtaydee
Wednesday	mercoledì	mehrkoalaydee
Thursday	giovedì	oavaydee
Friday	venerdì	vaynayrdee
Saturday	sabato	saabahtoa
January	gennaio	jehnnaaeeoa
February	febbraio	fehbbraaeeoa
March	marzo	mahrtsoa
April	aprile	ahpreelay
May	maggio	mahdjoa
June	guigno	jooñoa
July	luglio	loolyoa
August	agosto	ahgoastoa
September	settembre	sayttehmbray
October	ottobre	oattoabray
November	novembre	noavehmbray
December	dicembre	deechehmbray

NUMBERS, see page 110

Numbers *Numeri*

0	**zero**	**dzeh**roa
1	**uno**	**oo**noa
2	**due**	**doo**ay
3	**tre**	tray
4	**quattro**	**kwaht**troa
5	**cinque**	**cheeng**kooay
6	**sei**	**seh**ee
7	**sette**	**seht**tay
8	**otto**	**ot**toa
9	**nove**	**naw**vay
10	**dieci**	**deeai**chee
11	**undici**	**oon**deechee
12	**dodici**	**doa**deechee
13	**tredici**	**tray**deechee
14	**quattordici**	kwaht**tor**deechee
15	**quindici**	kooe**een**deechee
16	**sedici**	**say**deechee
17	**diciassette**	deechah**sseht**tay
18	**diciotto**	deech**ot**toa
19	**diciannove**	deechahn**naw**vay
20	**venti**	**vayn**tee
21	**ventuno**	vayn**too**noa
30	**trenta**	**trayn**tah
40	**quaranta**	kwah**rahn**tah
50	**cinquanta**	cheeng**kwahn**tah
60	**sesssanta**	says**sahn**tah
70	**settanta**	sayt**tahn**tah
80	**ottanta**	ot**tahn**tah
90	**novanta**	noa**vahn**tah
100	**cento**	**chehn**toa
1000	**mille**	**meel**lay
1,000,000	**un milione**	oon meel**yoa**nay
1,000,000,000	**un miliardo**	un meel**yahr**do
first	**primo**	**pree**moa
second	**secondo**	say**koan**doa
third	**terzo**	**tehr**tsoa
once	**una volta**	**oo**nah **vol**tah
twice	**due volte**	**doo**ay **vol**tay
a half	**un mezzo**	oon **mehd**dzoa
a quarter	**un quarto**	oon **kwahr**toa
a third	**un terzo**	oon **tehr**tsoa

Emergency *Emergenza*

Call the police	**Chiami la polizia**	keeaamee lah poaleetseeah
Get a doctor	**Chiami un medico**	keeaamee oon maideekoa
Go away	**Se ne vada**	say nay vaadah
HELP	**AIUTO**	aheeootoa
I'm ill	**Mi sento male**	mee sayntoa maalay
I'm lost	**Mi sono perso(a)**	mee soanoa pehrsoa(ah)
Leave me alone	**Mi lasci in pace**	mee laashee een paachay
LOOK OUT	**ATTENZIONE**	ahttayntseeoanay
STOP THIEF	**AL LADRO**	ahl laadroa
My... has been stolen.	**Mi hanno rubato ...**	mee ahnnoa roobaatoa
I've lost my ...	**Ho perso ...**	oa pehrsoa
handbag	**la mia borsetta**	lah meeah boarsayttah
wallet	**il mio portafogli**	eel meeoa portahfoalyee
passport	**il mio passaporto**	eel meeoa pahssahpoartoa
Where can I find a doctor who speaks English?	**Dove posso trovare un medico che parla inglese?**	doavay possoa troavaaray oon maideekoa kay pahrlah eengglaysay

Guide to Italian pronunciation *Pronuncia*

Consonants

Letter	Approximate pronunciation	Symbol	Example	
b, d, f, k, l, m, n, p, q, t, v	as in English			
c	1) before e and i, like ch in chip	ch	**cerco**	chayrkoa
	2) elsewhere, like c in cat	k	**conto**	koantoa
ch	like c in cat	k	**che**	kay
g	1) before e and i, like j in jet	j	**valigia**	vahleejah
	2) elsewhere, like g in go	g	**grande**	grahnday

TELEPHONING, see page 108

gh	like **g** in **go**	g	**ghiaccio**	gee**ah**tchoa
gl	like **lli** in million	ly	**gli**	lyee
gn	like **ni** in onion	ñ	**bagno**	**bah**ñoa
h	always silent		**ha**	ah
r	trilled like a Scottish **r**	r	**deriva**	deh**ree**vah
s	1) generally like **s** in **sit**	s	**questo**	koo**ay**stoa
	2) sometimes like **z** in zoo	z	**viso**	**vee**zoa
sc	1) before **e** and **i**, like **sh** in **shut**	sh	**uscita**	oo**shee**tah
	2) elsewhere, like **sk** in **sk**in	sk	**scarpa**	**skahr**pah
z/zz	1) generally like **ts** in hi**ts**	ts	**grazie**	**graat**seeay
	2) sometimes like **ds** in roa**ds**	dz	**romanzo**	roa**mahn**dzoa

Vowels

a	1) short, like **a** in **car**, but shorter	ah	**gatto**	**gah**ttoa
	2) long, like **a** in **car**	aa	**casa**	**kaa**sah
e	1) can always be pronounced like **ay** in **way**, but without moving tongue or lips	ay	**sera**	**sayr**ah
	2) in correct speech, it is sometimes pronounced like **e** in **get** or, when long, more like **ai** in **hair**	eh	**bello**	**behl**loa
i	like **ee** in **meet**	ee	**vini**	**vee**nee
o	1) can always be pronounced like **oa** in **goat**, but without moving tongue or lips	oa	**sole**	**soa**lay
	2) in correct speech, it is sometimes pronounced like **o** in **ingot**, or when long, more like **aw** in **law**	o	**notte**	**not**tay
		aw	**rosa**	**raw**zah
u	like **oo** in **foot**	oo	**fumo**	**foo**moa

Italiano

Norwegian

Basic expressions *Vanlyige uttrykk*

Yes/No.	**Ja/Nei.**	yaa/næi
Please.	**Vær (så) snill å .../ ..., takk.**	vǣ (saw) snil aw/ ... tahk
Thank you.	**Takk.**	tahk
I beg your pardon?	**Unnskyld?**	ewnshewl

Introductions *Presentasjon*

Good morning.	**God morgen.**	goomawer'n
Good afternoon.	**God dag.**	goodaag
Good night.	**God natt.**	goonaht
Hello/Hi.	**Hallo/Hei!**	hahlōō/hæi
Goodbye.	**Adjø.**	ahdyūr
My name is...	**Mitt navn er ...**	mit nahvn ær
Pleased to meet you.	**Hyggelig å treffes.**	hewgerli aw trehferss
What's your name?	**Hva heter du?**	vah hāyterr dew
How are you?	**Hvordan står det til?**	voo'dahn stawr deh til
Fine thanks. And you?	**Bare bra, takk. Og med deg?**	baarer braa tahk. o(g) meh(d) dæi
Where do you come from?	**Hvor kommer du fra?**	voor kommer dew fraa
I'm from...	**Jeg er fra ...**	yæi ær fraa
Australia	**Australia**	oustraaleeah
Canada	**Kanada**	kahnahdah
Great Britain	**Storbritannia**	stoorbrittahneeah
United States	**USA**	ēw-ehss-aa
I'm with my...	**Jeg er her med ...**	yæi æ hǣr meh(d)
wife/husband	**min kone/mann**	meen kōōner/mann
family	**min familie**	meen fahmeelyer
boyfriend/girlfriend	**min venn/venninne**	meen vehn/vehninner
I'm here on business/vacation.	**Jeg er her i forretninger/ på ferie.**	yæi ær hǣr ee forrehtingerr/ paw fāyryer

PRONUNCIATION, see page 127/EMERGENCIES, page 126

Questions *Spørsmål*

When?	**Når?**	nor
How?	**Hvordan/Hvor?**	voo'dahn/voor
What?/Why?	**Hva?/Hvorfor?**	vaa/**voor**for
Who?/Which?	**Hvem?/Hvilken?**	vehm/**vil**kern
Where is/are …?	**Hvor er …?**	voor ær
Where can I find …?	**Hvor finner jeg …?**	voor **finn**err yæi
Where can I get …?	**Hvor kan jeg få tak i …?**	voor kahn yæi faw taak ee
How far?	**Hvor langt?**	voor lahngt
How long?	**Hvor lenge?**	voor **leh**nger
How much/many?	**Hvor mye/mange?**	voor **mew**er/**mahng**er
Can I have …?	**Kan jeg få …?**	kahn yæi faw
Can you help me?	**Kan du hjelpe meg?**	kahn dew **yehl**per mæi
What does this mean?	**Hva betyr dette?**	vaa ber**tewr deh**ter
I understand.	**Jeg forstår.**	yæi fo**shtawr**
I don't understand.	**Jeg forstår ikke.**	yæi fo**shtawr ikk**er
Can you translate this for me?	**Kan du oversette dette for meg?**	kahn dew **aw**vershehter **deh**ter for mæi
Do you speak English?	**Snakker du engelsk?**	**snah**kerr dew **ehng**erlsk
I don't speak (much) Norwegian.	**Jeg snakker ikke (så bra) norsk.**	yæi **snah**kerr **ikk**er (saw braa) noshk

A few more useful words *Noen flere nyttige ord*

better/worse	**bedre/verre**	**bay**drer/**væ**er
big/small	**stor/liten**	stoor/**lee**tern
cheap/expensive	**billig/dyr**	**bill**i/**dewr**
early/late	**tidlig/sen**	**teel**i/**sayn**
good/bad	**bra/dårlig**	braa/**daw**'li
hot/cold	**varm/kald**	vahrm/kahl
near/far	**nær/fjern**	næer/fyæ'n
old/new	**gammel/ny**	**gah**merl/**new**
right/wrong	**riktig/feil**	**rik**ti/fæil
vacant/occupied	**ledig/opptatt**	**lay**di/**op**taht

Hotel–Accommodation *Hotell*

I have a reservation.	**Jeg har bestilt rom.**	yæi haar ber**stilt** room
Do you have any vacancies?	**Har dere noen ledige rom?**	haar da̅y̅rer no̅o̅ern la̅y̅deeyer room
I'd like a …	**Jeg vil gjerne ha et …**	yæi vil yæ̅'ner **haa** eht
single room	**enkeltrom**	**ehng**kerltroom
double room	**dobbeltrom**	**dobb**erltroom
with twin beds	**med to senger**	meh(d) to̅o̅ **sehng**err
with a double bed	**med dobbeltseng**	meh(d) **dobb**erltsehng
with a bath/shower	**med bad/dusj**	meh(d) baad/dewsh
We'll be staying …	**Vi blir …**	vee bleer
overnight only	**bare natten over**	**baa**rer **naht**ern **aw**verr
a few days	**et par dager**	eht pahr **daa**gerr
a week	**en uke (minst)**	ehn **e̅w̅**ker (minst)
Is there a camp site near here?	**Er det en camping-plass i nærheten?**	ær deh ehn **kæm**ping-plahss ee **nær**hehtern

Decision *Beslutning*

May I see the room?	**Kan jeg få se rommet?**	kahn yæi faw sa̅y̅ **room**mer
That's fine. I'll take it.	**Det er bra. Jeg tar det.**	deh ær braa. yæi taar deh
No. I don't like it.	**Nei. Jeg liker det ikke.**	næi. yæ **lee**kerr deh **ikk**er
It's too …	**Det er for …**	deh ær for
dark/small/noisy	**mørkt/lite/støyende**	murrkt/**lee**ter/**stoy**erner
Do you have any-thing …?	**Har dere noe …?**	haar da̅y̅rer no̅o̅er
better/bigger	**bedre/større**	**ba̅y̅**drer/**stu̅r**rer
cheaper	**rimeligere**	**ree**merleeyerrer
quieter	**roligere**	**ro̅o̅**leeyerrer
May I have my bill, please?	**Kan jeg få regnin-gen?**	kahn yæi faw **ræi**ningern
It's been a very enjoyable stay.	**Det har vært et meget hyggelig.**	deh haar væ't eht **ma̅y̅**gert **hew**gerli **op**hol

Eating out *Mat og drikke*

I'd like to reserve a table for 4.	**Jeg vil gjerne bestille et bord til 4.**	yæi vil y**æ'**ner berst**i**ller eht b**oo**r til 4
We'll come at 8.	**Vi kommer kl. 8.**	vee k**o**mmerr kl**o**kkern 8
I'd like breakfast/ lunch/dinner.	**Jeg vil gjerne ha frokost/lunsj/ middag.**	yæi vil y**æ'**ner haa fr**oo**kost/lurnsh m**i**ddah(g)
What would you recommend?	**Hva anbefaler du?**	vaa **a**hnberfaalerr dew
Do you have any vegetarian dishes?	**Har dere noen vegetariske retter?**	haar d**ay**rer n**oo**ern vehger**taa**risker r**e**hterr

Breakfast *Frokost*

I'll have some...	**Jeg tar...**	yæi taar
bread	**litt brød**	lit br**ur**
butter	**litt smør**	lit smurr
cheese	**ost**	oost
ham and eggs	**egg og skinke**	ehg o(g) sh**i**ngker
jam	**syltetøy**	**sew**ltertoy
rolls	**et rundstykke**	eht r**ewn**stewker

Starters and soups *Forretter og supper*

betasuppe	b**ay**tahsewper	thick meat and vegetable soup
blomkålsuppe	blomkawlsewper	cauliflower soup
fiskesppe	fiskersewper	fish soup
froskelår	froskerlawr	frog's legs
gåselever	gawsserlehverr	goose liver
hummersuppe	h**oo**mmerrsewper	lobster soup
neslesuppe	nehshlersewper	nettle soup
snegler	sn**æ**ilerr	snails

Fish and seafood *Fisk og skalldyr*

cod	**torsk**	toshk
crab	**krabbe**	**krah**ber
eel	**ål**	awl
haddock	**kolje**	**kol**yer
herring	**sild**	sil
lobster	**hummer**	**hoo**mmerr
mussels	**blåskjell**	**blaw**shehl
oysters	**østers**	**urs**tersh
sole	**sjøtunge**	sh**ur**toonger
trout	**ørret**	**ur**reht

NUMBERS, see page 126

baked/boiled	bakt/kokt	bahkt/kookt
fried/grilled	stekt/grillet	stehkt/grillert
roasted	ovnsstekt	ovnsstehkt
underdone (rare)	råstekt	rawstehkt
medium	medium stekt	maydiewm stehkt
well-done	godt stekt	got stehkt

Meat *Kjøtt*

I'd like some...	**Jeg vil gjerne ha...**	yæi vil yæ^rner haa
beef	**oksekjøtt**	ookserkhurt
chicken/duck	**kylling/and**	khewling/ahn
lamb	**lammekøtt**	lahmerkhurt
pork	**svinekjøtt**	sveenerkhurt
veal	**kalvekjøtt**	kahlverkhurt
fårikål	fawrikawl	lamb and cabbage stew
benløse fugler	baynlūrsser fewlerr	veal or beef stuffed with forcemeat
stekt juleribbe/ribbe	stehkt yewlerribber/ribber	roast spareribs with sweet and sour cabbage

Vegetables *Grønnsaker*

beans	**bønner**	burnerr
cabbage	**kål**	kawl
carrots	**gulrøtter**	gewlrurterr
cauliflower	**blomkål**	blomkawl
mushrooms	**sopp**	sop
onions	**løk**	lūrk
peas	**erter**	æ^rterr
potatoes	**poteter**	pootayterr
tomatoes	**tomater**	toomaaterr

Fruit and dessert *Frukt og dessert*

apple	**eple**	ehpler
banana	**banan**	bahnaan
cherries	**kirsebær**	khisherbær
lemon	**sitron**	sitrōon
orange	**appelsin**	ahperlseen
pear	**pære**	pærer
plums	**plommer**	ploommerr
strawberries	**jordbær**	yoorbær

Hoffdessert	hofdehssǣr	layered meringue and cream with chocolate sauce
is(krem)	eess(krāym)	ice-cream
jordbær-	yoorbǣr	strawberry
vanilje-	vahnilyer	vanilla
sjokoladepudding	shookoolaaderpewding	chocolate mousse
vafler med syltetøy	vahflerr meh(d) sewltertoy	waffles with jam

Drinks *Drikkevarer*

beer	**en øl**	ehn url
(hot) chocolate	**(varm) sjokolade**	(vahrm) shookoolaader
coffee	**kaffe**	kahfer
a pot of	**en kanne**	ehn kahner
with cream	**med fløte**	meh(d) flurter
fruit juice	**en juice**	ehn yēwss
(glass of) milk	**(et glass) melk**	(eht glahss) mehlk
mineral water	**naturlig mineralvann**	nahtēwrʹli minerraalvahn
tea	**te**	tāy
wine	**vin**	veen
red/white	**rødvin/hvitvin**	rūrveen/veetveen

Complaints and paying *Klager og regningen*

This is too...	**Dette er for...**	dehter ær for
bitter/sweet	**beskt/søtt**	behskt/surt
salty	**salt**	sahlt
That's not what I ordered.	**Dette er ikke det jeg bestilte.**	dehter ær ikker deh yæi berstilter
I'd like to pay.	**Jeg vil gjerne betale.**	yæi vil yǣʹner bertaaler
I think there's a mistake in this bill.	**Jeg tror det er en feil på regningen.**	yæi trōor deh ær ehn fæil paw ræiningern
Can I pay with this credit card?	**Kan jeg betale med dette kredittkortet?**	kahn yæi bertaaler meh(d) dehter krehditkoʹter
Is everything included?	**Er alt inkludert?**	ær ahlt inklewdāyʹt
We enjoyed it, thank you.	**Det var meget godt.**	deh vaar māygert got

NUMBERS, see page 126

Travelling around *På reise*

Plane *Fly*

Is there a flight to...?	**Går det et fl til...?**	gawr eh eht flew til
What time should I check in?	**Når må jeg sjekke inn?**	nor maw yæi **shehk**er in
I'd like to... my reservation.	**Jeg vil gjerne... reservasjonen.**	yæi vil yǣˊner... rehssævahshōōnern
cancel	**annullere**	ahnew**lay**rer
change	**endre**	**ehn**drer
confirm	**bekrefte**	ber**krehf**ter

Train *Tog*

I'd like a ticket to...	**Jeg vil gjerne ha en billett til...**	yæi vil yǣˊner haa ehn bill**eht** til
single (one-way)	**enkeltbillett**	**ehng**kerltbilleht
return (round trip)	**tur-returbillett**	tewr-reh**tewr**billeht
first class	**første klasse**	**fursh**ter **klah**sser
second class	**andre/annen klasse**	**ahn**drer/**aa**ern **klah**sser
When's the... train to...?	**Når går... tog til...?**	nor gawr... tawg til
first/next/last	**første/neste/siste**	**fursh**ter/**neh**ster/**sis**ter
Is this the train to...?	**Er dette toget til...?**	ær **deh**ter **taw**ger til

Bus–Tram (streetcar) *Buss–Trikk*

Which tram goes to the town centre?	**Hvilken trikk går til sentrum?**	**vil**kern trik gawr til **sehn**trewm
How much is the fare to...?	**Hvor mye koster det til...?**	voor **mew**er **kos**terr deh til
Will you tell me when to get off?	**Kan du si fra når jeg skal gå av?**	kahn dew see fraa nor yæi skahl gaw ahv

Taxi *Drosje/Taxi*

How much is the fare to...?	**Hva koster det til...?**	vaa **kos**terr deh til
Take me to this address.	**Kjør meg til denne adressen.**	khūrr mæi til **deh**ner ah**drehs**sern
Please stop here.	**Stans her.**	stahnss hǣr

TELLING THE TIME, see page 125

Could you wait for me?	**Kan du vente på meg?**	kahn dew **vehn**ter paw mæi

Car hire (rental) *Bilutleie*

I'd like to hire (rent) a car.	**Jeg vil gjerne leie en bil.**	yæi vil **yæ**'ner **læ**ier ehn beel
I'd like it for...	**Jeg vil ha den...**	yæi vil haa dehn
a day	**en dag**	ehn daag
a week	**en uke**	ehn **ew**ker
Where's the nearest filling station?	**Hvor er nærmeste bensinstasjon?**	voor ær **nær**mehster behn**seen**stah**shoon**
Fill it up, please.	**Full tank, takk.**	fewl tahngk tahk
Give me... litres of petrol (gasoline).	**... liter bensin, takk.**	... **lee**terr behn**seen** tahk
How do I get to...?	**Hvordan kommer jeg til...?**	**voo**'dahn **kom**merr yæi til
this place	**dette stedet**	**deh**ter **stay**der
this address	**denne adressen**	**deh**ner ah**dreh**ssern
I've had a break-down at...	**Jeg har fått motor-stopp ved...**	yæi haar fot **moo**tooshtop veh(d)
Can you send a mechanic?	**Kan du sende en mekaniker?**	kahn dew **seh**ner ehn meh**kaa**nikkerr
Can you mend this puncture (fix this flat)?	**Kan du reparere denne punkte-ringen?**	kahn dew reh**pah**ræyrer **deh**ner poong**tay**-ringern

---

Du har kjørt feil.	You're on the wrong road.
Kjør rett frem.	Go straight ahead.
Det er der borte til...	It's down there on the...
høyre/venstre	left/right
midt imot/bak...	opposite/behind...
ved siden av/etter...	next to/after...
nord/sør/øst/vest	north/south/east/west

NUMBERS, see page 126

Sightseeing *Sightseeing*

Where's the tourist office?	Hvor er turist-kontoret?	voor ær tewrist-koontoorer
Is there an English-speaking guide?	Fins det en engelsk-talende guide der?	finss deh ehn ehngerlsk-taalerner "guide" dær
Where is/are the...?	Hvor er...?	voor ær
art gallery	kunstgalleriet	kewnstgahlerreeyer
castle	slottet	shlotter
cathedral/church	domkirken/kirken	domkhirkern/khirkern
city centre	sentrum	sehntrewm
exhibition	utstillingen	ewtstillingern
harbour	havnen	hahvnern
market	torghandelen	torghahnderlern
museum	museet	mewssäyer
shopping area	handlestrøket	hahndlerstrürker
square	plassen/torget	plahssern/torgger
tower	tårnet	taw'ner
When is it open?	Når er det åpent?	nor ær deh awpernt
When does it close?	Når stenger det?	nor stehngerr deh
How much is the entrance fee?	Hva koster inn-gangsbilletten?	vah kosterr ingahngs-billehtern

Relaxing *Underholdning*

What's playing at the... Theatre?	Hva spilles på... Theatret?	vah spillerss paw ... täyaatrer
Are there any tickets for tonight?	Fins det fremdeles billetter til i kveld?	finss eh frehmdäylerss billehterr til ee kvehl
How much are the tickets?	Hvor mye koster billettene?	voor mëwer kosterr billehterner
Would you like to go out with me tonight?	Skal vi gå ut i kveld?	skahl vee gaw ewt ee kvehl
Is there a discoteque in town?	Fins det et diskotek i byen?	finss deh eht diskootäyk ee bëwern
Would you like to dance?	Skal vi danse?	skahl vee dahnser
Thank you, it's been a wonderful evening.	Takk, det har vært en veldig hyggelig kveld.	tahk deh haar væ't ehn vehldi hewgerli kvehl

TELLING THE TIME/DAYS OF THE WEEK, see page 125

Shops, stores and services Butikker og servicenæringer

Where's the nearest...?	Hvor er nærmeste...?	voor ær nærmehster
bakery	et bakeri	eht baakerree
bookshop/store	en bokhandel	ehn bookhahnderl
butcher's	en slakter	ehn shlahkterr
chemist's/drugstore	et apotek	eht ahpootayk
dentist	en tannlege	ehn tahnlayger
department store	et stormagasin	eht stoormahgahsseen
grocery	en matvarehandel	ehn maatvaarerhahnderl
hairdresser	en frisør	ehn frissurr
liquor store	et vinmonopol	eht veenmoonoopool
newsstand	en aviskiosk	ehn ahveeskhyosk
post office	et postkontor	eht postkoontoor
supermarket	et supermarked	eht sewperrmahrkerd
toilets	toalettet	tooahlehter

General expressions Vanlige uttrykk

Where's the main shopping area?	Hvor er det største handlestrøket?	voor ær deh stursher hahndlerstrurker
Do you have any...?	Har du noen...?	har dew nooern
Can you show me...?	Kan du vise meg...?	kahn dew veesser mæi
this/that	dette/det	dehter/deh
Don't you have anything...?	Har du ikke noe...?	haar dew ikker nooer
cheaper/better	rimeligere/bedre	reemerleeyerrer/baydrer
larger/smaller	større/mindre	sturrer/mindrer
Can I try it on?	Kan eg få prøve den?	kahn yæi faw prurver dehn
How much is this?	Hvor mye koster dette?	voor mewer kosterr dehter
Please write it down.	Kan du skrive det?	kahn dew skreever deh
I don't want to spend more than... kroner.	Jeg vil ikke gi mer enn... kroner.	yæi vil ikker yee mayr ehn... kroonerr
No, I don't like it.	Nei, jeg liker det ikke.	næi yæi leekerr deh ikker
I'll take it.	Jeg tar det.	yæi taar deh
Do you accept credit cards?	Tar dere kreditt-kort?	taar dayrer krehditko't
Can you order it for me?	Kan du bestille det til meg?	kahn dew berstiller deh til mæi

NUMBERS, see page 126

black	**svart**	svah'̱t
blue	**blå**	blaw
brown	**brun**	brēwn
green	**grønn**	grurn
orange	**oransje**	oo**rah**ngsh
red	**rød**	rūr
white	**hvit**	veet
yellow	**gul**	gēwl
light...	**lyse-**	lēwsser-
dark...	**mørke-**	murrker

I'd like a/an/some...	**Jeg vil gjerne ha...**	yæi vil yæ'̱ner haa
aspirin	**aspirin**	ahspir**ree**n
battery	**et batteri**	eht bahter**ree**
bottle opener	**en flaskeåpner**	ehn **flah**skerawpnerr
bread	**litt brød**	lit brūr
newspaper	**en avis**	ehn ah**vee**ss
American	**amerikansk**	ahm(eh)ri**kaa**nsk
English	**engelsk**	**ehng**erlsk
postcard	**et postkort**	eht **post**ko'̱t
shampoo	**en sjampo**	ehn **shah**mpoo
soap	**en såpe**	ehn **saw**per
sun-tan oil	**en sololje**	ehn **sōō**lolyer
toothpaste	**en tannpasta**	ehn **tahn**pahstah
half a kilo of tomatoes	**en halv kilo toma-ter**	ehn hahl **khee**loo too**maa**terr
litre of milk	**en liter melk**	ehn **lee**terr mehlk
I'd like a film for this camera.	**Jeg vil gjerne ha en film til dette apparatet.**	yæi vil yæ'̱ner haa ehn film til **deh**ter ahpah**raa**ter
black and white	**svart-hvitt**	svah'̱t-vit
colour	**farge**	**fah**rgger
I'd like a hair-cut, please.	**Klipping, takk.**	**kli**ping tahk

Souvenirs *Suvenirer*

I'd like a...	**Jeg vil gjerne ha...**	yæi vil yæ'̱ner haa
doll in native costume	**en dukke med bunad**	ehn **dew**ker meh(d) **bēw**nahd
drinking horn	**et drikkehorn**	eht **drik**kerhōō'̱n
troll	**et troll**	eht trol
Viking ship	**et vikingskip**	eht **vee**kingsheep
wooden figurine	**en trefigur**	ehn **trāy**figgēwr

At the bank / banken

Where's the nearest bank/currency exchange office?	Hvor er nærmeste bank/vekslings- kontor?	voor ær **nærm**ehster bahngk/**vehk**shlings- koont**oo**r
I want to change some dollars/pounds.	Jeg vil gjerne veksle noen dollar/ pund.	yæi vil y**æ**'ner **vehk**shler n**oo**ern **doll**ahr/ pewn
What's the exchange rate?	Hva er vekslings- kursen?	vaa ær **vehk**shlings- k**ew**shern
I want to cash a traveller's cheque.	Jeg vil gjerne løse inn en reisesjekk.	yæi vil y**æ**'ner l**ur**sser in ehn **ræi**ssershehk

At the post office / postkontoren

I'd like to send this by...	Jeg vil gjerne sende dette...	yæi vil y**æ**'ner **seh**ner **deh**ter
airmail	med fly	meh(d) fl**ew**
express	ekspress	**ehk**sprehss
A...-kroner stamp please.	Et... -kroners frimerke, takk.	eht... -kr**oo**nersh **free**mærker tahk
What's the postage for a letter/postcard to the U.S.?	Hva er portoen for et brev/postkort til USA?	vah ær poo'tooern for eht br**ā**yv/**post**ko't til **ew**-ehss-**aa**
Is there any post/ mail for me?	Har det kommet noe post til meg?	har deh **kom**mert n**oo**er post til mæi
My name is...	Mitt navn er...	mit nahvn ær

Telephoning Telefon

Where's the nearest telephone booth?	Hvor er nærmeste telefonkiosk?	voor ær **nærm**ehster tehler**foon**khyosk
May I use your phone?	Kan jeg få låne telefonen?	kahn yæi faw **law**ner tehler**foo**nern
Hello. This is...	Hallo. Dette er...	hahl**oo**. **deh**ter ær
I'd like to speak to...	Kan jeg få snakke med...?	kahn yæi faw **snah**ker meh(d)
When will he/she be back?	Når kommer han/ hun tilbake?	nor **kom**mer hahn/ hewn til**baa**ker
Will you tell him that I called?	Kan du si til ham at jeg har ringt?	kahn dew see til hahm aht yæi haar ringt

Days and date *Dager og dato*

It's...	Den er...	dehn ær
five past one	**fem over ett**	fehm awverr eht
quarter past three	**kvart over tre**	kvah't awverr trāy
twenty past four	**tjue over fire/**	khēwerr awverr feerer/
	ti på halv fem	tee paw hahl fehm
half-past six	**halv sju**	hahl shēw
twenty-five to seven	**fem over halv sju**	fehm awverr hahl shēw
ten to ten	**ti på ti**	tee paw tee
noon/midnight	**klokken tolv/mid-**	klokkern tol/**mid**naht
	natt	
in the morning	**om morgenen**	om **maw'**nern
in the afternoon	**om ettermiddagen**	om ehterrmiddaagern
in the evening	**om kvelden**	om kvehlern
during the day	**om dagen**	om **daa**gern
at night	**om natten**	om **nah**tern
yesterday	**i går**	ee gawr
today	**i dag**	ee daag
tomorrow	**i morgen**	ee mawer'n
spring	**vår**	vawr
summer	**sommer**	sommerr
autumn (fall)	**høst**	hurst
winter	**vinter**	vinterr

Sunday	**søndag**	**surn**dah(g)
Monday	**mandag**	**mahn**dah(g)
Tuesday	**tirsdag**	**teesh**dah(g)
Wednesday	**onsdag**	**oons**dah(g)
Thursday	**torsdag**	**tawsh**dah(g)
Friday	**fredag**	**frāy**dah(g)
Saturday	**lørdag**	**lur'**dah(g)
January	**januar**	yahnewaar
February	**februar**	fehbrewaar
March	**mars**	mahsh
April	**april**	ah**preel**
May	**mai**	maay
June	**juni**	**yew**nee
July	**juli**	**yew**lee
August	**august**	ou**gewst**
September	**september**	sehp**tehm**berr
October	**oktober**	ok**taw**berr
November	**november**	noo**vehm**berr
December	**desember**	deh**ssehm**berr

NUMBERS, see page 126

Numbers *Tall*

0	**null**	newl
1	**en**	āyn
2	**to**	tōo
3	**tre**	trāy
4	**fire**	feerer
5	**fem**	fehm
6	**seks**	sehkss
7	**sju**	shew
8	**åtte**	otter
9	**ni**	nee
10	**ti**	tee
11	**elleve**	ehlver
12	**tolv**	tol
13	**tretten**	trehtern
14	**fjorten**	fyoo'tern
15	**femten**	fehmtern
16	**seksten**	sæistern
17	**sytten**	surtern
18	**atten**	ahtern
19	**nitten**	nittern
20	**tjue**	khēwer
30	**tretti**	trehti
40	**førti**	fur'ti
50	**femti**	fehmti
60	**seksti**	sehksti
70	**sytti**	surti
80	**åtti**	otti
90	**nitti**	nitti
100	**hundre**	hewndrer
1,000	**tusen**	tēwssern
first	**første**	furshter
second	**annen/andre**	aaern/ahndrer
once/twice	**en gang/to ganger**	ehn gahng/tōo gahngerr
a half	**en halv**	ehn hahl

Emergency *Nødsfall*

Call the police	**Ring til politiet**	ring til poolitteeyer
Get a doctor	**Hent en lege**	hehnt ehn lāyger
Go away	**Gå vekk**	gaw vehk
HELP	**HJELP**	yehlp
I'm ill	**Jeg er syk**	yæi ær sēwk
STOP THIEF	**STOPP TYVEN**	stop tēwvern
My ... has been stolen.	**... er blitt stjålet.**	... ær blit styawlert

127

I've lost my...	**Jeg har mistet...**	yæi haar mistert
handbag	**håndvesken**	honvehskern
wallet	**lommeboken**	loommerbōōkern
passport/baggage	**passet/bagasjen**	pahsser/bahgaashern
Where can I find	**Hvor kan jeg få**	voor kahn yæi faw
a doctor who speaks	**tak i en lege som**	taak ee ehn layger som
English?	**snakker engelsk?**	snahkerr ehngerlsk

Guide to Norwegian pronunciation *Uttale*

Consonants

Letter	Approximate pronunciation	Symbol	Example	
b, c, d, f, h, l, m, n, p, q, t, v, x	as in English			
g	1) before **ei, i** and **y**, generally like **y** in yes	y	**gi**	yee
	2) before **e** and **i** in some words of French origin, like **sh** in **sh**ut	sh	**geni**	sheh**nee**
	3) like **g** in go	g	**gått**	got
gj	like **y** in yes	y	**gjest**	yehst
j	like **y** in yes	y	**ja**	yaa
k	1) generally like **ch** in German ich (like **h** in huge)	kh	**kino**	khee**noo**
	2) like **k** in kit	k	**kaffe**	kah**fer**
kj	like **ch** in German ich	kh	**kjøre**	kh**ūrrer**
r	rolled near the front of the mouth	r	**rare**	raa**rer**
rs	like **sh** in **sh**ut	sh	**norsk**	noshk
s	like **s** in sit	s/ss	**spise**	spee**sser**
sj	generally like **sh** in **sh**ut	sh	**stasjon**	stah**shōōn**
sk	1) before **i, y** and **ø**, generally like **sh** in **sh**ut	sh	**ski**	shee
	2) elsewhere, like **sk** in **sk**ate	sk	**skole**	sk**ōō**ler
skj	like **sh** in **sh**ut	sh	**skje**	sh**āy**
w	like **v** in vice	v	**whisky**	vis**ki**
z	like **s** in sit	s	**zoom**	s**ōōm**

Vowels

a	1) long, like **a** in car	aa	**dag**	daag
	2) when short, between **a** in car and **u** in cut	ah	**takk**	tahk

e	1) long, like **ay** in s**ay**	ay̅	**sent**	sa̅y̅nt
	2) when followed by **r**, often like **a** in m**a**n	æ	**her**	hær
			herre	**hæ**rer
	3) short, like **e** in g**e**t	eh	**penn**	pehn
	4) unstressed, like **a** in **a**bout	er	**betale**	bert**aa**ler
i	1) long, like **ee** in b**ee**	ee	**hit**	heet
	2) short, like **i** in s**i**t	i	**sitt**	sit
o	1) when long, often like **oo** in s**oo**n, but with the lips more tightly rounded	o̅o̅	**ord**	o̅o̅rd
	2) short, like **oo** in f**oo**t	oo	**ost**	oost
	3) long, like **aw** in s**aw**	aw	**tog**	tawg
	4) short, like **o** in g**o**t (British pronunciation)	o	**stoppe**	**stop**per
u	1) someting like **ew** in f**ew**, or Scottish **oo** in g**oo**d (long or short)	e̅w̅	**mur**	me̅w̅r
		oo	**busk**	bewsk
	2) like **oo** in f**oo**t	oo	**nummer**	**noom**merr
y	very much like the sound described under **u** (1) above (long or short)	e̅w̅	**by**	be̅w̅
		ew	**bygge**	**bew**ger
æ	like **a** in **a**ct (long or short)	æ̅	**lære**	**læ̅**rer
ø	like **ur** in f**ur**, but with the lips rounded (long or short)	u̅r	**dør**	du̅r
		ur	**sønn**	surn
å	1) when long, like **aw** in s**aw**	aw	**såpe**	**saw**per
	2) when short, like **o** in g**o**t (British pronunciation)	o	**sånn**	son

Diphthongs

au	rather like **ou** in l**ou**d, though the first part is the Norwegian **æ**-sound	ou	**sau**	sou
ei, eg, egn	like **ai** in w**ai**t, though first part is the Norwegian **æ**-sound	æi	**geit**	yæit
			jeg	yæi
øy	rather like **oy** in b**oy**, though the first part is the Norwegian **ø**-sound	oy	**gøy**	goy

Portuguese

Basic expressions *Expressões correntes*

Yes/No.	**Sim/Não.**	seeng/nahng^w
Please.	**Por favor/Se faz favor.**	poor fer**voar**/ser fahsh fer**voar**
Thank you.	**Obrigado(a).**	oabrig**gah**doo(er)
I beg your pardon?	**Como disse?**	**koa**moo **dees**ser

Introductions *Apresentações*

Good morning.	**Bom dia.**	bawng **dee**er
Good afternoon.	**Boa tarde.**	boaer **tahr**der
Good night.	**Boa noite.**	boaer **noy**ter
Good-bye.	**Adeus.**	erde**hoosh**
My name is...	**Chamo-me...**	**sher**moo mer
Pleased to meet you.	**Muito prazer em conhecê-lo(-la).**	**moong^y**too prer**zayr** ahng^y koonyers**say** loo(ler)
What's your name?	**Como se chama?**	**koa**moo ser **sher**mer
How are you?	**Como está?**	**koa**moo ish**tah**
Fine thanks. And you?	**Bem, obrigado(-a). E o Senhor [a Senhora]?**	bahng^w oabrig**gah**doo(-er). ee oo sinny**oar** [er sinny**oar**er]
Where do you come from?	**Donde é?**	**dawng**der eh
I'm from...	**Sou de...**	soa der
Australia	a Austrália	er owsh**trah**lyer
Canada	o Canadá	oo kerner**dah**
Great Britain	a Grã-Bretanha	er grahng brer**ter**nyer
United States	os Estados Unidos	oosh ish**tah**doosh oo**nee**doosh
I'm with my...	**Estou com...**	ish**toa** kawng
wife	a minha mulher	er **mee**nyer moo**lyehr**
husband	o meu marido	oo **meh**oo mer**ree**doo
family	a minha família	er **mee**nyer fer**mee**lyer
boyfriend	o meu namorado	oo **meh**oo nermoo**rah**doo
girlfriend	a minha namorada	er **mee**nyer nermoo**rah**der
I'm here on vacation.	**Estou aqui de férias.**	ish**toa** er**kee** der **feh**ryersh

PRONUNCIATION, see page 143/EMERGENCIES, page 142

Questions *Perguntas*

When?	Quando?	kwahngdoo
How?	Como?	koamoo
What?/Why?	O quê/Porquê?	oo kay/poorkay
Who?/Which?	Quem?/Qual?	kahng^y/kwahl
Where is ...?	Onde é/fica ...?	awngder eh/feeker
Where are ...?	Onde são/ficam ...?	awngder sahng^w/feekahng^w
Where can I find/get ...?	Onde posso encontrar/arranjar ...?	awngder possoo ayngkawngtrahr/errahngzhahr
How far?	A que distância?	er ker dishtahngsyer
How long?	Quanto tempo?	kwahngtoo tayngpoo
How much/many?	Quanto/Quantos?	kwahngtoo/kwahngtoosh
May I?	Pode ...?	podder
Can I have ...?	Pode dar-me ...?	podder dahr mer
Can you help me?	Pode ajudar-me?	podder erzhoodahr mer
What does this/that mean?	O que quer dizer isto/aquilo?	oo ker kehr dizzayr eeshtoo/erkeeloo
I understand.	Compreendo.	kawngpryayngdoo
I don't understand.	Não compreendo.	nahng^w kawngpryayngdoo
Can you translate this for me?	Pode traduzir-me isto?	podder trerdoozeer mer eeshtoo
Do you speak English?	Fala inglês?	fahler eengglaysh
I don't speak (much) Portuguese.	Não falo (bem) português.	nahng^w fahloo (bahng^y) poortoogaysh

A few more useful words *Outras palavras úteis*

better/worse	melhor/pior	millyor/pyor
big/small	grande/pequeno	grahngder/perkaynoo
cheap/expensive	barato/caro	berrahtoo/kahroo
early/late	cedo/tarde	saydoo/tahrder
good/bad	bom/mau	bawng/mow
hot/cold	quente/frio	kayngter/freeoo
near/far	perto/longe	pehrtoo/lawngzher
old/new	velho/novo	vehlyoo/novoo
right/wrong	certo/errado	sehrtoo/irrahdoo
vacant/occupied	livre/ocupado	leevrer/okkoopahdoo

Hotel–Accommodation *Hotel*

I have a reservation.	**Mandei reservar.**	mahng**day** rerzerr**vahr**
We've reserved two rooms.	**Reservámos dois quartos.**	rerzerr**vah**moosh doysh **kwahr**toosh
Do you have any vacancies?	**Tem quartos vagos?**	tahng^y **kwahr**toosh **vah**goosh
I'd like a . . . room.	**Queria um quarto . . .**	ker**reeer** oong **kwahr**too
single	**individual**	eeng**di**vvi**dwahl**
double	**duplo**	**doo**ploo
with twin beds	**com duas camas**	kawng **doo**ersh **ker**mersh
with a double bed	**de casal**	der ker**zahl**
with a bath/shower	**com banho/duche**	kawng **ber**nyoo/**doo**sher
We'll be staying . . .	**Ficamos . . .**	fi**kker**moosh
overnight only	**só esta noite**	saw **ehsh**ter **noy**ter
a few days	**alguns dias**	ahl**goongsh deeer**sh
a week	**uma semana**	**oo**mer ser**mer**ner
Is there a campsite near here?	**Há um parque de campismo aqui perto?**	ah oong **pahr**ker der kahng**peezh**moo er**kee pehr**too

Decision *Decisão*

May I see the room?	**Posso ver o quarto?**	**poss**oo vayr oo **kwahr**too
That's fine. I'll take it.	**Está bem. Fico com ele.**	ish**tah** bahng^y. **feek**oo kawng **ay**ler
No. I don't like it.	**Não, não gosto dele.**	nahng^w nahng^w **gosh**too **day**ler
It's too . . .	**É muito . . .**	eh **moong**^ytoo
dark/small	**escuro/pequeno**	ish**koo**roo/per**kay**noo
Do you have anything . . . ?	**Tem alguma coisa . . . ?**	tahng^y ahl**goo**mer **koy**zer
better/bigger	**melhor/maior**	mill**yor**/**may**or
cheaper	**mais barata**	mighsh ber**rah**ter
quieter	**mais sossegada**	mighsh soosser**gah**der
May I have my bill, please?	**Pode dar-me a conta, por favor?**	**pod**der dahr mer er **kawng**ter poor fer**voar**
It's been a very enjoyable stay.	**Tivemos uma estadia muito agradá-vel.**	tiv**veh**moosh **oo**mer ish**ter**deeer **moong**^ytoo ergrer**dah**vehl

Eating out *Restaurante*

I'd like to reserve a table for four.	Queria reservar uma mesa para quatro pessoas.	kerreeer rerzerrvahr oomer mayzer perrer kwahtroo perssoaersh
We'll come at 8.	Viremos às 8.	virraymoosh ahsh 8
I'd like…	Queria tomar…	kerreeer toomahr
breakfast	o pequeno almoço	oo perkaynoo ahlmoassoo
lunch	o almoço	oo ahlmoassoo
dinner	o jantar	oo zhahngtahr
What do you recommend?	O que me reco-menda?	oo ker mer rerkoomayngder
Do you have any vegetarian dishes?	Tem pratos vegetarianos?	tahng^y prahtoosh verzherterryernoosh

Breakfast *Pequeno almoço*

May I have some…?	Pode trazer-me…?	podder trerzayr mer
bread	pão	pahng^w
butter	manteiga	mahngtayger
cereal	cereais	serryighsh
ham and eggs	ovos estrelados com presunto	ovvoosh ishtrerlahdoosh kawng prerzoongtoo
jam	doce de fruta	doasser der frooter
rolls	papo-secos	pahpoo saykoosh

Starters and soups *Acepipes e sopas*

carnes frias	kahrnersh freeersh	assorted cold cuts
canja	kahngzher	chicken soup with rice
espargos	ishpahrgoosh	asparagus
pipis	pippeesh	spicy giblet stew
sopa à pescador	soaper ah pishkerdoar	fish soup
sopa de abóbora	soaper der erbobboorer	pumpkin soup
sopa de feijão frade	soaper der fayzhahng^w frahder	black-eyed bean soup
sopa de grão	soaper der grahng^w	chick-pea soup

caldo verde
(kahldoo vayrder)   thick potato and kale soup with sausage

chouriço
(shoareessoo)   smoked pork sausage with paprika and garlic

gaspacho
(gershpahshoo)   chilled soup with tomatoes, peppers, onions, cucumber and croutons

TELLING THE TIME, see page 141/NUMBERS, page 142

Fish and seafood *Peixes e mariscos*

crab	**caranguejo**	kerrahng**gay**zhoo
lobster	**lavagante**	lerver**gahng**ter
prawns	**gambas**	**gahng**bersh
sardines	**sardinhas**	serr**dee**nyersh
sole	**linguado**	leeng**gwah**doo
squid	**lulas**	**loo**lersh
tuna	**atum**	er**toong**

caldeirada	various fish simmered with onions, tomatoes,
(kahldayra**rah**der)	potatoes and olive oil

baked	**no forno**	noo **foar**noo
boiled	**cozido**	koo**zee**doo
fried/roast	**frito/assado**	**free**too/er**ssah**doo
grilled	**grelhado**	grill**yah**doo
stewed	**guisado**	giz**zah**doo
underdone (rare)	**mal passado**	mahl perr**ssah**doo
medium	**meio passado**	**may**oo perr**ssah**doo
well-done	**bem passado**	bahng^y perr**ssah**doo

Meat *Carnes*

I'd like some...	**Queria...**	ker**ree**er
bacon	**toucinho**	toa**ssee**nyoo
beef	**carne de vaca**	**kahr**ner der **vah**ker
chicken/duck	**frango/pato**	**frahng**goo/**pah**too
lamb	**borrego**	boo**rray**goo
pork	**carne de porco**	**kahr**ner der **poar**koo
sausage	**salsicha**	sahl**see**sher
steak	**bife**	"beef"
turkey	**peru**	per**roo**
veal	**vitela**	vit**teh**ler

churrasco misto	mixed barbecue (beef, sausage, pork)
(shoor**rahsk**oa **mees**toa)	

Vegetables *Legumes*

beans (green)	**feijão verde**	fay**zhahng**^{w} **vayr**der
carrots	**cenouras**	ser**noa**rersh
mushrooms	**cogumelos**	koo**goo**meh**loosh**
onions	**cebolas**	ser**boa**lersh
peas	**ervilhas**	irr**vee**lyersh
potatoes	**batatas**	ber**tah**tersh
spinach	**espinafres**	ish**pinnah**frersh
tomatoes	**tomates**	too**mah**tish

Fruit–Dessert–Pastries *Frutas–Sobremesas–Pastelaria*

apple	**maçã**	mer**ssahng**
cherries	**cerejas**	serray**zhersh**
lemon	**limão**	lim**mahng**ʷ
orange	**laranja**	ler**rahng**zher
pear	**pêra**	**pay**rer
plums	**ameixas**	er**may**shersh
strawberries	**morangos**	moo**rahng**goosh
arroz doce	er**roash doa**sser	rice pudding
bolinhos de canela	boo**lee**nyoosh der **ker**nehler	cinnamon biscuits
pastel de nata/de Belém	persh**tehl** der **nahter**/der ber**lahng**ʸ	small cream tart
pudim flam	poo**deeng** flahng	creme caramel
tarte de amêndoa	**tahr**ter der er**mayng**dwer	almond tart

Drinks *Bebidas*

beer	**cerveja**	serr**vay**zher
coffee	**um café**	oong ker**feh**
black	**sem leite**	sahngʸ **lay**ter
with milk	**com leite**	kawng **lay**ter
fruit juice	**um sumo de fruta**	oong **soo**moo der **froo**ter
(glass of) milk	**(um copo de) leite**	(oong **kop**poo der) **lay**ter
mineral water	**uma água mineral**	**oo**mer **ah**gwer minner**rahl**
tea	**um chá**	oong shah
wine	**vinho**	**vee**nyoo
red/white	**tinto/branco**	**teeng**too/**brahng**koo

Complaints and paying *Reclamações e a conta*

This is too…	**Isto está…**	**eesh**too ish**tah**…
	demais.	der**mighsh**
bitter/sweet	**amargo/doce**	er**mahr**goo/**doa**sser
That's not what I ordered.	**Não é o que eu encomendei.**	nahngʷ eh oo ker **eh**oo ayng**koo**mayng**day**
I'd like to pay.	**Queria pagar.**	ker**reeer** per**gahr**
I think there's a mistake in this bill.	**Creio que se enganou na conta.**	**kray**oo ker ser aynng**ger**noa ner **kawng**ter
Can I pay with this credit card?	**Posso pagar com este cartão de crédito?**	**poss**oo per**gahr** kawng **aysh**ter kerr**tahng**ʷ der **kreh**dittoo
We enjoyed it, thank you.	**Gostámos muito, obrigado(a).**	goosh**tah**moosh **moong**ʸtoo oabri**ggah**doo (er)

Travelling around *Excursões*

Plane *Avião*

Is there a flight to...?	**Há um voo para o...**	ah oong **voa**oo **per**rer oo
What time should I check in?	**A que horas devo apresentar-me?**	er ker **or**rersh **day**voo erprerzayng**tar** mer
I'd like to... my reservation.	**Queria... a marcação do meu lugar.**	ker**reeer**... er merrker-**ssahng**ʷ doo **meh**oo loo**gahr**
cancel	**anular**	ernoo**lahr**
change	**mudar**	moo**dahr**
confirm	**confirmar**	kawngfirr**mahr**

Train *Comboio (trem)*

I'd like a ticket to....	**Quero um bilhete para...**	**keh**roo oon bil**lyay**ter **per**rer
single (one-way)	**ida**	**ee**der
return (round trip)	**ida e volta**	**ee**der ee **voll**ter
first/second class	**primeira/segunda classe**	prim**may**rer/ser**goong**der **klahs**ser
How long does the journey (trip) take?	**Quanto tempo demora a viagem?**	**kwahng**too **tayng**poo der**mor**rer er **vyah**zhahngʸ
When is the... train to...?	**Quando é o... comboio para...?**	**kwahng**doo eh oo... kawng**boy**oo **per**rer
first/next/last	**primeiro/próximo/último**	prim**may**roo/**pros**simmoo/**oolt**immoo

Bus–Tram (streetcar) *Autocarro–Eléctrico*

Which tram goes to the town centre?	**Qual é o eléctrico que vai para o centro da cidade?**	kwahl eh oo il**leh**trikkoo ker vigh **per**rer oo **sayng**troo der **sidd**ahder
How much is the fare to...?	**Qual é o preço do bilhete para...?**	kwahl eh oo **prays**soo doo bil**lyay**ter **per**rer
Will you tell me when to get off?	**Pode avisar-me quando devo descer?**	**pod**der ervizz**ahr** mer **kwahng**doo **day**voo dish**sayr**

TELLING THE TIME, see page 141/NUMBERS, page 142

Taxi *Táxi*

How much is the fare to...?	**Qual é o preço do percurso para...?**	kwahl eh oo **prayss**oo doo perr**koor**soo **per**rer
Take me to this address.	**Leve-me a este endereço.**	**leh**ver mer er **aysh**ter ayng**der**raysoo
Please stop here.	**Páre aqui, por favor.**	**pah**rer er**kee** poor fer**voar**
Could you wait for me?	**Pode esperar por mim?**	**pod**der ishper**rahr** poor meeng

Car hire (rental) *Aluguer de automóveis*

I'd like to hire (rent) a car.	**Queria alugar um automóvel.**	ker**reeer** erloo**gahr** oong owtoo**mov**vehl
I'd like it for...	**Queria-o por...**	ker**reeer** oo poor
a day	**um dia**	oong **deeer**
a week	**uma semana**	oong ser**mer**ner
Where's the nearest filling station?	**Qual é a estação de serviço mais próxima?**	kwahl eh er ishter**ssahng**ʷ der serr**vees**soo mighsh **pros**simmer
Give me... litres of petrol (gasoline).	**Dê-me... litros de gasolina.**	day mer... **lee**troosh der gerzoo**lee**ner
How do I get to...?	**Como se vai para...?**	**koa**moo ser vigh **per**rer
I've broken down at...	**Tive uma avaria em...**	**tee**ver **oo**mer erver**ree**er ahngʷ
Can you send a mechanic?	**Pode mandar-me um mecânico?**	**pod**der mahng**dahr** mer oong mer**ker**nikkoo
Can you mend this puncture (fix this flat)?	**Pode consertar este furo?**	**pod**der kawngserr**tahr** **aysh**ter **foo**roo

---

Enganou-se na estrada.	You're on the wrong road.
Vá sempre em frente.	Go straight ahead.
É ali...	It's down there on the...
à esquerda/à direita.	left/right
ao lado de/depois de...	next to/after...
norte/sul/(l)este/oeste	north/south/east/west

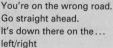

EMERGENCIES, see page 143

Português

Sightseeing *Visitas turísticas*

Where's the tourist office?	**Onde é o turismo?**	awngder eh oo tooreezhmoo
Is there an English-speaking guide?	**Há algum guia que fale inglês?**	ah ahlgoong gheeer ker fahler eengglaysh
Where is/are...?	**Onde fica/ficam...?**	awngder feeker/feekahngᵂ
art gallery	**o galeria de arte**	er gerlerreeer der ahrter
castle	**o castelo**	oo kershtehloo
cathedral	**a sé/catedral**	er seh/kerterdrahl
church	**a igreja**	er iggrayzher
city centre	**o centro da cidade**	oo sayngtroo der siddahder
exhibition	**a exposição**	er ishpoozissahngᵂ
harbour	**o porto**	oo poartoo
market	**o mercado**	oo merrkahdoo
museum	**o museu**	oo moozehoo
shopping area	**a zona comercial**	er zoaner koomerrsyahl
square	**a praça**	er prahsser
tower	**a torre**	er toarrer
zoo	**o jardim zoológico**	oo zherrdeeng zoolozhikkoo
What are the opening hours?	**Quais são as horas de abertura?**	kwighsh sahngᵂ ersh orrersh der erberrtoorer
When does it close?	**A que horas fecha?**	er ker orrersh faysher
How much is the entrance fee?	**Quanto custa a entrada (o ingresso)?**	kwahngtoo kooshter er ayngtrahder (oo eenggrehssoa)

Relaxing *Distracções*

What's playing at the... Theatre?	**O que está em cena no teatro...?**	oo ker ishtah ahngᵛ sayner noo tyahtroo
Are there any seats for tonight?	**Há ainda bilhetes para hoje à noite?**	ah ereengder billyaytish perrer oazher ah noyter
How much are the seats?	**Qual é o preço dos lugares?**	kwahl eh oo prayssoo doosh loogahrersh
Would you like to go out with me tonight?	**Quer sair comigo hoje à noite?**	kehr sereer koomeegoo oazher ah noyter
Is there a discotheque in town?	**Há alguma discoteca na cidade?**	ah ahlgoomer dishkootehker ner siddahder
Would you like to dance?	**Quer dançar?**	kehr dahngsahr
Thank you, it's been a wonderful evening.	**Obrigado(a), passei uma noite maravilhosa.**	oabriggahdoo(er) perssay oomer noyter merrervillyozzer

DAYS OF THE WEEKDAYS OF THE WEEK, see page 142

Shops, stores and services *Lojas e serviços*

Where's the nearest...?	Onde é... mais próximo(-a)?	awngder eh... mighsh prossimmoo(-er)
bakery	o padaria	er pahderreeer
bookshop	a livraria	er livvrerreeer
butcher's	o tahlo	oo tahlyoo
chemist/drugstore	a farmácia	er ferrmahssyer
dentist	o dentista	oo dayngteeshter
department store	o grande armazém	oo grahngder ahrmerzahng^y
grocery	a mercearia	er merrsyerreeer
hairdresser	o cabeleireiro	oo kerberlayrayroo
post office	a estação de correios	er ishterssahng^w der koorrayoosh
supermarket	o supermercado	oo soopehrmerrkahdoo
toilets/restrooms	as cases de banho (os banheiros)	ersh kahzersh der bernyoo (oass bahnyayroass)

General expressions *Expressões gerais*

Where's the main shopping area?	Onde é a zona comercial?	awngder eh er zoaner koomerrsyahl
Do you have any...?	Tem...?	tahng^y
Can you show me this/that?	Pode mostrar-me isto/aquilo?	podder mooshtrahr mer eeshtoo/erkeeloo
Haven't you anything...?	Não tem nada...?	nahng^w tahng^y nahder
cheaper	mais barato	mighsh berrahtoo
better/larger	melhor/maior	millyor/mayor
smaller	mais pequeno	mighsh perkaynoo
Can I try it on?	Posso provar?	possoo proovahr
How much is this?	Quanto custa isto?	kwahngtoo kooshter eeshtoo
Please write it down.	Pode escrever num papel?	podder ishkrervayr noong perpehl
I don't want to spend more than...escudos.	Não quero gastar mais que... escudos.	nahng^w kehroo gershtahr mighsh ker... ishkoodoosh
No, I don't like it.	Não, não gosto.	nahng^w nahng^w goshtoo
I'll take it.	Fico com ele.	feekoo kawng ayler
Do you accept credit cards?	Aceitam cartões de crédito?	erssaytahng^w kerrtawng^{y}sh der krehdittoo
Can you order it for me?	Pode encomendarmo?	podder ayngkoomayngdahrmoo

NUMBERS, see page 142

black	preto	praytoo
blue	azul	erzool
brown	castanho	kershternyoo
green	verde	vayrder
grey	cinzento	seengzayngtoo
orange	cor-de-laranja	koar der lerrahngzher
red	vermelho	verrmaylyoo
white	branco	brahngkoo
yellow	amarelo	ermerrehloo
light...	... claro	... klahroo
dark...	... escuro	... ishkooroo

I want to buy a/an/ some...	Quero comprar...	kehroo kawngprahr
aspirin	aspirinas	ershpirreenersh
bottle-opener	um abre-garrafas	oong ahbrer gerrahfersh
newspaper American/English	um jornal americano/inglês	oong zhoornahl ermerri-kkernoo/eengglaysh
postcard	um bilhete postal	oong billyayter pooshtahl
shampoo	um shampoo	oong shahngpoa
soap	um sabonete	oong serboonayter
sun-tan cream	um creme para bronzear	oong krehmer perrer brawngzyahr
toothpaste	uma pasta de dentes	oomer pahshter der dayngtish
a half-kilo of tomatoes	meio-quilo de tomates	mayoo keeloo der toomahtish
a litre of milk	um litro de leite	oong leetroo der layter
I'd like a film for this camera.	Queria um rolo para esta máquina.	kerreeer oong roaloo perrer ehshter mahkinner
black and white	a preto e branco	er praytoo ee brahngkoo
colour	a cores	er koarersh
I'd like a hair-cut, please.	Quero cortar o cabelo, por favor.	kehroo koortahr oo kerbayloo poor fervoar

Souvenirs *Lembranças*

china	a porcelana	er poorserlerner
corkware	os artigos de cortiça	oosh errteegoosh der koorteesser
lace	as rendas	ersh rayngdersh
pottery	a loiça de barro	er loysser der bahrroo
tiles	os azulejos	oosh erzoolayzhoosh

At the bank *Banco*

Where's the nearest bank/currency exchange office?	Onde é o banco/a agência de câmbio mais próximo/a?	awngder eh oo bahngkoo/er erzhayngsyer der kahngbyoo mighsh prossimmoo/er
I want to change some dollars/pounds.	Quero trocar dólares/libras.	kehroo trookahr dollersh/leebrersh
What's the exchange rate?	A como está o câmbio?	er koamoo ishtah oo kahngbyoo
I want to cash a traveller's cheque.	Quero levantar um cheque de viagem.	kehroo lervahngtahr oong shehker der vyahzhahng^y

At the post office *Correio*

I want to send this by...	Quero mandar isto...	kehroo mahngdahr eeshtoo
airmail	por avião	poor ervyahng^w
express	por expresso	poor ishprehssoo
A... escudo stamp, please.	Um selo de... escudos, por favor.	oong sayloo der... ishkoodoosh poor fervoar
What's the postage for a postcard/letter to United States?	Qual é a franquia de um bilhete postal/uma carta para os Estados Unidos?	kwahl eh er frahngkeeer der oong billyayter pooshtahl/oomer kahrter perrer oosh ishtahdoosh ooneedoosh
Is there any post/mail for me?	Há correio para mim?	ah koorrayoo perrer meeng

Telephoning *Telefones*

Where is the nearest telephone booth?	Onde fica e cabine telefónica mais próxima?	awngder feeker er kahbeener terlerfonnikker mighsh prossimmer
I want to reverse the charges (call collect).	Quero uma comunicação pagá vel no destino.	kehroo oomer koomoonikkerssahng^w pergahvehl noo dishteenoo
May I use your phone?	Posso utilizar o seu telefone?	possoo ootillizzahr oo sehoo terlefonner
Hello. This is... speaking.	Está. Aqui fala...	ishtah. erkee fahler
I'd like to speak to...	Queria falar com...	kerreeer ferlahr kawng
When will he/she be back?	Quando é que ele/ela estará de volta?	kwahngdoo eh ker ayler/ehler ishterrah der vollter

Time and date *Horas e data*

English	Portuguese	Pronunciation
It's one o'clock.	É uma hora.	eh **oo**mer orrer
It's two o'clock.	São duas horas.	sahng^w **doo**ersh orrersh
five past...	... e cinco	... ee **seeng**koo
quarter past...	... e um quarto	... ee oong **kwahr**too
twenty past...	... e vinte	... ee **veeng**ter
half past	... e meia	... ee **may**er
twenty-five to ...	vinte e cinco para as ...	**veeng**ter ee **seeng**koo **perr**er ersh ...
ten to...	dez para as...	dehsh **perr**er ersh...
noon/midnight	meio-dia/meia-noite	**may**oo **dee**er/**may**er **noy**ter
in the morning/ afternoon/evening	da manhã/da tarde/da noite	der mer**nyahng**/der **tahr**der/der **noy**ter
during the day	durante o dia	door**ahng**ter oo **dee**er
at night	à noite	ah **noy**ter
yesterday/today	ontem/hoje	**awng**tahng^y/**oa**zher
tomorrow	amanhã	ahmer**nyahng**
spring	a Primavara	er primmer**veh**rer
summer	o Verão	oo ver**rahng**^w
autumn (fall)	o Outono	oo oa**toa**noo
winter	o Inverno	oo eeng**vehr**noo

Sunday	domingo	doo**meeng**goo
Monday	segunda-feira	ser**goong**der **fay**rer
Tuesday	terça-feira	**tayr**ser **fay**rer
Wednesday	quarta-feira	**kwahr**ter **fay**rer
Thursday	quinta-feira	**keeng**ter **fay**rer
Friday	sexta-feira	**saysh**ter **fay**rer
Saturday	sábado	**sah**berdoo
January	Janeiro	zher**nay**roo
February	Fevereiro	ferver**ray**roo
March	Março	**mahr**soo
April	Abril	er**breel**
May	Maio	**migh**oo
June	Junho	**zhoon**yoo
July	Julho	**zhool**yoo
August	Agosto	er**goash**too
September	Setembro	ser**tayng**broo
October	Outubro	oa**too**broo
November	Novembro	noo**vayng**broo
December	Dezembro	der**zayng**broo

NUMBERS, see page 142

Numbers *Números*

0	**zero**	**zeh**roo
1	**um, uma**	oong **oo**mer
2	**dois, duas**	doysh **doo**ersh
3	**três**	**tray**sh
4	**quatro**	**kwah**troo
5	**cinco**	**seeng**koo
6	**seis**	saysh
7	**sete**	**seh**ter
8	**oito**	**oy**too
9	**nove**	**no**vver
10	**dez**	dehsh
11	**onze**	**awng**zer
12	**doze**	**do**azer
13	**treze**	**tray**zer
14	**catorze**	ker**to**arzer
15	**quinze**	**keeng**zer
16	**dezasseis**	derzer**ssay**sh
17	**dezassete**	derzer**sseh**ter
18	**dezoito**	der**zoy**too
19	**dezanove**	derzer**no**vver
20	**vinte**	**veeng**ter
21	**vinte e um**	**veeng**ter ee oong
30	**trinta**	**treeng**ter
40	**quarenta**	kwer**rayng**ter
50	**cinquenta**	seeng**kwayng**ter
60	**sessenta**	serss**ayng**ter
70	**setenta**	ser**tayng**ter
80	**oitenta**	oy**tayng**ter
90	**noventa**	noo**vayng**ter
100	**cem/cento**	sahng^{y}/**sahng**^{y}too
1,000	**mil**	meel
first	**primeiro**	prim**may**roo
second	**segundo**	ser**goong**doo
once/twice	**uma vez/duas vezes**	**oo**mer vaysh/**doo**ersh **vay**zersh
a half	**uma metade**	**oo**mer mer**tah**der

Emergency *Urgências*

Call the police	**Chame a polícia**	**sher**mer er poo**lee**ssyer
Get a doctor	**Chame um médico**	**sher**mer oong **meh**dikkoo
Go away	**Vá-se embora**	vah ser ayng**bor**rer
HELP	**SOCORRO**	soo**koar**roo
I'm ill	**Estou doente**	ishto**a dwayng**ter
I'm lost	**Perdi-me**	perr**dee** mer
LOOK OUT	**ATENÇÃO**	er**tayng**sahng^{w}

TELEPHONING, see page 140

My...has been stolen.	**Roubaram-me...**	roabahrahng^w mer
I've lost my...	**Perdi...**	perrdee
handbag	**a mala de mão**	er **mah**ler der mahng^w
wallet	**a minha carteira**	er **mee**nyer kerr**tay**rer
passport	**o passaporte**	o persser**porr**ter
luggage	**a minha bagagem**	er **mee**nyer ber**gah**zhahng^y
Where can I find a doctor who speaks English?	**Onde posso encontrar um médico que fale inglês?**	awngder **pos**soo ayngkawng**trahr** oong **meh**dikkoo ker **fah**ler eeng**glaysh**

Guide to Portuguese pronunciation *Pronúncia*

Consonants

Letter	Approximate pronunciation	Symbol	Example	
f, l, p, t, v	as in English			
b	as in English, but less decisive	b	**boca**	**bo**aker
c	1) before **a, o, u** or consonant, as in kill	k	**casa**	**kah**zer
	2) before **e, i**, like sit	s	**cedo**	**say**doo
ç	like **s** in sit	s	**começar**	koomer**ssahr**
ch	like **sh** in shut	sh	**chamar**	sher**mahr**
d	as in English but less decisive	d	**dia**	**dee**er
g	1) like **g** in go	g/gh	**garfo**	**gahr**foo
			guia	**ghee**er
	2) like **s** in pleasure	zh	**gelo**	**zhay**loo
h	always silent		**homem**	**o**mmahng^y
j	like **s** in pleasure	zh	**já**	zhah
lh	like **lli** in million	ly	**olho**	**oa**lyoo
m	1) like **m** in met	m	**mais**	mighsh
	2) nasalizes preceeding vowel; usually silent	ng ng^y	**tempo** **tem**	**tayng**poo tayng^y
n	1) like **n** in no	n	**novo**	**no**avoo
		ng	**branco**	**brahng**koo
	2) nasalizes preceeding vowel; usually silent	ng^y	**homens**	**o**mmahng^ysh
nh	like **ni** in onion	ny	**vinho**	**vee**nyoo
q	like **k** in kill	k	**querer**	ker**rayr**
r	strongly trilled	r	**rua**	**roo**er
s	1) like **s** in sit	s/ss	**saber**	ser**bayr**
	2) like **z** in razor	z	**casa**	**kah**zer
	3) like **sh** in shut	sh	**país**	per**eesh**
	4) like **s** in pleasure	zh	**cisne**	**seezh**ner

PORTUGUESE

x	1) like **sh** in **sh**ut	sh	**baixo**	**bigh**shoo
	2) like **z** in ra**z**or	z	**exacto**	i**zz**ahtoo
	3) like **x** in e**x**it	ks	**táxi**	**tah**ksi
z	1) like **z** in ra**z**or	z	**zero**	**z**ehroo
	2) like **sh** in **sh**ut	sh	**feliz**	ferlee**sh**
	3) like **s** in plea**s**ure	zh	**luz da**	loo**zh** der

Vowels

a	1) mix of c**u**t and p**a**rty	ah	**nado**	**nah**doo
	2) like **a** in **a**bout	er	**porta**	**port**er
e	1) like **e** in g**e**t	eh	**perto**	**peh**rtoo
	2) like **a** in l**a**te	ay	**cabelo**	ker**bay**loo
	3) like **er** in oth**er**	er	**pesado**	per**zah**doo
	4) like **i** in h**i**t	i	**exacto**	i**zz**ahtoo
é	like **e** in g**e**t	eh	**café**	ker**feh**
ê	like **a** in l**a**te	ay	**mês**	**may**sh
i	1) like **ee** in s**ee**d	ee	**riso**	**ree**zoo
	2) as **o** in c**o**ming	i	**final**	fi**nnahl**
o	1) like **o** in r**o**d	o	**fora**	**forr**er
	2) like **o** in n**o**te	oa	**voltar**	voal**tahr**
	3) like **oo** in f**oo**t	oo	**caso**	**kah**zoo
ô, ou	like n**o**te, but not diphthong	oa	**pôs**	**poa**sh
u	1) like **oo** in s**oo**n	oo	**número**	**noo**merroo
	2) silent in **gu, qu** before **e, i**		**querer**	ker**rayr**

Nasal vowels

ã, am, an	like **ung** in l**ung** or **an** in French d**an**s	ahng	**maçã**	mer**ssahng**
em, en	mix of **ing** in s**ing** and **a** in l**a**te	ayng	**cento**	**sayng**too
im, in	nasalized **ee** as in f**ee**t	eeng	**cinco**	**seeng**koo
om, on	like **orn** in c**orn**cob or **on** in French b**on**	awng	**bom**	bawng
um, un	nasalized **oo** in f**oo**t	oong	**um**	oong

Semi-nasalized diphthongs

em, final **en(s)**, usually final **em** as **ã** followed by **y** in y**e**t	ahng^y	**sem**	sahng^y
ão, final unstressed **am** as **ã** followed by **w**	ahng^w	**mão**	mahng^w
õe	as **on** in French b**on**, followed by **y** in y**e**t	awng^y	**põe**	pawng^y

Português

Spanish

Basic expressions *Expresiones generales*

Yes/No.	**Sí/No.**	see/noa
Please.	**Por favor.**	por fah**bhor**
Thank you.	**Gracias.**	**grah**thyahss
I beg your pardon?	**¿Perdóneme?**	payr**doa**naymay

Introductions *Presentaciones*

Good morning.	**Buenos días.**	**bway**noass **dee**ahss
Good afternoon.	**Buenas tardes.**	**bway**nahss **tahr**dayss
Good night.	**Buenas noches.**	**bway**nahss **noa**chayss
Good-bye.	**Adiós.**	ah**dhyoss**
My name is...	**Me llamo...**	may **lyah**moa
Pleased to meet you.	**Encantado(-a) de conocerle.**	aynkahn**tah**dhoa(-ah) day koanoa**thayr**lay
What's your name?	**¿Cómo de llama?**	**koa**moa say **lyah**mah
How are you?	**¿Cómo está usted?**	**koa**moa ay**stah** oo**staydh**
Fine thanks. And you?	**Bien, gracias. ¿Y usted?**	byayn **grah**thyahss. ee oo**staydh**
Where do you come from?	**¿De dónde es used?**	day **doan**day ayss oo**staydh**
I'm from...	**Soy de...**	soy day
Australia	**Australia**	ow**strah**lyah
Canada	**Canadá**	kahnah**dhah**
Great Britain	**Gran Bretaña**	grahn brah**tah**ñah
United States	**Estados Unidos**	ay**stah**dhoass oo**nee**dhoass
I'm with my...	**Estoy con mi...**	ay**stoy** kon mee
wife	**mujer**	moo**khehr**
husband	**marido**	mah**reed**hoa
family	**familia**	fah**meel**yah
boyfriend	**amigo**	ah**mee**goa
girlfriend	**amiga**	ah**mee**gah
I'm on my own.	**Estoy venido solo(-a).**	ay**stoy** bay**nee**dhoa **soa**loa(-ah)
I'm here on vacation.	**Estoy aquí para las vacaciones.**	ay**stoy** ah**kee** pah**rah** lahss bahkah**thyon**ayss

PRONUNCIATION/EMERGENCIES, page 159

Questions *Preguntas*

When?	¿Cuándo?	kwahndoa
How?	¿Cómo?	koamoa
What?/Why?	¿Qué/Por qué?	kay/por **kay**
Who?	¿Quién?	kyayn
Which?	¿Cuál/Cuáles?	kwahl/**kwah**layss
Where is...?	¿Dónde está...?	doanday aystah
Where are...?	¿Dónde están...?	doanday aystahn
Where can I find/ get...?	¿Dónde puedo encontrar...?	doanday pwaydhoa ayn-kontrahr
How far?	¿A qué distancia?	ah kay deestahnthyah
How long?	¿Cuánto tiempo?	kwahntoa tyaympoa
How much/many?	¿Cuánto/s?	kwahntoa/ss
May I?	¿Puedo?	pwaydhoa
Can I have...?	¿Puede darme...?	pwaydhay **dahr**may
Can you help me?	¿Puede usted ayu-darme?	pwaydhay oostaydh ahyoodharmay
I understand.	Comprendo/ Entiendo.	koam**praynd**oa/ aynt**yaynd**oa
I don't understand.	No comprendo.	noa koam**praynd**oa
Can you translate this for me?	¿Puede usted traducírmelo?	pwaydhay oostaydh trahdhoo**theer**mayloa
Do you speak English?	¿Habla usted inglés?	ahblah oostaydh eenglayss
I don't speak (much) Spanish.	No hablo (mucho) español.	noa **ah**bloa (**moo**choa) ayspah**ñol**

A few more useful words *Algunas palabras útiles*

better/worse	mejor/peor	mahkhor/pehor
big/small	grande/pequeño	grahnday/paykayñoa
cheap/expensive	barato/caro	bahrahtoa/kahroa
early/late	temprano/tarde	taymprahnoa/tahrday
good/bad	bueno/malo	bwaynoa/mahloa
hot/cold	caliente/frío	kahlyayntay/freeoa
near/far	cerca/lejos	thehrkah/lehkhoss
old/new	viejo/nuevo	byaykhoa/nwaybhoa
right/wrong	correcto/incorrecto	koarrehktoa/ eenkoarrehktoa
vacant/occupied	libre/occupado	leebray/oakoopahdhoa

Hotel–Accommodation *Hotel*

I have a reservation.	**He hecho una reserva.**	eh aychoa oonah reyssayrbah
We've reserved two rooms.	**Hemos reservado dos habitaciones.**	ehmoass rayssayrbahdhoa doss ahbheetahthyonayss
Do you have any vacancies?	**¿Tiene habitaciones libres?**	tyaynay ahbheetahthyonayss leebhrayss
I'd like a... room.	**Quisiera una habitacón...**	keessyayrah oonah ahbheetahthyon
single/double	**sencilla/doble**	sayntheelyah/doablay
with twin beds	**con dos camas**	kon doss kahmahss
with a double bed	**con una cama matrimonial**	kon oonah kahmah mahtreemoanyahl
with a bath/shower	**con baño/ducha**	kon bahñoa/doochah
We'll be staying...	**Nos quedaremos...**	noss kaydhahraymoass
overnight only	**sólo una noche**	soaloa oonah noachay
a few days	**algunos días**	ahlgoonoass deeahss
a week	**una semana**	oonah saymahnah

Decision *Decisión*

May I see the room?	**¿Puedo ver la habitación?**	pwaydhoa behr lah ahbheetahthyon
That's fine. I'll take it.	**Muy bien, la tomaré.**	mwee byayn lah toamahray
No. I don't like it.	**No, no me gusta.**	noa noa may goostah
It's too...	**Es demasiado...**	ayss deymahssyahdhoa
dark/small	**oscura/pequeña**	oskoorah/paykayñah
noisy	**ruidosa**	rweedhoassah
Do you have anything...?	**¿Tiene usted algo...?**	tyaynay oostaydh ahlgoa
better/bigger	**mejor/más grande**	mehkhor/mahss grahnday
cheaper	**más barato**	mahss bahrahtoa
quieter	**más tranquilo**	mahss trahnkeeloa
May I have my bill, please?	**Por favor, ¿puede darme mi cuenta?**	por fahbhor pwaydhay dahrmay mee kwayntah
It's been a very enjoyable stay.	**Ha sido una estancia muy agradable.**	ah seedhoa oonah aystahnthyah mwee ahgrahdhahblay

NUMBERS, see page 158/DAYS OF THE WEEK, see page 157

Eating out *Comidas y bebidas*

I'd like to reserve a table for four.	**Quiero reservar una mesa para cuatro.**	**kyay**roa rehssayr**bahr** **oo**nah **may**ssah **pah**rah **kwaht**roa
We'll come at 8.	**Vendremos a las ocho.**	bayn**dray**moass ah lahss **oa**choa
I'd like...	**Quisiera...**	kee**ssyay**rah
breakfast	**el desayuno**	ayl dayssah**yoo**noa
lunch	**el almuerzo**	ayl ahl**mwayr**thoa
dinner	**la cena**	lah **thay**nah
What do you recommend?	**¿Qué me aconseja?**	kay may ahkoan**seh**khah
Do you have any vegetarian dishes?	**¿Tiene platoas vegetarianos?**	**tyay**nay **plah**toass baykhaytah**ryah**noass

Breakfast *Desayuno*

May I have...	**Quisiera...**	kee**ssyay**rah
boiled egg	**huevo cocido**	**way**bhoa koa**thee**dhoa
bread	**pan**	pahn
butter	**mantequilla**	mahntay**kee**lyah
cereal	**cereales**	thayray**ah**layss
coffee	**café**	kah**fay**
jam	**mermelada**	mahrmay**lah**dhah
rolls	**panecillos**	pahnay**thee**lyoass
tea	**té**	tay

Starters (Appetizers) *Entremeses*

avocado	**aguacate**	ah wah**kah**tay
ham omelette	**tortilla de jamón**	toar**tee**lyah day kha**mon**
spiced meatballs	**albóndigas**	ahl**bon**dee ahss
spicy sausage	**chorizo**	choa**reet**hoa
squid	**calamares**	kahlah**mah**rayss

Soups *Sopas*

fish soup	**sopa de pescado**	**soa**pah day pays**kah**dhoa
onion soup	**sopa de cebolla**	**soa**pah day thay**boa**lyah
vegetable soup	**sopa de verduras**	**soa**pah day bayr**doo**rahss

caldo gallego
(**kahl**doa gah**lyeh**goa)
meat and vegetable broth

gazpacho
(gahth**pah**choa)
cold soup of tomato, cucumber, green pepper bread, onion and garlic

Fish and seafood *Pescado y mariscos*

cod	**bacalao**	bahkah**lah**oa
lobster	**langosta**	lahn**goas**tah
oysters	**ostras**	**os**trahss
snails	**caracoles**	kahrah**koa**layss
swordfish	**pez espada**	payth ays**pah**dhah
trout	**trucha**	**troo**chah
tuna (tunny)	**atún**	ah**toon**

zarzuela   spicy fish and seafood stew
(thahr**thway**lah)

baked	**al horno**	ahl **oar**noa
boiled	**hervido**	ayr**bhee**dhoa
fried/roast	**frito/asado**	**free**toa/ah**ssah**dhoa
grilled	**a la parrilla**	ah lah pahr**ree**lyah
stewed	**estofado**	aysto**afah**dhoa
underdone (rare)	**poco hecho**	**poa**koa **ay**choa
medium	**regular**	rehgoo**lahr**
well-done	**muy hecho**	mwee **ay**choa

Meat *Carne*

I'd like some…	**Quisiera**…	kees**syay**rah
bacon	**tocino**	toa**thee**noa
beef	**carne de buey**	**kahr**nay day bway
chicken/duck	**pollo/pato**	**poa**lyoa/**pah**toa
chops	**chuletas**	choo**lay**tahss
lamb	**carne de cordero**	**kahr**nay day koar**day**roa
pork	**carne de cerdo**	**kahr**nay day **thehr**doa
sausages	**salchichas**	sahl**chee**chahss
steak	**filete**	fee**lay**tay
veal	**carne de ternera**	day tehr**nay**rah

Vegetables *Verduras*

beans (green)	**judías verdes**	khoo**dhee**ahss **behr**dayss
cabbage	**repollo**	rey**poa**lyoa
lettuce	**lechuga**	lay**choo**gah
mushrooms	**setas**	**say**tahss
onions	**cebollas**	thay**boa**lyahss
potatoes	**patatas**	pah**tah**tahss
tomatoes	**tomates**	toa**mah**tayss

paella   golden saffron rice garnished with meat, fish,
(pah**ay**lyah   seafood and/or vegetables

Fruit and dessert *Fruta y postre*

apple	**manzana**	mahn**thah**nah
cherries	**cerezas**	thay**ray**tahss
lemon	**limón**	lee**mon**
orange	**naranja**	nah**rahn**khah
peach	**melocotón**	mayloakoa**ton**
pear	**pera**	**peh**rah
plums	**ciruelas**	theer**way**lahss
strawberries	**fresas**	**fray**sahss
crema catalana	**kray**mah kahtah**lah**nah	caramel pudding
fritos	**free**toass	fritters
helado	ay**lah**dhoa	ice-cream
pastel	pah**stayl**	cake
tarta de manzana	**tahr**tah day mahn**thah**nah	apple tart

Drinks *Bebidas*

beer	**cerveza**	thayr**bhay**thah
(hot) chocolate	**un chocolate (caliente)**	oon choakoa**lah**tay (kah**lyayn**tay)
coffee	**un café**	oon kah**fay**
black	**solo**	**soa**loa
with cream	**con crema**	kon **kray**mah
fruit juice	**un jugo de fruta**	oon **khoo**goa day **froo**tah
milk	**leche**	**lay**chay
mineral water	**agua mineral**	**ah**gwah meenay**rahl**
tea	**un té**	oon tay
wine	**vino**	**bee**noa
red/white	**tinto/blanco**	**teen**toa/**blahn**koa

Complaints and paying *Reclamaciones y la cuenta*

This is too...	**Esto está...**	**ays**toa ay**stah**
bitter/sweet	**amargo/dulce**	ah**mahr**goa/**dool**thay
salty	**salado**	sah**lah**dhoa
That's not what I ordered.	**Esto no es lo que he pedido.**	**ays**toa noa ayss loa kay ay peh**dhee**dhoa
I'd like to pay.	**Quisiera pagar.**	kees**syay**rah pah**gahr**
I think you made a mistake in this bill.	**Creo que se ha equivocado usted en esta cuenta.**	**kre**hoa kay say ah aykee-bhoa**kah**dhoa oo**staydh** ayn **ays**tah **kwayn**tah
Do you accept this credit card?	**¿Acepta esta tarjeta de crédito?**	ah**thayp**tah **ays**tah tahr-**khay**tah day **kray**dheetoa
We enjoyed it, thank you.	**Nos ha gustado, gracias.**	noss ah goo**stah**dhoa **grah**thyahss

Travelling around *Excursiones*

Plane *Avión*

Is there a flight to...?	¿Hay algún vuelo a...?	igh ahl**goon** bway**loa** ah
What time should I check in?	¿A qué hora debo presentarme?	ah kay **oar**ah **day**bhoa prayssayn**tahr**may
I'd like to... my reservation.	Quisiera... mi reserva.	kees**syay**rah... mee rayss**ayr**bah
cancel	anular	ahnoo**lahr**
change	cambiar	kahm**byahr**
confirm	confirmar	konfeer**mahr**

Train *Tren*

I'd like a ticket to...	Quiero un billete para...	**kyay**roa oon beel**yay**tay **pah**rah
single (one-way)	ida	**ee**dhah
return (roundtrip)	ida y vuelta	**ee**dhah ee **bwehl**tah
first/second class	primera/segunda clase	pree**may**rah/say**goon**dah **klahs**say
How long does the journey (trip) take?	¿Cuánto dura el viaje?	**kwahn**toa **doo**rah ayl **byah**khay
When is the... train to...?	¿A qué hora sale el ... tren para...?	ah kay **oar**ah **sah**lay ayl... trayn **pah**rah
first/next/last	primer/próximo/ último	pree**mayr**/**prok**seemoa/ **ool**teemoa
Is this the train to...?	¿Es éste el tren para...?	ayss **ay**stay ayl trayn **pah**rah

Bus *Autobús*

Which bus do I take for the town centre?	¿Qué autobús debo tomar para el cen-tro?	kay owtoa**bhooss day**bhoa toa**mahr pah**rah ayl **thayn**troa
How much is the fare to...?	¿Cuánto es la tarifa para...?	**kwahn**toa ayss lah tah**ree**fah **pah**rah
Will you tell me when to get off?	¿Me diría usted cuándo tengo que apearme?	may dee**ree**ah oos**taydh kwahn**doa **tayn**goa kay ahpay**ahr**may

Taxi *Taxi*

How much is the fare to...?	¿Cuánto es la tarifa a...?	**kwahn**toa ayss lah tah**ree**fah rah

NUMBERS, see page 158

Take me to this address.	Lléveme a estas señas.	**lyay**bhaymay ah **ays**tahss **say**ñahss
Please stop here.	Pare aquí, por favor.	**pah**ray ah**kee** por fah**bhor**
Could you wait for me, please?	¿Puede esperarme, por favor?	**pway**dhay ayspay-**rahr**may por fah**bhor**

Car hire (rental) *Alquiler de coches*

I'd like to hire/rent a car.	Quisiera alquilar un coche.	kee**ssyay**rah ahl**kee**lahr oon **koa**chay
I'd like it for...	Lo quisiera para...	loa kee**ssyay**rah **pah**rah
a day	un día	oon **dee**ah
a week	una semana	**oo**nah say**mah**nah
Where's the nearest filling station?	¿Dónde está la gasolinera más cercana?	**doan**day ays**tah** lah gahssoa**lee**nayrah mahss thehr**kah**nah
Full tank, please.	Llénelo, por favor.	**lyay**nayloa por fah**bhor**
Give me... litres of petrol (gasoline).	Déme... litros de gasolina.	**day**may... **lee**troass day gahssoa**lee**nah
How do I get to...?	¿Cómo se va a...?	**koa**moa say bah ah
I've broken down at...	Tengo un coche estropeado en...	**tayn**goa oon **koa**chay aystroapay**ah**dhoa ayn
Can you send a mechanic?	¿Puede usted mandar un mecánico?	**pway**dhay oos**taydh** mahn**dahr** oon may**kah**neekoa
Can you mend this puncture (fix this flat)?	¿Puede arreglar este pinchazo?	**pway**dhay ahrray**glahr ays**tay peen**chah**thoa

Se ha equivocado usted de carretera.	You're on the wrong road.
Siga todo derecho.	Go straight ahead.
Es hacia allí...	It's down there...
a la izquierda/derecha	on the left/right
junto a/después de...	next to/after...
norte/sur/este/oeste	north/south/east/west

EMERGENCIES, see page 158

Sightseeing *Visitas turísticas*

Where's the tourist office?	¿Dónde está la oficina de turismo?	doanday aystah lah oafeetheenah day tooreesmoa
Is there an English-speaking guide?	¿Hay algún guía que hable inglés?	igh ahlgoon geeah kay ahblay eenglayss
Where is/are ...?	¿Dónde está/están ...?	doanday aystah/aystahn
art gallery	la galería de arte	lah gahlayreeah day ahrtay
castle	el castillo	ayl kahsteelyoa
cathedral	la catedral	lah kahtaydrahl
church	la iglesia	lah eeglayssyah
city centre/downtown	el centro de la ciudad	ayl thayntroa day lah thyoodhahdh
harbour	el puerto	ayl pwayrtoa
market	el mercado	ayl mehrkahdhoa
museum	el museo	ayl moossayoa
square	la plaza	lah plahthah
tower	la torre	lah torray
When does it open/close?	¿A qué hora abren/cierran?	ah kay oarah ahbrayn/thyayrrahn
How much is the entrance fee?	¿Cuánto vale la entrada?	kwahntoa bahlay lah ayntrahdhah

Relaxing *Diversiones*

What's playing at the ...Theatre?	¿Qué ponen en el teatro ...?	kay poanehn ayn ayl tayahtroa
Are there any seats for tonight?	¿Quedan localidades para esta noche?	kaydhan loakahleedhahdhayss pahrah aystah noachay
How much are the seats?	¿Cuánto valen las localidades?	kwahntoa bahlayn lahss loakahleedhahdhayss
Would you like to go out with me tonight?	¿Quisiera usted salir conmigo esta noche?	keessyayrah oostaydh sahleer konmeegoa aystah noachay
Is there a discotheque in town?	¿Hay alguna discoteca en la ciudad?	igh ahlgoonah deeskoataykay ayn lah thyoodhahdh
May I have this dance?	¿Me permite este baile?	may payrmeetay aystay bighlay
Thank you for the evening. It was great.	Muchas gracias por la velada. Ha sido estupenda.	moochahss grahthyahss por lah baylahdhah. ah seedhoa aystoopayndah

TELLING THE TIME, see page 157

Shops, stores and services *Comercios y servicios*

Where's the nearest...	¿Dónde está... más cercano/cercana?	doanday aystah ... mahss thayrkahnoa/thayrkahnah
bakery	la panadería	lah pahnahdhayreeah
bookshop	la librería	lah leebrayreeah
butcher's	la carnicería	lah kahrneethayreeah
chemist/drugstore	la farmacia	lah fahrmahthyah
dentist	el dentista	ayl daynteestah
department store	los grandes almacenes	loss grahndayss ahlmahthaynayss
grocery	la tienda de comestibles	lay tyayndah day koamaysteeblayss
hairdresser (ladies)	la peluquería	lah paylookayreeah
news-stand	el quiosco de periódicos	ayl kyoskoa day payryodheekoass
post office	la oficina de correos	lah oafeetheenah day korrehoass
supermarket	el supermercado	ayl soopayrmayrkahdhoa
toilets/restrooms	los servicios	loass sayrbeethyoass

General expressions *Locuciones básicas*

Where's the main shopping area?	¿Dónde está la zona de tiendas más importante?	doanday aystah lah thoanah day tyayndahss mahss eempoartahntay
Do you have any...?	¿Tiene usted...?	tyaynay oostaydh
Haven't you anything...?	¿No tiene usted algo...?	noa tyaynay oostaydh ahlgoa
cheaper/better larger/smaller	más barato/mejor más grande/más pequeño	mahss bahrahtoa/mehkhor mahss grahnday/mahss paykayñoa
Can I try it on?	¿Puedo probármelo?	pwaydhoa probahrmayloa
How much is this?	¿Cuánto cuesta esto?	kwahntoa kwaystah aystoa
Please write it down.	Escríbamelo, por favor.	ayskreebhahmayloa por fahbhor
I don't want to spend more than...	No quiero gastar más de...	noa kyayroa gahstahr mahss day
No, I don't like it.	No, no me gusta.	noa noa may goostah
I'll take it.	Me lo llevo.	may loa lyaybhoa
Do you accept credit cards?	¿Acepta usted tarjetas de crédito?	ahthayptah oostaydh tahrkhaytahss day kraydheetoa

NUMBERS, see page 158

black	**negro**	**neh**groa
blue	**azul**	ah**thool**
brown	**marrón**	mah**rr**on
green	**verde**	**behr**day
orange	**naranja**	nah**rahn**khah
red	**rojo**	**ro**akhoa
white	**blanco**	**blahn**koa
yellow	**amarillo**	ahmah**ree**lyoa
light...	**... claro**	**klah**roa
dark...	**... oscuro**	oas**koo**roa

I want to buy...	**Quisiera comprar...**	kees**syay**rah kom**prahr**
aspirins	**unas aspirinas**	**oo**nahss ahspee**ree**nahss
bread	**pan**	pahn
newspaper	**un periódico**	oon payr**yo**dheekoa
American	**americano**	ahmayree**kah**noa
English	**inglés**	een**glayss**
postcards	**unas tarjetas postales**	**oo**nahss tahr**khay**tahss poas**tah**layss
shampoo	**un champú**	oon chahm**poo**
soap	**jabón**	khah**bhon**
sun-tan cream	**una crema solar**	**oo**nah **kray**mah soa**lahr**
toothpaste	**pasta de dientes**	**pah**stah day **dyayn**tayss
a half kilo of tomatoes	**medio kilo de tomates**	**may**dhyoa **kee**loa day toa**mah**tayss
a litre of milk	**un litro de leche**	oon **lee**troa day **lay**chay
I'd like a film for this camera.	**Quisiera un rollo para esta cámara.**	kees**syay**rah oon **ro**alyoa **pah**rah **ay**stah **kah**mahrah
black and white	**en blanco y negro**	ayn **blahn**koa ee **nay**groa
colour	**en color**	ayn koa**loar**
I'd like a haircut, please.	**Quiero un corte de pelo, por favor.**	**kyay**roa oon **kor**tay day **peh**loa por fah**bhor**

Souvenirs *Recuerdos*

castanets	**las castañuelas**	lahss kahstahn̄**way**lahss
copperware	**objetos de cobre**	oab**khay**toass day **koa**bray
doll	**la muñeca**	lah moo**ñay**kah
fan	**el abanico**	ayl ahbhah**nee**koa
guitar	**la guitarra**	lah gee**tah**rrah
lace	**los encajes**	loss ayn**kah**khayss
poncho	**el poncho**	ayl **pon**choa

At the bank *En el banco*

Where's the nearest currency exchange office?	¿Dónde está la oficina de cambio más cercana?	doanday aystah lah oafeetheenah day kahmbyoa mahss thehrkahnah
I want to change some dollars/pounds.	Quiero cambiar unos dólares/unas libras esterlinas.	kyayroa kahmbyahr oonoass doalahrayss/ oonahss leebrahss aystayrleenahss
What's the exchange rate?	¿A cómo está el cambio?	ah koamoa aystah ayl kahmbyoa
I want to cash a traveller's cheque.	Quiero cobrar un cheque de viajero.	kyayroa koabrahr oon chaykay day byahkhayroa

At the post office *Correos*

I want to send this ...	Quiero mandar esto ...	kyayroa mahndahr aystoa
airmail express	por correo aéreo urgente	por korrehoa ahayrehoa oorkhayntay
I want ... ...-peseta stamps.	Quiero ... sellos para ... pesetas.	kyayroa ... saylyoass pahrah ... payssaytahss
What's the postage for a letter to United States?	¿Cuál es el franqueo para una carta para los Estados Unidos?	kwahl ayss ayl frahnkayoa pahrah oonah kahrtah pahrah loass aysahd hoass ooneedhoass
Is there any post/mail for me? My name is ...	¿Hay correo para mí? Me llamo(-a) ...	igh korrehoa pahrah mee. may lyahmoa(-ah)

Telephoning *Teléfonos*

Where is the nearest telephone?	¿Dónde está el teléfono más cercano?	doanday aystah ayl taylayfoanoa mahss thehrkahnoa
May I use your phone?	¿Puedo usar su teléfono?	pwaydhoa oossahr soo taylayfoanoa
Hello. This is ... speaking.	Oiga. Aquí habla con ...	oyga. ahkee ahblah kon
I'd like to speak to ...	Quiero hablar con ...	kyayroa ahblahr kon
When will he/she be back?	¿Cuándo estará de vuelta?	kwahndoa aystahrah day bwayltah

NUMBERS, see page 158

Time and date *Horas y fechas*

It's…	Es/Son…	ayss/son
five past one	la una y cinco	lah **oo**nah ee **theen**koa
quarter past three	las tres y cuarto	lahss trayss ee **kwahr**toa
twenty past four	las cuatro y veinte	lahss **kwah**troa ee **bayn**tay
half past six	las seis y media	lahss sayss ee **may**dhyay
twenty-five to seven	las siete menos veinticinco	lahss **say**tay **may**noass bayntee**theen**koa
ten to ten	las diez menos diez	lahss dyayth **may**noass dyayth
twelve o'clock	las doce	lahss **doa**thay
in the morning	por la mañana	por lah mah**ñah**nah
in the afternoon	por la tarde	por lah **tahr**day
in the evening	por la tarde	por lah **tahr**day
during the day	durante el día	doo**rahn**tay ayl **dee**ah
at night	por la noche	por lah **noa**chay
yesterday/today	ayer/hoy	ah**yehr**/oy
tomorrow	mañana	mah**ñah**nah
spring	la primavera	lah preemah**bhay**rah
summer	el verano	ayl bay**rah**noa
autumn (fall)	el otoño	ayl o**toa**ñoa
winter	el invierno	ayl een**byayr**noa

Sunday	domingo	doa**meen**goa
Monday	lunes	**loo**nayss
Tuesday	martes	**mahr**tayss
Wednesday	miércoles	**myayr**koalayss
Thursday	jueves	**khway**bhayss
Friday	viernes	**byayr**nayss
Saturday	sábado	**sah**bhadhoa
January	enero	ay**nay**roa
February	febrero	feh**breh**roa
March	marzo	**mahr**thoa
April	abril	ah**breel**
May	mayo	**mah**yoa
June	junio	**khoo**nyoa
July	julio	**khool**yoa
August	agosto	ah**goas**toa
September	septiembre	sehp**tyaym**bray
October	octubre	ok**too**bray
November	noviembre	noa**bhyaym**bray
December	diciembre	deeth**yaym**bray

NUMBERS, page 158

Numbers *Números*

0	**cero**	**thay**roa
1	**uno**	**oon**oa
2	**dos**	**doss**
3	**tres**	**trayss**
4	**cuatro**	**kwah**troa
5	**cinco**	**theen**koa
6	**seis**	**sayss**
7	**siete**	**syay**tay
8	**ocho**	**oa**choa
9	**nueve**	**nway**bhay
10	**diez**	**dyayth**
11	**once**	**on**thay
12	**doce**	**doa**thay
13	**trece**	**tray**thay
14	**catorce**	kah**tor**thay
15	**quince**	**keen**thay
16	**dieciséis**	dyaythee**ssayss**
17	**diecisiete**	dyaythee**ssyay**tay
18	**dieciocho**	dyaythee**oa**choa
19	**diecinueve**	dyaytheen**way**bhay
20	**veinte**	**bayn**tay
21	**veintiuno**	baynteе**oon**oa
30	**treinta**	**trayn**tah
40	**cuarenta**	kwah**rayn**tah
50	**cincuenta**	theen**kwayn**tah
60	**sesenta**	sayss**ayn**tah
70	**setenta**	say**tayn**tah
80	**ochenta**	oa**chayn**tah
90	**noventa**	noab**hayn**tah
100	**cien/ciento**	**thyayn**/**thyayn**toa
1,000	**mil**	meel
10,000	**diez mil**	dyath meel
1,000,000	**un millón**	oon meel**yon**
first	**primero**	pree**may**roa
second	**segundo**	say**goon**doa
third	**tercero**	tehr**thay**roa
once	**una vez**	**oon**ah behth
twice	**dos veces**	doss **bay**thayss
a half	**una mitad**	**oon**ah meet**ahdh**
a quarter	**un cuarto**	oon **kwahr**toa
a third	**un tercio**	oon **tehr**thyoa

Emergency *Urgencia*

Call the police	Llama a la policía	lyahmah ah lah poaleetheeah
Get a doctor	Busque un doctor	booskay oon doaktor
Go away	Váyase	bahyahssay
HELP	SOCORRO	sokoarroa
I'm ill	Estoy enfermo(-a)	aystoy aynfehrmoa(ah)
I'm lost	Me he perdido	may ay payrdeedhoa
Leave me alone	Déjeme en paz	daykhaymay ayn pahth
LOOK OUT	CUIDADO	kweedhahdhoa
STOP THIEF	AL LADRÓN	ahl lahdron
My ... has been stolen.	Me han robado mi ...	may ahn roabhahdhoa mee
I've lost my ...	He perdido mi ...	ay pehrdeedhoa mee
handbag	bolso	boalsoa
luggage	equipaje	aykeepahkhay
passport	pasaporte	passahportay
wallet	cartera	kahrtayrah
Where can I find a doctor who speaks English?	¿Dónde puedo encontrar un médico que hable inglés?	doanday pwaydhoa aynkontrahr oon mehdheekoa kay ahblay eenglayss

Guide to Spanish pronunciation *Pronunciación*

Consonants

Letter	Approximate pronunciation	Symbol	Example	
f, k, l, m, n, p, t, x, y	as in English			
b	1) generally as in English	b	**bueno**	**bway**noa
	2) between vowels, a sound between **b** and **v**	bh	**bebida**	bay**bhee**dhah

c	1) before **e**, **i** like **th** in **thin**	th	**centro**	**thayn**troa
	2) like **k** in **kit**	k	**como**	**koa**moa
ch	as in English	ch	**mucho**	**moo**choa
d	1) like **d** in **dog** but weaker	d	**donde**	**doan**day
	2) between vowels and at end of word like **th** in **this**	dh	**edad**	ay**dhah**dh
g	1) before **e**, **i**, like **ch** in Scottish lo**ch**	kh	**urgente**	oor**khayn**tay
	2) between vowels, sometimes within word, weak version	g̱	**agua**	**ah**g̱wah
	3) like **g** in **go**	g	**ninguno**	neen**goo**noa
h	always silent		**hombre**	**om**bray
j	like **ch** in lo**ch**	kh	**bajo**	**bah**khoa
ll	like **lli** in mi**lli**on	ly	**lleno**	**lyay**noa
ñ	like **ni** in o**ni**on	ñ	**señor**	say**ñor**
qu	like **k** in **kit**	k	**quince**	**keen**thay
r	trilled, like Scottish **r**	r	**río**	**ree**oa
rr	strongly trilled	rr	**arriba**	ahr**ree**bhah
s	like **s** in **sit**, with a slight lisp	s/ss	**vista** **cuantos**	**bees**tah **kwahn**toass
v	1) like **b** in **bad** but lighter	b	**viejo**	**byayk**hoa
	2) between vowels like English **v**	bh	**rival**	ree**bhahl**
z	like **th** in **thin**	th	**brazo**	**brah**thoa

Vowels

a	like **ar** in c**ar**t, but fairly short	ah	**gracias**	**grah**thyahss
e	1) like **a** in l**a**te	ay	**de**	day
	2) like **e** in g**e**t	eh	**llover**	lyoa**bhehr**
i	like **ee** in f**ee**t	ee	**sí**	see
o	1) like **oa** in b**oa**t, but pronounced without a movement of tongue or lips	oa	**sopa**	**soa**pah
	2) like **o** in g**o**t	o	**dos**	doss
u	like **oo** in l**oo**t	oo	**una**	**oo**nah
y	like **ee** in f**ee**t, at end of word	ee	**y**	ee

Swedish

Basic expressions *Användbara uttryck*

Yes/No.	**Ja/Nej.**	yaa/nay
Please.	**Var snäll och.../ ..., tack.**	vaar snehl ok/ tahk
Thank you.	**Tack.**	tahk
I beg your pardon?	**Förlåt?**	fur'lawt

Introductions *Presentation*

Good morning.	**God morgon.**	goo(d) **mo**rron
Good afternoon.	**God middag.**	goo(d) **mi**ddah(g)
Good night.	**God natt.**	goo(d) naht
Good-bye.	**Adjö.**	ah**yūr**
My name is...	**Mitt namn är...**	mit nahmn ǣr
Pleased to meet you.	**Trevligt att träffas.**	**trāyv**lli(g)t aht **treh**fahss
What's your name?	**Vad heter ni/du?**	vaad **hāy**terr nee/dēw
How are you?	**Hur står det till?**	hēwr stawr dāy(t) til
Fine thanks. And you?	**Bra, tack. Och du?**	braa tahk. ok dēw
Where do you come from?	**Varifrån kommer du?**	**vaa**rifrawn **ko**mmer dēw
I'm from...	**Jag är från...**	yaa(g) ǣr frawn
Australia	**Australien**	aaew**straa**liern
Canada	**Kanada**	**kah**nahdah
Great Britain	**Storbritannien**	**stoo**rbrittahniern
United States	**USA**	**ēw**ehssaa
I'm with my...	**Jag är här med...**	yaa(g) ǣr hǣr māyd
wife	**min fru**	min frēw
husband	**min man**	min mahn
family	**min familj**	min fah**mil**y
boyfriend	**min pojkvän**	min **poyk**vehn
girlfriend	**min flickvän**	min **flik**vehn
I'm here on business/vacation.	**Jag är här i affärer/ på semester.**	yaa(g) ǣr hǣr ee ah**fǣ**rerr/paw seh**meh**sterr

GUIDE TO PRONUNCIATION/EMERGENCIES, page 175

SWEDISH

Questions *Frågor*

When?	**När?**	nær
How?	**Hur?**	hewr
What?/Why?	**Vad?/Varför?**	vaad/**vahr**furr
Who?	**Vem?**	vehm
Which?	**Vilken?**	**vil**kern
Where is/are...?	**Var är/Var finns/ Var ligger...?**	vaar ǣr/vaar finss/ vaar **lig**gerr
Where can I find...?	**Var hittar jag...?**	vaaar **hit**tahr yaa(g)
Where can I get...?	**Var kan jag få tag på...?**	vaar kahn yaa(g) faw taag paw
How far?	**Hur långt?**	hewr longt
How long?	**Hur länge?**	hewr **lehng**er
How much/many?	**Hur mycket/ många?**	hewr **mewk**er(t)/**mong**ah
Can I have...?	**Kan jag få...?**	kahn yaa(g) faw
Can you help me?	**Kan ni hjälpa mig?**	kahn nee **yehl**pah may
What does this mean?	**Vad betyder det här?**	vaa(d) ber**tew**derr dǟy(t) hǟr
I understand.	**Jag förstår.**	yaa(g) furr**stawr**
I don't understand.	**Jag förstår inte.**	yaa(g) furr**stawr** inter
Can you translate this for me?	**Kan ni översätta det här för mig?**	kahn nee **ūr**ver**r**sehtah dǟy(t) hǟr fürr may
Do you speak English?	**Talar ni engelska?**	**taal**ahr nee **ehng**erlskah
I don't speak (much) Swedish.	**Jag talar inte (så bra) svenska.**	yaa(g) **taal**ahr inter (saw braa) **svehn**skah

A few more useful words *Några fler användbara ord*

better/worse	**bättre/sämre**	**beht**rer/**sehm**rer
big/small	**stor/liten**	stōōr/**lee**tern
cheap/expensive	**billig/dyr**	**bil**li(g)/dewr
early/late	**tidig/sen**	**teed**i(g)/sǟyn
good/bad	**bra/dålig**	braa/**daw**li(g)
hot/cold	**varm/kall**	vahrm/kahl
near/far	**nära/långt (bort)**	**nǣr**ah/longt (bo`t)
old/new	**gammal/ny**	**gah**mahl/new
right/wrong	**rätt/fel**	reht/**fayl**
vacant/occupied	**ledig/upptagen**	**lay**di(g)/**ewp**taagern

Svensk

Hotel–Accommodation *Hotell*

I/We have a reservation.	Jag/Vi har beställt rum.	yaa(g)/vee haar ber**stehlt** rewm
Do you have any vacancies?	Har ni några lediga rum?	har nee **naw**grah **lay**diggah rewm
I'd like a ..	Jag skulle vilja ha ett ...	yaa(g) **skew**ler **vil**yah haa eht
single room	enkelrum	**ehn**kerlrewm
double room	dubbelrum	**dew**berlrewm
with twin beds	med två sängar	mayd tvaw **sehng**ahr
with a double bed	med dubbelsäng	mayd **dew**berlsehng
with a bath/shower	med bad/dusch	mayd baad/dewsh
We'll be staying ...	Vi tänker stanna ...	vee **tehn**kerr **stah**nah
overnight only	bara över natten	**baa**rah **ur**verr **nah**tern
a few days	några dagar	**naw**grah **daa**(gah)r
a week	en vecka	ehn **veh**kah
Is there a camp site near here?	Finns det någon campingplats i närheten?	finss day(t) **naw**gon **kahm**pingplahtss ee **naer**haytern

Decision *Beslut*

May I see the room?	Kan jag få se på rummet?	kahn yaa(g) faw say paw **rew**mert
That's fine. I'll take it.	Det är bra. Jag tar det.	day(t) aer braa. yaa(g) taar day(t)
No. I don't like it.	Nej. Jag tycker inte om det.	nay. yaa(g) **tew**kerr **in**ter om day(t)
It's too ...	Det är för ...	day(t) aer furr
dark/cold	mörkt/kallt	murrkt/kahlt
Do you have anything ...?	Har ni något ...?	haar nee **naw**got
better/bigger	bättre/större	**beht**rer/**stur**rer
cheaper	billigare	**bil**liggahrer
quieter	tystare	**tews**tahtrer
May I have my bill, please?	Kan jag få räkningen, tack?	kahn yaa(g) faw **raik**ningern tahk
It's been a very enjoyable stay.	Det har varit en mycket trevlig vistelse.	day(t) haar **vaa**rit ehn **mew**ker(t) **trayv**li(g) **vis**terlser

DAYS OF THE WEEK, see page 172/NUMBERS, see page 173

Eating out *Mat och dryck*

I'd like to reserve a table for 4.	Jag skulle vilja beställa ett bord för 4.	yaa(g) skewler vilyah berstehlah eht boo'd fürr 4
We'll come at 8.	Vi kommer klockan 8.	vee kommerr klokkahn 8
I'd like some...	Jag skulle vilja ha...	yaa(g) skewler vilyah haa
breakfast/lunch/ dinner	frukost/lunch/ middag	frewkost/lewnsh/ middah(g)
What would you recommend?	Vak rekommen- derar ni?	vaad rehkommerndayrahr nee
Do you have any vegetarian dishes?	Har ni några vegetariska rätter?	haar nee nawgrah vehgertaariskah rehterr

Breakfast *Frukost*

May I have some...	Kan jag få...?	kahn yaa(g) faw
bread	lite bröd	leeter brürd
butter	lite smör	leeter smürr
cheese	ost	oost
ham and eggs	skinka och ägg	shinkah ok ehg
jam	lite sylt	leeter sewlt
rolls	ett småfranska	eht smawfrahnskah

Starters *Förrätter*

färska räkor	fæ'skah raikoor	unshelled prawns with toast and butter
grodlår	groodlawr	frog's legs
gåslever	gawslayverr	goose liver
smör, ost och sill	smürr, oost ok sil	herring with bread, butter and cheese

Soups *Sopper*

buljong	bewlyong	consommé
grönsakssoppa	grürnsaakssoppah	vegetable soup
kålsoppa	kawlsoppah	cabbage soup
nässelsoppa	nehsserlsoppah	nettle soup
ärtsoppa	æ'tsoppah	yellow pea soup

Fish and seafood *Fisk och skaldjur*

cod	**torsk**	to'sk
crab	**krabba**	**krah**bah
eel	**ål**	awl
herring	**sill**	sil
lobster	**hummer**	**hew**merr
mullet	**multe**	**mewl**ter
oysters	**ostron**	**oos**tron
smoked herring	**böckling**	**burk**ling

gubböra (**gewb**rūrrah)	marinated sprats, onions and hard-boiled eggs, fried
lättrökt lax (**lehtr**ūrkt lahks)	smoked salmon with creamed spinach and poached egg
sotare (**sōō**tahrer)	Baltic herring grilled until black, with dill butter

baked	**ugnstekt**	**ewngn**stāykt
boiled	**kokt**	kookt
fried	**stekt**	stāykt
grilled (broiled)	**halstrad, grillad**	**hahl**strahd, **gri**llahd
roasted	**helstekt**	**hayl**stāykt
underdone (rare)	**blodig**	**bloo**dig
medium	**medium**	**may**deeyewn
well-done	**genomstekt**	**yay**nomstāykt

Meat *Kött*

I'd like some...	**Jag skulle vilja ha...**	yaa(g) **skew**ler **vil**yah haa
beef/lamb	**oxkött/lamm**	**ooks**khurt/lahm
chicken/duck	**kyckling/anka**	**khewk**ling/**ahn**kah
pork/veal	**fläskkött/kalv**	**flehsk**khurt/kahlv
dillkött	**dil**khurt	veal in lemon and dill sauce
lövbiff	**lūrv**bif	fried sliced beef and onions
slottsstek	**slots**stāyk	pot roast with sprats and golden syrup

Vegetables *Grönsaker*

beans	**böner**	**bū**rnoor
carrots	**morötter**	**mōō**rurterr
mushrooms	**svamp**	svahmp
onions	**lök**	lūrk

peas	**ärtor**	æ'toor
potatoes	**potatis**	pootaatiss
tomatoes	**tomater**	toomaaterr

Fruit and dessert *Frukt och Efterrätter*

apple	**äpple**	ehpler
banana	**banan**	bahnaan
cherries	**bigarråer**	biggahrawerr
lemon	**citron**	sitroon
orange	**apelsin**	ahperlseen
pear	**päron**	pæron
plums	**plommon**	ploomon
strawberries	**jordgubbar**	yoo'dgewbahr

Drinks *Drycker*

apple juice	**äppeljuice**	ehperlyooss
beer	**öl**	url
(hot) chocolate	**(varm) choklad**	(vahrm) shoklaa(d)
coffee	**kaffe**	kahfer
a pot of	**en kanna**	ehn kahnah
with cream	**med grädde**	mayd grehder
milk	**mjölk**	myurlk
mineral water	**mineralvatten**	minerraalvahtern
tea	**te**	tay
wine	**vin**	veen
red/white	**rött/vitt**	rurt/vit

Complaints and paying *Klagomål och notan*

This is too...	**Det här är för...**	day(t) hær ær furr
bitter/sweet	**beskt/sött**	behskt/surt
salty	**salt**	sahlt
That's not what I ordered.	**Det där har jag inte beställt.**	day(t) dær haar yaa(g) inter berstehlt
I'd like to pay.	**Får jag betala.**	fawr yaa(g) bertaalah
I think there's a mistake in this bill.	**Jag tror att det är ett fel på notan.**	yaa(g) troor aht day(t) ær eht fayl paw nootahn
Can I pay with this credit card?	**Kan jag betala med det här kreditkortet?**	kahn yaa(g) bertaalah mayd day(t) hær krehdeetkoo'tert
Is everything included?	**Är allting inräknat?**	ær ahlting inraiknaht
We enjoyed it, thank you.	**Det var mycket gott.**	day(t) vaar mewker(t) got

SWEDISH

Travelling around *På resa*

Plane *Flyg*

Is there a flight to...?	**Finns et något flyg till...?**	finss dāy(t) **naw**got flew̄g til
What time should I check in?	**Hur dags måste jag checka in?**	hew̄r dahgss **mos**ter yaa(g) **kheh**kah in
I'd like to... my reservation.	**Jag skulle vilja... min reservation.**	yaa(g) **skew**ler **vil**yah min rehsehrvah**shōōn**
cancel	**annullera**	ahnew**lay**rah
change	**ändra**	**ehn**drah
confirm	**bekräfta**	ber**krehf**tah

Train *Tåg*

I'd like a ticket to...	**Jag skulle vilja ha en bilett till...?**	yaa(g) **skew**ler **vil**yah haa ehn bil**yeht** til
single (one-way)	**enkel**	**ehn**kerl
return (round trip)	**tur och retur**	tew̄r ok reh**tew̄r**
first/second class	**första/andra klass**	**fur**'stah/**ahn**drah klahss
What time does the train arrive in...?	**Hur dags är tåget framme i...**	hew̄r dahgss **ær tawg**ert **frah**mer ee
When is the... train to...?	**När går... tåget till...?**	nær gawr... **tawg**ert til
first/last/next	**första/sista/nästa**	**fur**'stah/**sis**tah/**nehs**tah
Is this the train to...?	**Är det här tåget till...?**	**ær** dāy(t) hær **tawg**ert til

Bus–Tram (streetcar) *Buss–Spårvagn*

Which tram goes to the town centre?	**Vilken spårvagn går till centrum?**	**vil**kern **spawr**vahngn gawr til **sehn**trewm
How much is the fare to...?	**Hur mycket kostar det till...?**	hew̄r **mew**ker(t) **kos**tahr dāy(t) til
Will you tell me when to get off?	**Kan ni säga till när jag skall stiga av?**	kahn nee **seh**yah til nær yaa(g) skah(l) **stee**gah aav

Taxi *Taxi*

How much is the fare to...?	**Hur mycket kostar det till...?**	hew̄r **mew**ker(t) **kos**tahr dāy(t) til
Take me to this address.	**Kör mig till den här adressen.**	khūr may til dehn hær ah**dreh**ssern
Please stop here.	**Var snäll och stanna här.**	vaar snehl ok **stah**nah hær

TELLING THE TIME, see page 172/NUMBERS, page 173

Svensk

Car hire (rental) *Biluthyrning*

I'd like to hire (rent) a car.	**Jag skulle vilja hyra en bil.**	yaa(g) **skew**ler **vil**yah **hew**rah ehn beel
I'd like it for...	**Jag vill ha den...**	yaa(g) vil haa dehn
a day/a week	**en dag/en vecka**	ehn daa(g)/ehn **veh**kah
Where's the nearest filling station?	**Var ligger närmaste bensin- station?**	vaar **liggerr nærm**ahster behn**seen**stahsh**oon**
Fill it up, please.	**Full tank, tack.**	fewl tahnk tahk
Give me... litres of petrol (gasoline).	**Kan jag få... liter bensin.**	kahn yaa(g) faw... **leet**err behn**seen**
How do I get to this place/this address?	**Hur kommer jag till den här platsen/ adressen?**	**hewr kommerr** yaa(g) til dehn **här plaht**sern/ ah**dreh**ssern
I've had a break- down at...	**Jag har fått motorstopp vid...**	yaa(g) haar fot **moo**to'stop veed
Can you send a mechanic?	**Kan ni skicka en mekaniker?**	kahn nee **shik**kah ehh meh**kaa**nikkerr
Can you mend this puncture (fix this flat)?	**Kan ni laga den här punkteringen?**	kahn nee **laa**gah dehn här pewng**tay**ringern

---

Ni har kört fel.	You're on the wrong road.
Kör rakt fram.	Go straight ahead.
Det är där nere till...	It's down there on the...
vänster/höger	left/right
bredvid/efter...	next to/after...
norr/söder/öster/väster	north/south/east/west

Sightseeing *Sightseeing*

Where's the tourist office?	**Var ligger turistbyrån?**	vaar **liggerr** tew**rist**b**ew**rawn
Is there an English- speaking guide?	**Finns det någon engelsktalande guide?**	finss **day**(t) **naw**gon **ehng**erlsktaalahnder "guide"
Where is/are the...?	**Var ligger...?**	vaar **liggerr**
art museum	**konstmuseet**	**konst**mewss**ay**ert
castle	**slottet**	**slott**ert

cathedral	**domkyrkan**	**doom**khewrkahn
church	**kyrkan**	**khewr**kahn
city centre/downtown	**(stads)centrum**	**(stahds)sehn**trewm
harbour	**hamnen**	**hahm**nern
museum	**museet**	mewss**ay**ert
square	**torget**	**tor**yert
tower	**tornet**	**too'**nert
When is it open?	**När är det öppet?**	nǣr ǣr dāy(t) **ur**pert
When does it close?	**När stänger det?**	nǣr **stehng**err dāy(t)
How much is the entrance fee?	**Vad kostar det i inträde?**	vaad **kos**tahr dāy(t) ee **in**traider

Relaxing *Nöjen*

What's playing at the ... Theatre?	**Vad går det på ... teatern?**	vad gawr dāy(t) paw ... tāy**aa**ter'n
Are there any tickets for tonight?	**Finns det några biletter till i kväll?**	finss dāy(t) **naw**grah bil**yeh**terr til ee kvehl
How much are the seats?	**Hur mycket kostar biljetterna?**	hēwr **mew**ker(t) **kos**tahr bil**yeh**ter'nah
Would you like to go out with me tonight?	**Skall vi gå ut i kväll?**	skah(l) vee gaw ēwt ee kvehl
Would you like to dance?	**Skall vi dansa?**	skah(l) vee **dahn**sah
Thank you, it's been a wonderful evening.	**Tack, det har varit en underbar kväll.**	tahk dāy(t) haar **vaa**rit ehn **ewn**derrbaar kvehl

Shops, stores and services *Affärer och service*

Where's the nearest ...?	**Var ligger närmaste ...?**	vaar **ligg**err **nǣr**mahster
bakery	**ett bageri**	eht baager**ree**
bookshop	**en bokhandel**	ehn **bōōk**hahnderl
butcher's	**en slaktare**	ehn **slahk**tahrer
chemist's/drugstore	**ett apotek**	eht ahpoo**tāyk**
dentist	**en tandläkare**	ehn **tahn(d)**laikahrer
department store	**ett varuhus**	eht **vaa**rewhēwss
grocery	**en livsmedelsaffär**	ehn **livs**māyderlsahfǣr
hairdresser	**en frisör**	ehn fri**sur**r
newsstand	**en tidningskiosk**	ehn **tee(d)**ningskhiosk
post office	**ett postkontor**	eht **post**kontōōr
supermarket	**ett snabbköp**	eht **snahb**khȗrp
toilets	**toaletten**	tooah**leh**tern

TELLING THE TIME, see page 172

General expressions *Allmänna uttryck*

Where's the main shopping area?	**Var ligger affärscentrum?**	vaar **lig**gerr ahf**æ'**ssehntrewm
Do you have any...?	**Har ni några...?**	haar nee **naw**grah
Don't you have anything...?	**Har ni inter någonting...?**	haar nee **in**ter **naw**gonting
cheaper/better larger/smaller	**billigare/bättre större/mindre**	**bil**liggahrer/**beh**trer **stur**rer/**min**drer
Can I try it on?	**Kan jag få prova den?**	kahn yaa(g) faw **prōō**vah dehn
Where's the changing room?	**Var är provhytten?**	vaar ǣr **prōōv**hewtern
How much is this?	**Hur mycket kostar det här?**	hēwr **mew**ker(t) **kos**tahr dāy(t) hǣr
Please write it down.	**Kan ni skriva det?**	kahn nee **skree**vah dāy(t)
I don't want to spend more than... crowns.	**Jag vill inte lägga ut mer än... kroner.**	yaa(g) vil **in**ter **leh**gah ēwt māyr ehn... **krōō**ner
No, I don't like it.	**Nej, jag tycker inte om det.**	nay yaa(g) **tew**kerr **in**ter om dāy(t)
I'll take it.	**Jag tar det.**	yaa(g) taar dāy(t)
Do you accept credt cards?	**Tar ni kreditkort?**	taar nee kreh**deet**kooᵗ

black	**svart**	svahᵗ
blue	**blå**	blaw
brown	**brun**	brēwn
green	**grön**	grurn
orange	**orange**	orahnsh
red	**röd**	rūrd
white	**vit**	veet
yellow	**gul**	gēwl
light...	**ljus...**	yēwss
dark...	**mörk...**	murrk

I want to buy a/an/some...	**Jag skulle vilja köpa...**	yaa(g) **skew**ler **vil**yah **khūr**pah
aspirin	**aspirin**	ahspi**reen**
battery	**batteri**	bahter**ree**
newspaper	**en dagstidning**	ehn **dahg**stee(d)ning
American	**amerikansk**	ahm(eh)ri**kaansk**
English	**engelsk**	**eng**erlsk

NUMBERS, see page 173

postcard	**ett vykort**	eht v̄ewkoo't
shampoo	**ett shampo**	eht **shahm**poo
soap	**en tvål**	ehn tvawl
sun-tan oil	**en sololja**	ehn **s̄ōōl**olyah
toothpaste	**en tandkräm**	ehn **tahn(d)**kraim
half-kilo of tomatoes	**ett halvt kilo tomater**	eht hahlft **khee**loo too**maa**terr
litre of milk	**en liter mjölk**	ehn **lee**terr myurlk
I'd like a ... film for this camera.	**Jag skulle vilja ha film till den här kameran.**	yaa(g) **skew**ler **vil**yah haa film til dehn hǣr **kaam**(er)rahn
black and white	**svart-vit**	svah't-veet
colour	**färg**	fǣry

Souvenirs *Souvenirer*

I'd like a/some ...	**Jag skulle vilja ha ...**	yaa(g) **skew**ler **vil**yah haa
ceramics	**keramik**	khehrah**meek**
glassware	**glas**	glaass
Lapp handicrafts	**sameslöjd**	**saa**merslur̄yd
silverware	**något i silver**	**naw**got ee **sil**verr
woodwork	**något i trä**	**naw**got ee trǣ

At the bank *Bank*

Where's the nearest bank/currency exchange office?	**Var ligger närmaste bank/växelkontor?**	vaar **lig**gerr **nǣr**mahster bahnk/**veh**kserlkont̄ōōr
I want to change some dollars/pounds.	**Jag skulle vilja växla några dollar/pund.**	yaa(g) **skew**ler **vil**yah **vehks**lah **naw**grah **dol**lahr/pewnd
What's the exchange rate?	**Vilken är växelkursen?**	**vil**kern ǣr **veh**kserlkew'sern
I want to cash a traveller's cheque.	**Jag skulle vilja lösa in en resecheck.**	yaa(g) **skew**ler **vil**yah **lur**ssah in ehn **r̄ay**sserkhehk

At the post office *Post*

I'd like to send this by ...	**Jag vil skicka det här ...**	yaa(g) vil **shik**kah d̄ay(t) hǣr
airmail	**med flyg**	m̄ayd flewg
express	**express**	ehk**sprehss**

A...-öres stamp, please.	Ett... -öres frimärke, tack.	eht... ūrrerss freemærker tahk
What's the postage for a letter/postcard to the U.S.A.?	Vad är portot för ett brev/vykort till USA?	vaad ær po'tot fūrr eht brāyv/vewkoo't til ēwehssaa
Is there any post (mail) for me?	Finns det någon post till mig?	finss dāy(t) nawgon post til may.
My name is...	Mitt namn är...	mit nahmn ær

Telephoning *Telefon*

Where's the nearest telephone booth?	Var finns närmaste telefonkiosk?	vaar finss nærmahster tehlehfawnkhiosk
May I use your phone?	Får jag låna telefonen?	fawr yaa(g) lawnah tehlehfawnern
Hello. This is...	Hallå, det här är...	hahlaw dāy(t) hær ær
I'd like to speak to...	Kan jag få tala med...?	kahn yaa(g) faw taalah māyd
When will he/she be back?	När kommer han/hon tillbaka?	nær kommerr hahn/ hoon tilbaakah
Will you tell him/her that I called?	Kan ni tala om för honom/henne att jag har ringt?	kahn nee taalah om fūrr honnom/hehner aht yaa(g) haar ringt

Time and date *Klockan och datum*

It's...	Den är...	dehn ær
five past one	fem över ett	fehm ūrverr eht
quarter past three	kvart över tre	kvah't ūrverr trāy
twenty past four	tjugo över fyra	khewgoo ūrverr fewrah
half-past six	halv sju	hahlv shēw
twenty-five to seven	fem över halv sju	fehnm ūrverh hahlv shēw
ten to ten	tio i tio	teeoo ee teeoo
twelve o'clock	klockan tolv	klokkahn tolv
in the morning	på morgonen	paw morronern
in the afternoon	på eftermiddagen	paw ehfterniddahn
in the evening	på kvällen	paw kvehlern
during the day	under dagen	ewnderr daagern
at night	på natten	paw nahtern
yesterday	i går	ee gawr
today	idag	eedaa(g)
tomorrow	i morgon	ee morron
spring/summer	vår/sommar	vawr/sommahr
autumn (fall)/winter	höst/vinter	hurst/vinterr

NUMBERS, see page 173

Sunday	**söndag**	surndaa(g)
Monday	**måndag**	mondaa(g)
Tuesday	**tisdag**	teesdaa(g)
Wednesday	**onsdag**	oonsdaa(g)
Thursday	**torsdag**	too'sdaa(g)
Friday	**fredag**	frāydaa(g)
Saturday	**lördag**	lūr'daa(g)
January	**januari**	yahnewaari
February	**februari**	fahbrewaari
March	**mars**	mah'ss
April	**april**	ahpril
May	**maj**	mahy
June	**juni**	yēwni
July	**juli**	yēwli
August	**augusti**	ahgewsti
September	**september**	sehptehmberr
October	**oktober**	oktōoberr
November	**november**	noovehmberr
December	**december**	dehssehmberr

Numbers *Räkneord*

0	**noll**	nol
1	**ett**	eht
2	**två**	tvaw
3	**tre**	trāy
4	**fyra**	fēwrah
5	**fem**	fehm
6	**sex**	sehks
7	**sju**	shēw
8	**åtta**	ottah
9	**nio**	neeoo
10	**tio**	teeoo
11	**elva**	ehlvah
12	**tolv**	tolv
13	**tretton**	trehton
14	**fjorton**	fyōo'ton
15	**femton**	fehmton
16	**sexton**	sehkston
17	**sjutton**	shewton
18	**arton**	aa'ton
19	**nitton**	nitton
20	**tjuggo**	khēwgoo
30	**trettio**	trehti
40	**fyrtio**	fur'ti

SWEDISH

Svensk

50	**femtio**	fehmti
60	**sextio**	sehksti
70	**sjuttio**	shewti
80	**åttio**	otti
90	**nittio**	nitti
100	**(ett)hundra**	(eht)hewndrah
1,000	**(ett)tusen**	(eht)tewssern
first	**första**	fur'stah
second	**andra**	ahndrah
once/twice	**en gång/två gånger**	ehn gong/tvaw gongerr
a half	**eh halva**	ehn hahlvah

Emergency Nödsituation

Call the police	**Ring polisen**	ring poleessern
Get a doctor	**Hämta en läkare**	hehmtah ehn laikahrer
Go away	**Ge er i väg**	yāy āyr ee vaig
HELP	**HJÄLP**	yehlp
I'm ill	**Jag är sjuk**	yaa(g) ær shewk
I'm lost	**Jag har gått vilse**	yaa(g) haar got vilser
LOOK OUT	**SE UPP**	sāy ewp
STOP THIEF	**STOPPA TJUVEN**	stoppah khēwvern
My ... has been stolen.	**... har stulits.**	... haar stewlitss
I've lost my ...	**Jag har tappat ...**	yaa(g) haar tahpaht
handbag	**min handväska**	min hahn(d)vehskah
passport	**mitt pass**	mit pahss
wallet	**min plånbok**	min plawnbōōk
Where can I find a doctor who speaks English?	**Var kan jag få tag på en läkare som talar engelska?**	vaar kahn yaa(g) faw taag paw ehn laikahrer som taalahr engerlskah

Guide to Swedish pronunciation Uttal

Consonants

Letter	Approximate pronunciation	Symbol	Example	
b, c, d, f, h, l, m, n, p, v, w, x	as in English			
ch	at the beginning of words borrowed from French, like **sh** in shut	sh	**chef**	shāyf
g	1) before stressed **i, e, y, ä, ö**, and sometimes after **l** or **r**, like **y** in yet	y	**ge**	yāy

TELEPHONING, see page 172

	2) before **e** and **i** in words of French origin, like **sh** in **sh**ut	sh	**geni**	sha͞ynee
	3) elsewhere, like **g** in **go**	g	**gaffel**	**gah**ferl
j, dj, **g, lj,** **hj**	at the beginning of words always like **y** in **yet**	y	**ja** **ljus**	yaa ye͞wss
k	1) before stressed **i, e,** **y, ä, ö,** generally like **ch** in Scottish lo**ch**, but pronounced in the front of the mouth	kh	**köpa**	**khu͞r**pah
	2) elsewhere, like **k** in **k**it	k	**klippa**	**kli**ppah
kj	like **ch** in lo**ch**, but pronounced in the front of the mouth	kh	**kjol**	kho͞ol
qu	like **k** in **k**it followed by **v** in **v**at	kv	**Lindquist**	**lin**(d)kvist
r	rolled near the front of the mouth	r	**ryka**	**re͞w**kah
s	1) in the ending **-sion** like **sh** in **sh**ut	sh	**mission**	mi**sho͞on**
	2) elsewhere, like **s** in **so**	s/ss	**ses**	sa͞yss
	3) the groups **sch, skj,** **sj, stj** are pronounced like **sh** in **sh**ut	sh	**schema**	**sha͞y**mah
sk	1) before stressed **e, i,** **y, ä, ö,** like **sh** in **sh**ut	sh	**skänk**	shehnk
	2) elsewhere, like **sk** in **sk**ip	sk	**skola**	**sko͞o**la
t	1) in the ending **-tion** like **sh** in **sh**ut or **ch** in **ch**at	sh tsh	**station** **nation**	stah**sho͞on** nah**tsho͞on**
	2) elsewhere, like **t** in **t**op	t	**tid**	teed
tj	like **ch** in Scottish lo**ch**, but pronounced in the front of the mouth; sometimes with a **t**-sound at the beginning	kh	**tjäna**	**khai**nah
z	like **s** in **so**	s	**zenit**	**sa͞y**nit

Vowels

a	1) long, like **a** in car	aa	**dag**	daa(g)
	2) short, between **a** in cat and **u** in cut	ah	**tack**	tahk
e	1) long, like **ay** in say	$\overline{ay}$	**sen**	$s\overline{ay}n$
	2) when followed by **r**, like **a** in man	ӕ	**erfara**	$\overline{ӕ}$rfaarah
	3) short, like **e** in get	eh	**beck**	behk
	4) like **a** in about	er	**betala**	ber**taa**lah
ej	like **a** in mate	ay	**nej**	nay
i	1) long, like **ee** in bee	ee	**vit**	veet
	2) when short, between **ee** in meet and **i** in hit	i	**hinna**	**hi**nnah
	3) like **a** in mate	ay	**mig**	may
o	1) when long, often like **oo** in soon, but with the lips more tightly rounded	$\overline{oo}$	**sko**	sk$\overline{oo}$
	2) the same sound can be short	oo	**solid**	soo**leed**
	3) when long, sometimes like **aw** in raw, but with the tongue a little higher	aw	**son**	sawn
	4) like **o** in hot	o	**korrekt**	korr**ehkt**
u	1) when long, like Swedish **y**, but with the tongue a little lower in the mouth	$\overline{ew}$	**hus**	h$\overline{ew}$ss
	2) when short, a little more like the **u** of put	ew	**full**	fewl
y	like French **u** in une; round your lips and try to say **ee** as in bee	$\overline{ew}$	**vy**	v$\overline{ew}$
		ew	**syster**	**sew**sterr
å	1) when long, like **aw** in raw, but with the tongue a little higher in the mouth	aw	**gå**	gaw
	2) short, like **o** in hot	o	**sång**	song
ä	1) when followed by **r**, like **a** in man	$\overline{ӕ}$	**ära**	$\overline{ӕ}$rah
		ӕ	**värka**	**vӕr**kah
	2) like **e** in get; long or short	ai	**läsa**	**lais**sah
		eh	**bäst**	behst
ö	like **ur** in fur, but with the lips rounded and without any r-sound	$\overline{ur}$	**röd**	r$\overline{ur}$d
		ur	**köld**	khurld
			öra	$\overline{ur}$rrah

Turkish

Basic expressions *Önemli deyimler*

Yes/No.	**Evet/Hayır.**	ehveht/hahır
Please.	**Lütfen.**	lewtfehn
Thank you.	**Teşekkür ederim.**	tehshehkkewr ehdehreem
I beg your pardon?	**Efendim?**	ehfehndeem

Introductions *Tanıştırmak*

Good morning.	**Günaydın.**	gewnahdın
Good afternoon.	**İyi günler.**	eeyee gewnlehr
Good night.	**İyi geceler.**	eeyee gehjehlehr
Good-bye.	**Allahaısmarladık.***	ahllahhahısmahrlahdık.
	Güle güle.**	gewleh gewleh
My name is...	**Adım ... 'dir.**	ahdım ...deer
Pleased to meet you.	**Memnum oldum.**	mehmnoom oldoom
What's your name?	**Adınız ne?**	ahdınız neh
How are you?	**Nasılsınız?**	nahsılsınız
Fine thanks.	**İyiyim, teşekkür ederim.**	eeyeeyeem tehshehkkewr ehdehreem
And you?	**Siz nasılsınız?**	seez nahsılsınız
Where do you come from?	**Nerelisiniz?**	nehrehleesseeneez
I'm from...	**... denim/danım.**	... dehneem/dahnım
Australia	**Avustralya**	ahvoostrahlyah
Canada	**Kanada**	kahnahdah
Great Britain	**Büyük Britanya**	bewyewk breetahnyah
United States	**Amerika Birleşik Devletleri**	ahmehreekah beerlehsheek dehvlehtlehree
I'm with my...	**... beraberim.**	... behrahbehreem
wife	**Karımla**	kahrımlah
husband	**Kocamla**	kojahmlah
family	**Ailemle**	aheelehmleh
friend	**Arkadaşımla**	ahrkahdahshımlah
I'm here on vacation.	**Burada izindeyim.**	boorahdah eezeendeheem

* said by the one who is leaving; ** said by the one who remains.

PRONUNCIATION, see page 191/EMERGENCIES, see page 190

Questions *Sorular*

When?	**Ne zaman?**	neh zah**mahn**
How?	**Nasıl?**	**nah**ssıl
What?/Why?	**Ne?/Neden?**	neh/**neh**dehn
Who?	**Kim?**	kʸeem
Which?	**Hangi?**	hahngʸee
Where is...?	**... nerededir?**	... **neh**rehdehdeer
Where are...?	**... nerededir?**	... **neh**rehdehdeer
Where can I find/get...?	**Nerede ... bulabilirim/alabilirim?**	**neh**rehdeh ... boolahbeeleer**eem**/ahlahbeeleer**eem**
How far?	**Ne uzaklıktadır?**	neh oozahklıktahdır
How long?	**Ne kadar zaman?**	neh kahdahr zah**mahn**
How much/many?	**Ne kadar?/Kaç tane?**	neh kahdahr/kahch **tah**neh
Can I have...?	**... rica edebilir miyim?**	... reejah ehdehbee**leer** meeyeem
Can you help me?	**Yardım edebilir misiniz?**	**yahr**dım ehdehbee**leer** meesseeneez
What does this/that mean?	**Bu/Şu ne demek?**	boo/shoo neh deh**mehk**
I understand.	**Anlıyorum.**	ahnlı**yo**room
I don't understand.	**Anlamıyorum.**	ahnlahmı**yo**room
Do you speak English?	**İngilizce biliyor musunuz?**	eengʸeeleezjeh beeleeyor moossoonooz
I don't speak (much) Turkish.	**(İyi) Türkçe bilmem.**	(eeyee) tewrk**cheh** beelmehm

A few more useful words *Birkaç önemli kelime*

better/worse	**daha iyi/daha kötü**	dahhah eeyee/dahhah kʸurtew
big/small	**büyük/küçük**	bewyewk/kʸewchewk
cheap/expensive	**ucuz/pahalı**	oojooz/pahhahlı
early/late	**erken/geç**	ehrkʸehn/gʸehch
good/bad	**iyi/kötü**	eeyee/kʸurtew
hot/cold	**sıcak/soğuk**	sıjahk/sawook
near/far	**yakın/uzak**	yahkın/oozahk
old/new	**eski/yeni**	ehskʸee/yehnee
vacant/occupied	**serbest/meşgul**	sehrbehst/meshgool

Hotel–Other accommodation *Otel*

I have a reservation.	**Rezervasyonum var.**	rehzehrvahsyonoom **vahr**
We've reserved two rooms.	**İki odayı rezerve ettik.**	eekee odah^yı rehz**e**hrveh **e**htteek
Do you have any vacancies?	**Boş odanız var mı?**	bosh odahnız **vahr** mı
I'd like a... room.	**... bir oda istiyorum.**	... beer odah eesteey**o**room
single	**Tek yataklı**	tehk yaht**a**hklı
double	**Çift yataklı**	cheeft yaht**a**hklı
with twin beds	**İki yataklı**	eek^yee yaht**a**hklı
with a double bed	**Çift kişilik**	cheeft k^yeesheeleek
with a bath/shower	**Banyolu/Duşlu**	bahnyol**oo/do**oshloo
We'll be staying...	**... kalacağız.**	... kahlahjaaız
overnight only	**Sadece bir gece**	sahdehjeh beer g^yehjeh
a few days	**Birkaç gün**	**bee**rkahch g^yewn
a week	**Bir hafta**	beer h**a**hftah

Decision *Karar*

May I see the room?	**Odayı görebilir miyim?**	odah^yı g^yurrehbeel**ee**r meey**e**em
That's fine. I'll take it.	**İyi. Alıyorum.**	eeyee. ahlıy**o**room
No. I don't like it.	**Hayır, beğenmedim.**	hah^yır bayehnm**e**hdeem
It's too...	**Çok...**	chok
dark	**karanlık**	kahr**a**hnlık
small	**küçük**	k^yewch**e**wk
noisy	**gürültülü**	g^yewrewlt**e**wlew
Do you have anything...?	**... birşeyiniz var mı?**	... **bee**rsheh^yeeneez vahr mı
better	**Daha iyi**	**da**hhah eeyee
bigger	**Daha büyük**	**da**hhah bewy**e**wk
cheaper	**Daha ucuz**	**da**hhah ooj**o**oz
quieter	**Daha sakin**	**da**hhah sahk^y**e**en
May I have my bill, please?	**Lütfen hesabı istiyorum?**	**lew**tfehn hehss**a**hbı eesteey**o**room
It's been a very enjoyable stay.	**Burada çok hoş zaman geçirdik.**	**boo**rahdah chok hosh zahm**a**hn g^yehcheerd**ee**k

Eating out *Dışarda yemek*

I'd like to reserve a table for 4.	**Dört kişi için bir masa ayırtmak istiyorum.**	durrt k^yeeshee eecheen beer mahssah ah^yırtmahk eesteeyoroom
We'll come at 8.	**Saat 8 de geliriz.**	sahaht 8 deh g^yehleereez
I'd like...	**... istiyorum**	... eesteeyoroom
breakfast	**Kahvaltı**	kahhvahltı
lunch	**Öğle yemeği**	urleh yehmayee
dinner	**Akşam yemeği**	ahkshahm yehmayee
What do you recommend?	**Ne tavsiye edersiniz?**	neh tahvsseyeh ehdehrseeneez
Do you have any vegetarian dishes?	**Etsiz yemeğiniz var mı?**	ehtseez yehmayeeneez vahr mı

Breakfast *Kahvaltı*

May I have some...	**... alabilir miyim?**	... ahlahbeeleer meeyeem
bread	**Ekmek**	ehkmehk
butter	**Tereyağ**	tehrehyaa
cheese	**Peynir**	peh^yneer
ham and eggs	**Jambon ve yumurta**	zhahmbon veh yoomoortah
jam	**Reçel**	rehchehl
rolls	**Küçük ekmek**	k^yewchewk ehkmehk

Starters *Antreler*

chickpea dip	**humus**	hoomoos
creamed red caviar	**tarama**	tahrahmah
marinated artichoke	**enginar**	ehng^yeenahr
mussels	**midye**	meedyeh
oysters	**istiridye**	eesteereedyeh
sardines	**sardalya**	sahrdahlyah
seafood cocktail	**deniz mahsulleri kokteyli**	dehneez mahhssoollehree kokteh^ylee

Soup *Çorba*

chicken consomme	**tavuk suyu**	tahvook sooyoo
consomme	**et suyu (konsome)**	eht sooyoo (konsomeh)
French onion soup	**gratine soğan çorbası**	grahteeneh sawahn chorbahssı
noodle soup	**erişteli çorba**	ehreeshtehlee chorbah
tomato soup	**domates çorbası**	domahtehss chorbahssı
vegetable soup	**sebze çorbası**	sehbzeh chorbahssı

NUMBERS, see page 189

Fish and seafood *Balık ve deniz hayvanları*

lobster	**ıstakoz**	ıstahkoz
plaice	**pisi**	peessee
prawns	**karides**	k^yehreedehss
salmon	**som balığı**	som bahlıı
sole	**dil balığı**	deel bahlıı
trout	**alabalık**	ahlahbahlık
tuna	**ton balığı**	ton bahlıı

baked	**fırında**	fırındah
boiled	**haşlama**	hahshlahmah
fried	**tavada kızarmış**	tahvahdah kızahrmısh
grilled	**ızgara**	ızgahrah
roast	**kızarmış**	kızahrmısh
stewed	**yahni**	yahnee
underdone (rare)	**az pişmiş**	ahz peeshmeesh
medium	**orta pişmi**	ortah peeshmeesh
well-done	**iyi pişmiş**	eeyee peeshmeesh

Meat *Et*

I'd like some...	**... istiyorum.**	... eesteeyoroom
beef/lamb	**Sığır/Kuzu**	sııır/koozoo
pork/veal	**Domuz/Dana**	domooz/dahnah
chicken/steak	**Tavuk/Biftek**	tahvook/beeftehk
fried meatballs	**kuru köfte**	kooroo k^yurfteh
lamb chops	**kuzu pirzolası**	koozoo peerzolahssı
stew	**haşlama**	hahshlahmah

kuzu dolması lamb stuffed with savoury rice, liver and pis-
(koozoo dolmahssı) tachios

Vegetables *Sebzeler*

beans	**fasulye**	fahssoolyeh
cabbage	**lâhana**	laahahnah
carrots	**havuç**	hahvooch
mushrooms	**mantar**	mahntahr
onions	**soğan**	sawahn
peas	**bezelye**	behzehlyeh
potatoes	**patates**	pahtahtehss
tomatoes	**domates**	domahtehss
... dolması	dolmahssı	stuffed...
biber	beebehr	peppers
patlıcan	pahtlıjahn	aubergine (eggplant)
yaprak	yahprahk	vine leaves

Fruit/dessert *Meyve/Tatlılar*

apple	**elma**	ehlmah
banana	**muz**	mooz
lemon	**limon**	leemon
melon	**kavun**	kahvoon
orange	**portakal**	portahkahl
pear	**armut**	ahrmoot
strawberries	**çilek**	cheelehk
baklava	bahklahvah	pastry with chopped nuts and syrup
börek	burrehk	fried pastry strips in sugar
kaymaklı ve sütlü dondurma	kah^ymahklı veh sewtlew dondoormah	ice-cream
lokum	lokoom	Turkish delight
peşmelba	**pehsh**mehlbah	peach melba
turtalar	**toort**ahlahr	tarts

Drinks *İçkiler*

beer	**bira**	beerah
coffee without sugar	**sade kahve**	sah**deh** kahhveh
fruit juice	**meyve suyu**	meh^yveh sooyoo
milk	**süt**	sewt
mineral water fizzy/still	**maden suyu gazlı/sade**	mahdehn sooyoo gahzlı/sahdeh
tea	**çay**	chah^y
wine red/white	**ğarap kırmızı/beyaz**	shahrahp kırmızı/beh^yahz
a bottle	**bir şişe**	beer sheesheh
a glass	**bir bardak**	beer bahrdahk

Complaints and paying *Şikayetler–Hesap*

This is too …	**Bu çok …**	boo chok
bitter/sweet	**acı/tatlı**	ahjı/tahtlı
That's not what I ordered.	**Bunu ısmarlamamıştım.**	boonoo ısmahrlahmahmıshtım
I'd like to pay.	**Ödemek istiyorum.**	urdehmehk eesteeyoroom
I think there's a mistake in this bill.	**Bu hesapta bir hata var galiba.**	boo hehssahptah beer hahtah vahr gahleebah
Can I pay with this credit card?	**Bu kredi kartı ile ödeyebilir miyim?**	boo **kreh**dee kahrti eeleh urdeh^yehbeel**leer** meeyeem
We enjoyed it, thank you.	**Hoşumuza gitti, teşekkür ederiz.**	hoshoomoozah g^yeettee tehsheh**kk**^yewr ehdehreez

Travelling around *Yolculukta*

Plane *Uçak*

Is there a flight to Antalya?	**Antalya'ya uçuş var mı?**	ahntahlyahyah oochoosh vahr mı
What time do I have to check in?	**Bagajların kaydını saat kaçta yapmam gerek?**	bahgahzhlahrın kah^ydını sahaht kahchtah yahpmahm g^yehrehk
I'd like to ... my reservation.	**Rezervasyonumu ... istiyorum.**	rehzehrvahsyomoo ... eesteeyoroom
cancel	**iptal etmek**	eeptahl ehtmehk
change	**değiştirmek**	dayeeshteermehk
confirm	**konfirme etmek**	konfeermeh ehtmehk

Train *Tren*

I'd like a ticket to ...	**... 'ya bir bilet istiyorum.**	yah beer beeleht eesteeyoroom
single (one-way)	**gidiş**	g^yeedeesh
return (round trip)	**gidiş-dönüş**	g^yeedeesh-durnewsh
first class	**birinci mevki**	beereenjee mehvk^yee
second class	**ikinci mevki**	eek^yeenjee mehvk^yee
How long does the journey (trip) take?	**Yolculuk ne kadar zaman sürer?**	yoljoolook neh kahdahr zahmahn sewrehr
When is the ... train to Eskisehir?	**Eskişehir'e ... tren ne zaman?**	ehskeeshehheereh ... trehn neh zahmahn
first	**ilk**	eelk
next	**gelecek**	g^yehlehjehk
last	**son**	son
Is this the train to ...?	**... treni bu mudur?**	trehnee boo moodoor

Bus *Otobüs*

Which bus goes to the town centre?	**Şehir merkezine hangi otobüs gider?**	shehheer mehrk^yehzeeneh hahng^yee otobewss g^yeedehr
How much is the fare to Erzurum?	**Erzurum'a yolculuk kaça?**	ehrzooroomah yoljoolook kahchah
Will you tell me when to get off?	**Ne zaman inmem gerektiğini söyler misiniz?**	neh zahmahn eenmehm g^yehrehkteeeenee surlehr meesseeneez

TELLING THE TIME, see page 188/NUMBERS, see page 189

Taxi *Taksi*

How much is the fare to...?	... a/e ücret ne kadardır?	... ah/eh ewjreht neh kahdahrdır
Take me to this address.	Beni bu adrese götürün.	behnee boo ahdrehsseh g^{y}urtewrewn
Please stop here.	Durabilir miyiz, lütfen?	doorahbeeleer meeyeez lewtfehn
Could you wait for me?	Lütfen beni bekler misiniz.	lewtfehn behnee behklehr meesseeneez

Car hire (rental) *Araba kiralama*

I'd like to hire (rent) a car.	Bir araba kiralamak istiyorum.	beer ahrahbah k^{y}eerahlah-mak eesteeyoroom
I'd like it for a day/a week.	Bir gün/Bir hafta için istiyorum.	beer g^{y}ewn/beer hahftah eecheen esteeyoroom
Where's the nearest filling station?	En yakın benzin istasyonu nerededir?	ehn yahkın behnzeen eestahssyonoo nehrehdehdeer
Fill it up, please.	Doldurun, lütfen.	doldooroon lewtfehn
Could you give me... litres of petrol (gasoline).	... litre benzin verir misiniz?	... leehtreh behnzeen vehrer meesseeneez
How do I get to...?	... 'e nasıl gide-bilirim?	... eh nahssıl g^{y}eedehbee-leereem
I've broken down at...	... 'da/de arabam arızalandı.	... dah/deh ahrahbahm ahrızahlahndı
Can you send a mechanic?	Bir araba tamircisi gönderir misiniz?	beer ahrahbah tahmeer-jeessee g^{y}urndehreer meesseeneez

Yanlış yoldasınız.	You're on the wrong road.
Doğru gidin.	Go straight ahead.
Orada ileride...	It's down there on the...
solda/sağda	left/right
... ın yanında	next to
... den/dan sonra	after...
kuzey/güney/doğu/batı	north/south/east/west

Sightseeing *Gezi*

Where's the tourist office?	Turizm bürosu nerededir?	tooreezm bewrossoo nehrehdehdeer
Is there an English-speaking guide?	İngilizce bilen bir rehber var mı?	eengᵛeeleezjeh beelehn beer rehhbehr vahr mı
Where is/are the...?	... nerededir?	... nehrehdehdeer
art gallery	Sanat galerisi	sahnaht gahlehreessee
botanical gardens	Botanik bahçesi	botahneek bahhchehssee
castle	Şato	shahto
city centre/downtown	Şehir merkezi	shehheer mehrkᵛehzee
harbour	Liman	leemahn
market	Pazar	pahzahr
mosque	Câmi	jaamee
museum	Müze	mewzeh
square	Meydan	mehᵛdahn
tower	Kule	kooleh
zoo	Hayvanat bahçesi	hahᵛvahnaht bahh-chehssee
What are the opening hours?	Habgi saatlerde açıktır?	hahngᵛee sahahtlehrdeh ahchıktır
When does it close?	Ne zaman kapanır?	neh zahmahn kahpahnır
How much is the entrance fee?	Giriş ücreti ne kadar?	gᵛeereesh ewjrehtee neh kahdahr

Relaxing *Eğlence*

What's playing at the...Theatre?	... tiyatrosunda ne oynuyor?	... teeyahtrossoondah neh oynooyor
Are there any seats for tonight?	Bu akşam için yer var mı?	boo ahkshahm eecheen yehr vahr mı
How much are the tickets?	Biletler ne kadar?	beelehtlehr neh kahdahr
Would you like to go out with me tonight?	Bu akşam benimle çıkar mısınız?	boo ahkshahm behneemleh chıkahr mıssınız
Is there a disco-theque in town?	Şehirde diskotek var mı?	shehheerdeh deeskotehk vahr mı
Would you like to dance?	Dans eder misiniz?	dahns ehdehr meesseeneez
Thank you, it's been a wonderful evening.	Teşekkür ederim, fevkalâde bir akşam geçirdim.	tehshehkkᵛewr ehdehreem fehvkahlaadeh beer ahkshahm gᵛehcheerdeem

TELLING THE TIME, see page 188/NUMBERS, see page 189

Shops, stores and services *Dükkânlar ve hizmet*

Where's the nearest...?	En yakın... nerededir?	ehn yahkın ... nehrehdehdeer
bakery	fırın	fırın
bookshop	kitabevi	kʸeetahbehvee
butcher's	kasap dükkânı	kahsahp dewkkaanı
chemist/drugstore	eczane	ehjzahneh
dentist	dişçi	deeshchee
department store	büyük mağaza	bewyewk maaahzah
grocery	bakkal dükkânı	bahkkahl dewkkaanı
hairdresser	kuaför/berber	kooahfurr/behrbehr
newsagent	gazeteci	gahzehtehjee
post office	postane	postahneh
supermarket	süpermarket	sewpehrmahrkʸeht
toilets	tuvaletler	toovahlehtlehr

General expressions *Genel tabirler*

Where's the main shopping area?	Asıl alış veriş merkezi nerededir?	ahssıl ahlısh vehreesh mahrkʸehzee nehrehdehdeer
Do you have any...?	... var mı?	... vahr mı
Haven't you anything...?	... birşey yok mu?	... beershehʸ yok moo
cheaper/better	Daha ucuz/Daha iyi	dahhah oojooz/dahhah eeyee
larger/smaller	Daha büyük/Daha küçük	dahhah bewyewk/dahhah kʸewchewk
Can I try it on?	Bunu deneyebilir miyim?	boonoo dehnehʸehbeeleer meeyeem
How much is this?	Bu ne kadar?	boo neh kahdahr
Please write it down.	Lütfen yazar mısınız.	lewtfehn yahzahr mıssınız
I don't want to spend more than... lira.	... liradan fazla harcamak istemiyorum.	... leerahdahn fahzlah hahrjahmahk eestehmeeyoroom
No, I don't like it.	Hayır, bunu beğenmedim.	hahʸır boonoo bayehnmehdeem
I'll take it.	Bunu alacağım.	boonoo ahlahjaaım
Do you accept credit cards?	Kredi kartı kabul eder misiniz?	krehdee kahrtı kahbool ehder meesseeneez
Can you order it for me?	Bunu benim için ısmarlar mısınız?	boonoo behneem eecheen ısmahrlahr mıssınız

black	**siyah**	seeyahh
blue	**mavi**	mahvee
brown	**kahverengi**	kahhvehrehng'ee
green	**yeşil**	yehsheel
orange	**portakal rengi**	portahkahl rehng'ee
red	**kırmızı**	kırmızı
white	**beyaz**	beh'ahz
yellow	**sarı**	sahrı
light...	**açık**	ahchık
dark...	**koyu**	koyoo

I want to buy a/an/some...	**... istiyorum**	... eesteeyoroom
aspirin	**Aspirin**	ahspeereen
newspaper	**Bir ... gazetesi**	beer ... gahzehtehssee
American/English	**Amerikan/İngiliz**	ahmehreekahn/eeng'eeleez
postcard	**Bir kartpostal**	beer kahrtpostahl
shampoo	**Şampuan**	shahmpooahn
soap	**Sabun**	sahboon
sun-tan cream	**Güneş kremi**	g'ewnehsh krehmee
toothpaste	**Diş macunu**	deesh mahjoonoo
a half kilo of tomatoes	**Yarım kilo domates**	yahrım k'eelo domah-tehss
a litre of milk	**Bir litre süt**	beer leetreh sewt
I'd like a film for this camera.	**Bu fotoğraf makinesi için film istiyorum.**	boo fotawrahf mahk'ee-nehssı eecheen feelm eesteeyoroom
black and white	**siyah-beyaz film**	seeyahbeh'ahz feelm
colour	**renkli film**	rehnklee feelm
I'd like a hair-cut, please.	**Lütfen saçımı kesin.**	lewtfehn sahchımı k'ehsseen

Souvenirs *Hatıra*

carpet	**halı**	hahlı
chocolate	**çukolata**	chookolahtah
crystal	**kristal**	kreestahl
hubble-bubble pipe	**nargile**	nahrg'eeleh
prayer mat	**namaz seccâdesi**	nahmahz sehjjaadehssee
Turkish delight	**lokum**	lokoom

NUMBERS, see page 189

At the bank *Banka*

Where's the nearest bank/currency exchange office?	En yakın banka/ kambiyo bürosu nerededir?	ehn yahkın **bahn**kah/ **kam**beeyo bewrossoo **neh**rehdehdeer
I want to change some dollars/pounds.	Birkaç dolar/sterlin çevirmek istiyorum.	**beer**kahch dolahr/ stehrleen chehveer**mehk** eesteeyoroom
What's the exchange rate?	Kambiyo kuru nedir?	**kahm**beeyo kooroo **neh**deer
I want to cash a traveller's cheque.	Traveller's çek bozdurmak istiyorum.	'traveller's' chehk bozdoor**mahk** eestee**yo**room

At the post office *Postane*

A...-lira stamp, please	... liralık posta pulu lütfen.	... leerahlık **pos**tah pooloo **lewt**fehn
What's the postage for a postcard/letter to United States?	Amerika Birleşik Devletleri'e kartpostal/mektup kaça gider?	ahmehreekah beerleh-**sheek** dehvlehtlehree'eh kahrtpostahl/mehktoop **kah**chah g^yeedehr
Is there any post/mail for me?	Benim için posta var mı?	behneem eecheen **pos**tah vahr mı

Telephoning *Telefon etmek*

Where is the nearest telephone?	En yakın telefon kulübesi nerededir?	ehn yahkın **teh**lehfon koolewbehssee **neh**rehdehdeer
Hello. This is...	Alo, ben...	ahlo behn
I'd like to speak to...	... ile konuşmak istiyorum.	... eeleh konooshmahk eestee**yo**room
When will he/she be back?	Ne zaman geri döner?	neh zahmahn g^yehree dur**nehr**

Time and date *Saat ve tarih*

It's...		
five past one	Biri beş geçiyor	bee**ree** behsh g^yehchee**yor**
quarter past three	Üçü çeyrek geçiyor	ewchew cheh^yrehk g^yehchee**yor**
twenty past four	Dördü yirmi geçiyor	durr**dew** yeermee g^yehchee**yor**
half past six	Altı buçuk	ahltı boochook
twenty-five to seven	Yediye yirmibeş var	yehdee**yeh** yeermeebehsh vahr

ten to ten	**Ona on var**	onah on vahr
noon/midnight	**Öğle/Gece yarısı**	urley/g'ehjeh yahrıssı
in the morning	**sabahları**	sahbahhlahrı
in the afternoon	**öğleden sonra**	urlehdehn sonrah
in the evening	**akşamları**	ahkshahmlahrı
during the day	**gündüzleri**	g'ewndewzlehree
at night	**geceleri**	g'ehjehlehree
yesterday/today	**dün/bugün**	dewn/**boog**'ewn
tomorrow	**yarın**	yahrın
spring/summer	**ilkbahar/yaz**	**eelk**bahhahr/yahz
autumn/winter	**sonbahar/kış**	**son**bahhahr/kısh

Sunday	**Pazar**	pah**zahr**
Monday	**Pazartesi**	pah**zahr**tehssee
Tuesday	**Salı**	sahlı
Wednesday	**Çarşamba**	chahrshahm**bah**
Thursday	**Perşembe**	pehrshehm**beh**
Friday	**Cuma**	**joo**mah
Saturday	**Cumartesi**	**joo**mahrtehssee
January	**Ocak**	ojahk
February	**Şubat**	shoobaht
March	**Mart**	mahrt
April	**Nisan**	neessahn
May	**Mayıs**	mah'ıss
June	**Haziran**	hahzeerahn
July	**Temmuz**	tehmmooz
August	**Ağustos**	aaoostos
September	**Eylül**	eh'lewl
October	**Ekim**	ehk'eem
November	**Kasım**	kahssım
December	**Aralık**	ahrahlık

Numbers *Sayılar*

0	**sıfır**	sıfir
1	**bir**	beer
2	**iki**	eek'ee
3	**üç**	ewch
4	**dört**	durrt
5	**beş**	behsh
6	**altı**	ahltı
7	**yedi**	yeh**dee**
8	**sekiz**	sehk'eez
9	**dokuz**	do**kooz**

10	**on**	on
11	**on bir**	on beer
12	**on iki**	on eek^yee
13	**on üç**	on ewch
14	**on dört**	on durrt
15	**on beş**	on behsh
16	**on altı**	on ahltı
17	**on yedi**	on yehdee
18	**on sekiz**	on sehk^yeez
19	**on dokuz**	on dokooz
20	**yirmi**	yeermee
21	**yirmi bir**	yeermee beer
30	**otuz**	otooz
40	**kırk**	kırk
50	**elli**	ehllee
60	**altmış**	ahltmısh
70	**yetmiş**	yehtmeesh
80	**seksen**	sehksehn
90	**doksan**	doksahn
100/1000	**yüz/bin**	yewz/been
first/second	**ilk/ikinci**	eelk/eek^yeenjee
once/twice	**bir kez/iki kez**	beer k^yehz/eek^yee k^yehz
a half	**yarım**	yahrım

Emergency *Tehlikeli durum*

Call the police	**Polis çağırın**	poleess chaaırın
Get a doctor	**Doktor çağırın**	doktor chaaırın
Go away	**Gidiniz**	g^yeedeeneez
HELP	**İMDAT**	eemdaht
I'm ill	**Hastayım**	hahstah^yım
I'm lost	**Kayboldum**	kah^yboldoom
LOOK OUT	**DİKKAT**	deekkaht
STOP THIEF	**HIRSIZI YAKA-LAYIN**	hırsızı yahkahlah^yın
My...has been stolen.	**... um/im/am çalındı.**	... oom/eem/ahm chahlındı
I've lost my...	**... kaybettim.**	... kah^ybehtteem
handbag	**El çantamı**	ehl chahntahmı
wallet	**Para cüzdanımı**	pahrah jewzdahnımı
passport	**Pasaportumu**	pahssahportoomoo
luggage	**Bagaj**	bahgahz
Where can I find a doctor who speaks English?	**İngilizce bilen bir doktor nerede bulabilirim?**	eeng^yeeleezjeh beelehn beer doktor nehrehdeh boolahbeeleereem

TELEPHONING, see page 188